*THE
TRADE UNION
AND
INDUSTRIAL RELATIONS
ACTS
OF IRELAND*

Australia
The Law Book Company
Sydney

Canada
The Carswell Company
Toronto, Ontario

India
N.M. Tripathi (Private) Ltd
Bombay

Eastern Law House (Private) Ltd
Calcutta

M P P House
Bangalore

Universal Book Traders
Delhi

Israel
Steimatzky's Agency Ltd
Tel Aviv

Pakistan
Pakistan Law House
Karachi

THE TRADE UNION AND INDUSTRIAL RELATIONS ACTS OF IRELAND

COMMENTARY BY

ANTHONY KERR

M.A. (Dub.), LL.M. (Lond.)
of King's Inn, Barrister,
Statutory Lecturer in Law,
University College, Dublin

LONDON
SWEET & MAXWELL
1991

Published in 1991
by
Sweet and Maxwell Ltd.
of
South Quay Plaza, 183 Marsh Wall, London, E14 9FT
Computerset by
MFK Typesetting Ltd., Hitchin, Herts.
Printed in Scotland

British Library Cataloguing in Publication Data

A catalogue record for this book is
available from the British Library

ISBN 0 421 44920 9

All rights reserved.
No part of this publication may be
reproduced or transmitted in any form
or by any means, electronic, mechanical, photocopying,
recording or otherwise, or stored in any retrieval system
of any nature, without the written permission
of the copyright holder and the publisher, application
for which shall be made to the publisher.

Acknowledgement:
The statutory material in
this book is reproduced
with the permission of the
Controller's Stationary Office, Dublin.

©
Anthony Kerr
1991

PREFACE

The Industrial Relations Act 1990 involves the most far-reaching changes in Irish Labour Law since the 1940s. It effects substantial modification of the law both in the area of trade disputes and industrial relations generally. The Trade Disputes Act 1906 is repealed in its entirety and a completely new institution—the Labour Relations Commission—is established to discharge a wide variety of functions. The 1990 Act, however, is not a consolidation statute. The principal Industrial Relations Act is still that of 1946, as amended in 1969 and 1976. The Trade Union Acts date back to 1871 and the four pre-Independence statutes that are still in force, along with the relevant statutory rules and orders, have in the main been repealed in the United Kingdom. Consequently this material is not readily available even to those with access to law libraries.

This book brings together longstanding but crucial provisions such as those in the Trade Union Act 1871 and the Conspiracy and Protection of Property Act 1875, presented in their up-to-date form, as well as the more recent Trade Union and Industrial Relations legislation. All textual amendments, adaptations and repeals are clearly shown and all the statutes are fully annotated. All relevant statutory instruments, including the rules governing the procedure before the Labour Court, are also included. It is hoped thereby to give a full picture of the law as it stands after the enactment of the 1990 Act and thus to provide some guidance and assistance to those who are concerned with, or interested in, the relationship between industrial relations and the law.

The proofs of the book were corrected largely by candlelight and readers will note that the temptation to amend the commentary to section 4 of the 1875 Act was resisted. Industrial peace, even in essential services, cannot be enforced by penal sanctions. Whether the proposed Code of Practice under section 42 of the 1990 Act will enable disputes in essential services to be avoided remains to be seen but it is much more likely that services can be maintained during such disputes by means of a voluntarily agreed code than by resort to the law.

Grateful appreciation is due to a large number of individuals for assistance provided and encouragement offered. In particular, thanks are due to Gerry Whyte, Declan Madden, Bob Clark, Patricia Garland, Liz Gleeson, Kevin Duffy, Muirean O Briain, Kevin Bonner and numerous officials of the Department of Labour, Paul O'Connor and other staff of the Labour Court, Michael M. Collins, Peter Kelly,

Preface

Rosario Cooney and Tony Eklof. The editorial staff of Sweet and Maxwell were extremely helpful and supportive and warrant special praise.

The commentary to the legislation is based on materials and information available to me at May 31, 1991. Consequently it was not possible to incorporate into the discussion of the 1990 Act the deep dissatisfaction expressed by delegates to the 1991 ICTU annual conference. Concern was expressed at the continued practice of the courts in granting labour injunctions almost automatically, with delegates saying that, unless the Act was changed substantially to provide a fairer balance between employer and union interests, it would fail in its objective of ensuring harmonious industrial relations. Delegates adopted a motion asking the executive council to examine restrictive provisions of the Act and to lobby to have it amended.

Nor was it possible to include any reference in the Trade Union Act 1975 to the Supreme Court's decision in *National Union of Journalists* v. *Sisk* June 20, 1991 in which the decision of Keane J. was overruled. The Supreme Court unanimously held that a foreign trade union, having a presence in and members belonging to it within the State and holding a negotiation licence, did come within the provisions of the 1975 Act. The Chief Justice said that it was of "significant importance" that section 2 of the Trade Union Act 1913, read in conjunction with section 1 of that Act, did not purport to define a trade union as being either a registered or a certified trade union, but defined it in relation to what it was and what its principal objects were. He added that the right of trade union members to vote in favour of a transfer of engagements by that trade union to another, whether one registered within the State or not, appeared to be a necessary and valuable expansion of the general right to form trade unions and belong to them.

In relation to section 12 of the 1990 Act readers should note that the House of Lords, in *Lonrho plc* v. *Fayed, The Independent*, July 3, 1991, have overruled *Metall und Rohstoff* and have held that, where conspirators use unlawful means to injure a plaintiff, the plaintiff, in seeking to establish the tort of conspiracy to injure, need not prove that the intention to injure him was the predominant purpose of the conspirators and that it is no defence for the conspirators to show that their primary purpose was to further or protect their own interests.

The publication of the *Report of the Registrar of Friendly Societies 1987–89* also came too late to amend the references to the 1985–86 Report. A number of matters referred to therein are worth noting however. In paragraph 3.8 the Registrar refers to his investigation into a complaint under section 10 of the Trade Union Act 1975 and states that, "where fundamental matters relative to the affairs of trade unions are concerned", it is strongly recommended that the notice

Preface

which is required to be issued to every member under section 3(1)(*d*) of the 1975 Act should be sent to the member's home address. The Registrar also recommended that this notice should indicate precisely where and when the ballots for transfers of engagements or amalgamations are due to take place. In paragraph 3.12 the Registrar reminds officers of trade unions that it is most desirable that rule books are available in as clear a format as possible to members and other interested parties. The Registrar went on to observe that the lack of clear, consolidated and up-to-date rules caused difficulties and delays in processing applications under the 1975 Act. Finally the Registrar in paragraph 3.13 signalled that, because some trade unions were very late in submitting their annual returns, he had decided to introduce a policy of prosecuting the more serious offenders. Consideration was also being given to the possibility of including officers of trade unions in such prosecutions.

Every effort has been made to ensure that the information given in this book is accurate. No legal responsibility, however, is accepted by the author or the publishers for any errors or omissions in that information or otherwise.

Tony Kerr
Dublin
Bastille Day 1991

CONTENTS

	Page
Preface	v
Table of Cases	xix

Trade Union Legislation

TRADE UNION ACT 1871

1.	Short title	1
2.	Trade union not criminal	1
3.	Trade union not unlawful for civil purposes	1
4.	Trade union contracts, when not enforceable	1
5.	Provisions not to apply to trade unions	2
6.	Registry of trade unions	3
7.	Buildings for trade unions may be purchased or leased	3
8.	Property of the trade unions vested in trustees	3
9.	Actions, etc. by or against trustees, etc.	4
10.	Limitation of responsibility of trustees	5
11.	Treasurers, etc. to account	5
12.	Punishment for withholding money, etc.	5
13.	Regulations for registry	6
14.	Rules of registered trade unions	7
15.	Registered office of trade unions	8
16.	Annual returns to be prepared as registrar may direct	8
17.	Registrars	9
18.	Circulating false copies of rules, etc. a misdemeanour	9
19.	Summary proceedings for offences, penalties, etc.	9
20.	Appeal to quarter sessions	10
21.	[. . .]	11
22.	Interested person not to act as a member of a court of appeal	11
23.	Definitions	12
24.	Repeal of Trades Unions Funds Protection Act 1869, as herein stated	13
	First Schedule	13
	Second Schedule	14

CONSPIRACY AND PROTECTION OF PROPERTY ACT 1875

1.	Short title	15
2.	[. . .]	15
3.	Amendment of law as to conspiracy in trade disputes	15
4.	Breach of contract by persons employed in supply of gas and water	16
5.	Breach of contract involving injury to persons or property	17

Contents

6.	Penalty for neglect by master to provide food, clothing, etc. for servant or apprentice	17
7.	Penalty for intimidation or annoyance by violence or otherwise	17
8.	Reduction of penalties	18
9.	Power for offender under this act to be tried on indictment and not by court of summary jurisdiction	19
10.	Proceedings before court of summary jurisdiction	19
11.	Regulations as to evidence	19
12.	Appeal to quarter sessions	19
13.	General definitions	20
14.	Definitions	21
15.	"Maliciously" in this Act construed as in Malicious Injuries to Property Act	21
16.	Saving as to sea service	21
17.	Repeal of Acts	21
18.	[...]	24
19.	[...]	24
20.	[...]	24
21.	Application to Ireland	25

TRADE UNION AMENDMENT ACT 1876

1.	Construction and short title	27
2.	Trade unions to be within [ss.62–67] of Friendly Societies Act [1896]	27
3.	Amendment of s.8 of Principal Act	27
4.	Provision in case of absence, etc. of trustee	27
5.	Jurisdiction in offences	28
6.	[...]	28
7.	Life Assurance Companies Acts not to apply to registered unions	29
8.	Withdrawal or cancelling of certificate	29
9.	Membership of minors	29
10.	Nomination	30
11.	[...]	30
12.	[...]	30
13.	[...]	30
14.	Dissolution	31
15.	Penalty for failure to give notice	31
16.	Definition of "trade union" altered	31

REGULATIONS AS TO THE REGISTRATION OF TRADE UNIONS DATED NOVEMBER 1, 1876   33

Recording of Rules already registered	34
Withdrawal or cancelling of certificate of registration	35
Registered office	35
Change of name	35
Transfer of stock	36
Dissolution	36
Amalgamation	36
Nominations	36
Fees	37
Authentication of documents by registrar	37

Contents

Form A	—Application for registry of trade union	37
Form B	—Certificate of registry of trade union	39
Form C	—Application for registry of partial registration of rules	39
Form D	—Declaration accompanying alteration of rules	40
Form E	—Certificate of registry of partial alteration of rules	40
Form F	—Form of application for registry of complete alteration of rules	41
Form G	—Certificate of registry of complete alteration of rules	42
Form J	—Request to withdraw or cancel certificate of registry	43
Form K	—Notice before withdrawal or cancelling of certificate of registry	43
Form L	—Withdrawal or cancelling of certificate of registry	44
Form M	—Notice of change of registered office	44
Form N	—Application for approval, and notice of change of name	45
Form O	—Declaration to accompany application for approval of change of name	46
Form P	—Application for direction to transfer stock	46
Form Q	—Declaration verifying statements in an application for direction to transfer stock	47
Form R	—Direction by the registrar to transfer stock	48
Form S	—Notice of dissolution	49

TRADE UNION ACT 1913

1.	Amendment of law as to objects and powers of trade unions	51
2.	Definition of trade union	51
3.	Restriction on application of funds for certain political purposes	53
4.	Approval of rules	55
5.	Notice of objection to contribute towards political objects	56
6.	Mode of giving effect to exemption from contributions to political fund	57
7.	[...]	57
8.	Short title and construction	57
	Schedule	57

TRADE UNION ACT 1941

1.	Short title and collective citation	59
2.	Definitions	59
3.	Regulation	59
4.	Expenses	60
5.	Definitions for the purposes of Part II	60
6.	Restrictions on carrying on of negotiations for fixing of wages, etc.	60
7.	Restrictions on grant and holding of negotiation licence	62
8.	Variation of Schedule to this Act	63
9.	Application for negotiation licence	63
10.	Grant of negotiation licence	63
11.	[...]	63
12.	Obligations of holder of negotiation licence where holder is a registered trade union	64
13.	Obligations of holder of negotiation licence where holder is not a registered trade union	65

Contents

14.	General provisions in relation to deposits under this Part of this Act	68
15.	Change of deposit consequent on change of number of members	68
16.	Payment of judgment debts out of deposits	69
17.	Revocation of negotiation licence	69
	Schedule	70

TRADE UNION ACT 1941 (APPLICATION FOR NEGOTIATION LICENCE) REGULATIONS 1942 — 71

Schedule — 71

TRADE UNION (INSPECTION OF REGISTER OF MEMBERS) REGULATIONS 1942 — 73

RULES OF THE SUPERIOR COURT 1986 — 75

Order 77, Part VIII — 75

Appendix P—Form 14	76
—Form 15	77
—Form 16	77
—Form 17	78
—Form 18	78
—Form 19	79

TRADE UNION ACT 1942

1.	Definitions	81
2.	Extension of "excepted body" in section 6 of the Act of 1941	81
3.	Exemption in certain cases from requirement of holding negotiation licence	81
4.	Inspection free of charge by officer of the Minister of register of members of trade union	82
5.	[...]	83
6.	Repeal of certain provisions of the Act of 1941	83
7.	Short title and citation	83

TRADE UNION ACT 1947

1.	Definitions	85
2.	Variation of Schedule to Act of 1941	85
3.	Repeal of section 8 of Act of 1941 and continuance of orders	86
4.	Short title and collective citation	86

TRADE UNION ACT 1952

1.	Act of 1947	87
2.	Appointed day	87
3.	Extension of section 2 of the Act of 1947	87
4.	Continuance of existing orders	87
5.	Short title and collective citation	88

Contents

TRADE UNION ACT 1971

1.	Definitions	89
2.	Grant of negotiation licence	89
3.	Application to the High Court	90
4.	Expenses	91
5.	Short title and collective citation	91
	Schedule	92

TRADE UNION ACT 1971 (NOTICE OF INTENTION TO APPLY FOR NEGOTIATION LICENCE) REGULATIONS 1972   93

	Schedule	93

TRADE UNION ACT 1975

1.	Interpretation	95
2.	Amalgamations of, and transfers of engagements by, trade unions	96
3.	Conditions for amalgamations or transfers	97
4.	Approval of documents by registrar	98
5.	Voting on resolution to approve amalgamation or transfer	98
6.	Registration of instrument of amalgamation or transfer	98
7.	Application of sections 2 to 6	98
8.	Power to alter rules for purpose of transfer of engagements	98
9.	Amalgamations and transfers by members of certain trade unions	99
10.	Complaints to Registrar regarding resolutions	100
11.	Disposal of property on amalgamation or transfer	101
12.	Change of name of trade union	102
13.	Regulations	102
14.	Saver for pending amalgamations, etc.	103
15.	Grants towards exceptional expenses of amalgamation or transfer	104
16.	Repeals	104
17.	Restriction on holding and grant of negotiation licence in case of certain trade unions	104
18.	Expenses	105
19.	Short title and collective citation	105
	Schedule	105

TRADE UNION AMALGAMATIONS REGULATIONS 1976   109

General	109
Approval of proposed instruments and notices	109
Contents of instrument of amalgamation or transfer	110
Contents of notice of vote	110
Application for registration of instruments	110
Registration of change of name	111

Contents

Schedule 1—Contents of instrument of amalgamation		111
Schedule 2—Contents of instrument of transfer		112
Schedule 3—Trade Union Acts 1871 to 1975		113

TRADE UNION (FEES) REGULATIONS 1983   115

Schedule   116

Industrial Relations Legislation

INDUSTRIAL RELATIONS ACT 1946   117

1. Short title — 117
2. Commencement — 117
3. Definitions generally — 117
4. [...] — 118
5. Regulations — 118
6. Laying of regulations before Houses of the Oireachtas — 118
7. Prosecutions by the Minister — 118
8. Repeals — 118
9. Expenses — 119
10. Establishment of the Labour Court — 119
11. [...] — 120
12. [...] — 121
13. Registrar and officers and servants of the Court — 121
14. Technical assessors — 121
15. Places for sitting of the Court and lodgment of documents — 121
16. [...] — 121
17. Finality of decisions of the Court — 122
18. Seal of the Court — 122
19. Proof of orders of the Court — 122
20. Procedure of the Court — 122
21. Power of the Court to summon witnesses, etc. — 124
22. Prohibition on disclosure of information — 125
23. Reports, etc. by Court — 125
24. Duty of Court to consider certain matters with regard to employment conditions referred to it by the Minister — 126
25. Definitions for the purpose of Part III — 126
26. Register of Employment Agreements — 127
27. Registration of employment agreements — 127
28. Variation of registered employment agreement — 128
29. Cancellation of registration — 129
30. Adaptation of contracts of service consequential upon registration of employment agreement — 130
31. Publication of particulars in relation to employment agreements and right to obtain copies thereof — 130
32. Breaches of registered employment agreements — 131
33. Interpretation of registered employment agreements — 132
34. Definitions for purposes of Part IV — 133
35. Power of the Court to establish joint labour committees — 134
36. Applications for establishment orders — 134
37. Restrictions on making establishment orders — 134
38. Inquiry into application for an establishment order — 135
39. Making of establishment orders — 136
40. Revocation and variation of establishment orders — 136

Contents

41.	[...]	137
42.	Proposals by joint labour committees in relation to remuneration and conditions of employment	137
43.	Making of employment regulation orders	137
44.	Adaptation of contracts of service consequential upon employment regulation orders	138
45.	Enforcement of employment regulation orders	139
46.	Permits authorising employment of infirm and incapacitated persons at less than the statutory minimum remuneration	140
47.	Computation of remuneration	141
48.	Employers not to receive premiums from apprentices or learners	141
49.	Records and Notices	142
50.	Criminal liabililty of agent and superior employer and special defence open to employer	143
51.	Inspectors	144
52.	Powers of inspectors	144
53.	Existing trade boards to become joint labour committees	146
54.	Existing orders under the Trade Boards Acts 1909 and 1918	146
55.	Pending notices of proposals varying minimum rates of wages under the Trade Boards Acts 1909 and 1918	146
56.	Adaptation of references to trade boards	146
57.	Determination of certain questions	146
58.	Standard wages for areas	147
59.	Definitions for purposes of Part V	147
60.	Register of Joint Industrial Councils	148
61.	Registration of joint industrial councils	148
62.	Cancellation of registration	148
63.	Inspection of rules of registered joint industrial council	149
64.	[...]	149
65.	Registered joint industrial council to be a body in respect of which section 3 of the Trade Union Act 1942 is applicable	149
66.	[...]	149
67.	[...]	149
68.	Recommendation by Court on trade dispute	150
69.	Mediation in trade dispute by conciliation officer	150
70.	Reference of trade dispute to arbitration	150
71.	[...]	150
72.	[...]	151
	First Schedule	151

LABOUR COURT PROVISIONAL (PART III) RULES 1946 — 153

Preliminary		153
A.	Procedure at formal sittings	153
B.	Registration of Employment Agreements (Section 27)	154
C.	Variation of registered Employment Agreement (Section 28)	155
D.	Cancellation of registered Employment Agreement (Section 29)	155
E.	Complaints under section 32 of the Act	156
F.	General	156

LABOUR COURT PROVISIONAL (PART VI) RULES 1946 — 157

Preliminary	157
Investigation of trade dispute under Part VI of the Act	157

Contents

INDUSTRIAL RELATIONS ACT 1946 REGULATIONS 1950   159

INDUSTRIAL RELATIONS ACT 1969

1.	Definitions	161
2.	Membership of the Court	161
3.	Divisions of the Court	161
4.	Deputy chairman of the Court	162
5.	Superannuation for chairman and ordinary members of the Court	163
6.	[...]	164
7.	Interpretation of employment agreements	164
8.	Investigation of trade dispute to be in private	164
9.	Inclusion of members of the Court on public service arbitration boards	165
10.	Breaches of registered employment agreements	165
11.	[...]	166
12.	Enforcement of sections 10 and 11	167
13.	Rights commissioners	168
14.	Prohibition on disclosure of information	170
15.	[...]	170
16.	[...]	171
17.	[...]	171
18.	[...]	171
19.	[...]	171
20.	Investigation of dispute by Court at request of parties	171
21.	Dissolution of Electricity Supply Board manual workers and general employees tribunals	172
22.	Laying of orders before Houses of Oireachtas	172
23.	Repeals	172
24.	Short title, construction and collective citation	172
	Schedule	173

INDUSTRIAL RELATIONS ACT 1976

1.	Definitions	175
2.	[...]	175
3.	[...]	175
4.	Establishment of joint labour committee for agricultural workers	176
5.	[...]	176
6.	Repeal of Agricultural Wages Acts 1936 to 1969	176
7.	Modification of section 49 of Principal Act	177
8.	Additional divisions of the Court	177
9.	[...]	177
10.	[...]	177
11.	Repeal of Agricultural Workers (Holidays) Acts 1950 to 1975	178
12.	Short title, construction and collective citation	178

Contents

INDUSTRIAL RELATIONS ACT 1990   179

1.	Short title	181
2.	Collective citations and construction	181
3.	Interpretation	181
4.	Increase of fines	182
5.	Summary proceedings for an offence	182
6.	Expenses	182
7.	Repeals	182
8.	Definitions for Part II	183
9.	Applications of provisions for Part II	186
10.	Acts in contemplation or furtherance of trade dispute	188
11.	Peaceful picketing	189
12.	Removal of liability for certain acts	193
13.	Restriction of actions of tort against trade unions	194
14.	Secret ballots	195
15.	Power to alter rules of trade unions	198
16.	Enforcement of rule for secret ballot	199
17.	Actions contrary to outcome of secret ballot	200
18.	Non-application of sections 14 to 17 to employers' unions	200
19.	Restriction of right to injunction	200
20.	Change of deposit consequent on change in number of members	202
21.	Amendment of section 2 of Trade Union Act 1971	203
22.	Amalgamations and transfers	204
23.	"Worker"	205
24.	Establishment of the Commission	207
25.	Functions of the Commission	208
26.	Investigation of dispute by Court	210
27.	Procedure of the Commission	211
28.	The chief executive	211
29.	Superannuation and gratuities for and in respect of the chief executive of the Commission	212
30.	Grants to the Commission and power to borrow	212
31.	Accounts and audits	212
32.	Staff of the Commission	213
33.	Industrial relations officers and advisory service	213
34.	Rights commissioners	213
35.	The Rights Commissioner Service	214
36.	Objections and appeals	214
37.	Equality officers	214
38.	Reference of dispute by Minister	215
39.	Review of joint labour committees	216
40.	Superannuation and gratuities for and in respect of chairman, deputy chairmen and ordinary members of the Court	216
41.	Divisions of Court	216
42.	Codes of practice	217
43.	Functions of Labour Court relating to codes of practice	218
44.	Constitution and proceedings of joint labour committees	218
45.	Making of establishment orders	219
46.	Exclusion from scope of joint labour committee	219
47.	Report for assistance of joint labour committee	219
48.	Proposals for employment regulation order	220
49.	Enforcement of employment regulation order by inspector by civil proceedings	221

Contents

50. Amendment of section 52(2)(d) of Industrial Relations Act 1946	221
51. Records	221
52. Powers of inspection for enforcement of registered employment agreement	222
53. Proof of registered employment agreement and related matters	222
54. Enforcement of registered employment agreement by inspector by civil proceedings	222
55. Amendment of section 12(2)(d) of Industrial Relations Act 1969	223
56. Evidence of failure to attend sitting of Court	223
First Schedule—Increase of fines	224
Second Schedule—Repeals	225
Third Schedule—Deposits	225
Fourth Schedule—Labour Relations Commission	226
Fifth Schedule—Constitution and Proceedings of Joint Labour Committees	227

Index   231

TABLE OF CASES

A.S.T.M.S. v. Parkin [1984] I.C.R. 127 55
Amalgamated Society of Railway Servants v. Osborne [1910] A.C. 87 51
Associated British Ports v. Transport and General Workers' Union [1989] I.R.L.R.
    291 185
Attorney General v. O'Brien (1936) 70 I.L.T.R. 101 18

Bayzana Ltd. v. Galligan [1987] I.R. 241 206
Becton Dickinson & Co. Ltd. v. Lee [1973] I.R. 1 .... 185, 193
Birch v. National Union of Railwaymen [1950] Ch. 602 55
Bork (P.) International A/S v. Foreningen af Arbejdsledere i Danmark (Case 101/
    87) [1988] E.C.R. 3057 192
Bradbury (J.) Ltd. v. Duffy (1984) 3 J.I.S.L.L. 86 184
Branigan v. Keady [1959] I.R. 283 122
Burke v. Minister for Labour [1979] I.R. 354 221

Cleary v. Coffey (1985) 4 J.I.S.L.L. 70 .... 184, 185
Coleman v. Post Office Employees Union [1981] I.R.L.R. 427 55
Crazy Prices (Northern Ireland) Ltd. v. Hewitt [1980] N.I. 150 .... 185, 189
Crowley v. Cleary [1968] I.R. 261 186

Doran v. Lennon [1945] I.R. 315 186
Drennan v. Beechey [1935] N.I. 74 4
Dunne v. Marks unreported, May 30, 1968 (High Court) 98
Dunne (Brendan) Ltd. v. Fitzpatrick [1958] I.R. 29 .... 184, 191

E.I. Co. Ltd. v. Kennedy [1968] I.R. 69 191
Esplanade Pharmacy Ltd. v. Larkin [1957] I.R. 285 .... 185, 189, 190
Examite Ltd. v. Whitaker [1977] I.R.L.R. 312 184
Express Newspapers Ltd. v. MacShane [1980] A.C. 672 .... 189, 195

Ferguson Ltd. v. O'Gorman [1937] I.R. 620 192
Fitzhenry v. Gallagher (Dublin) Ltd. UD 419/1986 170

Galt v. Philp [1984] I.R.L.R. 156 18
Goulding Chemicals Ltd. v. Bolger [1977] I.R. 211 .... 184, 185, 187, 191, 193, 200

Hadmor Productions Ltd. v. Hamilton [1983] 1 A.C. 191 194
Hayes v. Ireland [1987] I.L.R.M. 651 195
Hayes and Caffrey v. B & I Line Ltd. UD 192 and 193/1979 206
Health Computing Ltd. v. Meek [1981] I.C.R. 24 186

Iarnród Éireann v. Darby and O'Connor *Irish Times*, March 23, 1991 187
Inspector of Taxes' Association v. Minister for the Public Service unreported, March
    24, 1983 (High Court); [1986] I.L.R.M. 296 (Supreme Court) 207
Irish Aviation Executive Staff Association v. Minister for Labour [1981] I.L.R.M.
    350 91
Irish Transport and General Workers' Union v. Green [1936] I.R. 471 .... 28, 35, 195

Kennedy v. Cowie [1891] 1 Q.B. 771 21

Larkin v. Belfast Harbour Commissioners [1908] 2 I.R. 214 192
—— v. Long [1915] A.C. 814 186
Linaker v. Pilcher (1901) 17 T.L.R. 256 4

Table of Cases

Lonrho plc v. Fayed [1990] 2 Q.B. 490 194
Lyons (J.) & Sons v. Wilkins [1899] 1 Ch. 255 18

Mackendrick v. National Union of Dock Labourers in Great Britain and Ireland
    (1910) 48 Sc.L.R. 17 3
Maher v. Attorney General [1973] I.R. 110 .... 53, 82
McCafferty v. Irish Transport and General Workers' Union (1952) Report of the
    Registrar of Friendly Societies 37 55
McCusker v. Smith [1918] 2 I.R. 432 192
McDona v. Croker and Power [1941] Ir. Jur. Rep. 63 2
McDowell v. Dublin Corporation [1903] 2 I.R. 541 21
McElroy v. Mortished unreported, June 17, 1949 (High Court) 124
McGonagle v. McGonagle [1951] I.R. 12 19
McHenry Brothers Ltd. v. Carey (1984) 3 J.I.S.L.L. 80 184
McMahon v. Minister for Finance unreported, May 13, 1963 (High Court) 287
McNamara (Michael) & Co. Ltd. v. Lacken (High Court 1990 No. 17675P) 184
Metall und Rohstoff A.G. v. Donaldson Lufkin & Jenrette Inc. [1990] 1 Q.B. 391 188
Minister for Labour v. Costello [1988] I.R. 235 140
Murphy v. Minister for Social Welfare [1987] I.R. 295 120

N.W.L. Ltd. v. Woods [1979] I.C.R. 867 .... 185, 186
National Union of Journalists v. Sisk unreported, July 31, 1990 (High
    Court) 90, 96, 99–100
National Union of Railwaymen v. Sullivan [1947] I.R. 77 .... 70, 83
Newbridge Industries Ltd. v. Bateson (1988) 7 J.I.S.L.L. 191 193

O'Callaghan v. Cork Corporation UD 309/1978 206

Post Office Workers' Union v. Minister for Labour [1981] I.L.R.M. 355 91

Quigley v. Beirne [1955] I.R. 62 184

R. v. Jones [1974] I.C.R. 310 18
—— v. Lynch [1898] 1 Q.B. 61 21
Rayware Ltd. v. Transport and General Workers' Union [1989] I.C.R. 457 .. 192
Reeves v. Transport and General Workers' Union [1980] I.C.R. 728 55
River Valley Products Ltd. v. Strutt (High Court, 1991 No. 1670P) 194
Roundabout Ltd. v. Beirne [1959] I.R. 423 183
Ryan v. Cooke and Quinn [1938] I.R. 512 .... 186, 193

Sheriff v. McMullen [1952] I.R. 236 186
Smith v. Beirne (1954) 89 I.L.T.R. 24 185
State (Casey) v. Labour Court (1984) 3 J.I.S.L.L. 135 124
Stratford (J.T.) & Son Ltd. v. Lindley [1965] A.C. 269 194
Sutcliffe v. Pat Russell Haulage Ltd. [1991] E.L.R. 42 169

Talbot (Ireland) Ltd. v. Merrigan unreported April 30, 1981 (Supreme Court) ... 194
Taylor v. Smith unreported, July 5, 1990 (Supreme Court) 188
Thomas v. National Union of Mineworkers (South Wales Area) [1985] I.C.R. 886 191
Tierney v. Amalgamated Society of Woodworkers [1959] I.R. 254 65
Torquay Hotel Ltd. v. Cousins [1969] 2 Ch. 106 195

Universe Tankships Inc. of Monrovia v. International Transport Workers' Feder-
    ation [1980] I.R.L.R. 363 195

Ward Lock & Co. v. Operative Printers Assistants' Society (1906) 22 T.L.R. 327 18
Waterford Co-Op v. Murphy Irish Times, August 3, 1988 201
Westman Holdings Ltd. v. McCormack unreported, May 14, 1991 .... 191, 202

TRADE UNION
LEGISLATION

TRADE UNION ACT 1871

(34 & 35 Vict. c. 31)

An Act to amend the Law relating to Trade Unions.
[*29 June 1871*]

PRELIMINARY

Short title

1. This Act may be cited as "The Trade Union Act, 1871."

CRIMINAL PROVISIONS

Trade union not criminal

2. The purposes of any trade union shall not, by reason merely that they are in restraint of trade, be deemed to be unlawful so as to render any member of such trade union liable to criminal prosecution for conspiracy or otherwise.

Trade union not unlawful for civil purposes

3. The purposes of any trade union shall not, by reason merely that they are in restraint of trade, be unlawful so as to render void or voidable any agreement or trust.

Trade union contracts, when not enforceable

4. Nothing in this Act shall enable any court to entertain any legal proceeding instituted with the object of directly enforcing or recovering damages for the breach of any of the following agreements, namely,

 1. Any agreement between members of a trade union as such, concerning the conditions on which any members for the time being of such trade union shall or shall not sell their goods, transact business, employ, or be employed:
 2. Any agreement for the payment by any person of any subscription or penalty to a trade union:

3. Any agreement for the application of the funds of a trade union,—

   (a) To provide benefits to members; or
   (b) To furnish contributions to any employer or workman not a member of such trade union, in consideration of such employer or workman acting in conformity with the rules or resolutions of such trade union; or
   (c) To discharge any fine imposed upon any person by sentence of a court of justice; or

4. Any agreement made between one trade union and another; or,
5. Any bond to secure the performance of any of the above-mentioned agreements.

But nothing in this section shall be deemed to constitute any of the above-mentioned agreements unlawful.

COMMENTARY

In *McDona* v. *Croker and Power* [1941] Ir.Jur.Rep. 63 Judge Davitt allowed an action to recover death benefit from a trade union, despite section 4, on the ground that the union (the United Stationary Engine Drivers, Cranemen, Firemen, Motormen and Machinemen's Trade Union) was a lawful association at common law and that, even if some of its rules were in restraint of trade, those relating to the payments of benefits to members or their dependants were not. These were severable and consequently enforceable. On section 4 generally, see Kerr and Whyte, *Irish Trade Union Law* (1985) pp. 123–133.

Provisions not to apply to trade unions

5. The following Acts, that is to say,

   (1) The Friendly Societies [Act 1896] and the Acts amending the same;
   (2) The Industrial and Provident Societies Acts [1893–1977], and any Act amending the same; and
   (3) The Companies Acts [1963—1990]

shall not apply to any trade union, and the registration of any trade union under any of the said Acts shall be void, and the deposit of the rules of any trade union made under the Friendly Societies Acts 1852 and 1858, and the Acts amending the same, before the passing of this Act, shall cease to be of any effect.

COMMENTARY

Section 2 of the Trade Union Act Amendment Act 1876 provides that, notwithstanding anything in this section, a trade union which insures or pays money on

Trade Union Act 1871

the death of a child under 10 years of age shall be deemed to be within the provisions of what are now sections 62–67 of the Friendly Societies Act 1896. Section 3(4)(c) of the Companies Act 1963 provides that nothing in the 1963 Act shall affect the provisions of this section.

Registered Trade Unions

Registry of trade unions

6. Any seven or more members of a trade union may by subscribing their names to the rules of the union, and otherwise complying with the provisions of this Act with respect to registry, register such trade union under this Act, provided that if any one of the purposes of such trade union be unlawful such registration shall be void.

COMMENTARY

For the effect of registration see *Mackendrick v. National Union of Dock Labourers in Great Britain and Ireland* (1910) 48 Sc.L.R. 17, 19, *per* Lord Johnston. See also Kerr and Whyte, *Irish Trade Union Law* (1985) pp. 48–50.

Buildings for trade unions may be purchased or leased

7. It shall be lawful for any trade union registered under this Act to purchase or take upon lease in the names of the trustees for the time being of such union any land [...], and to sell, exchange, mortgage, or let the same, and no purchaser, assignee, mortgagee, or tenant shall be bound to inquire whether the trustees have authority for any sale, exchange, mortgage, or letting, and the receipt of the trustees shall be a discharge for the money arising therefrom; and for the purpose of this section every branch of a trade union shall be considered a distinct union.

COMMENTARY

The words in square brackets were deleted by section 1 of the Trade Union Act 1935.

Property of the trade unions vested in trustees

8. All real and personal estate whatsoever belonging to any trade union registered under this Act shall be vested in the trustees for the time being of the trade union appointed as provided by this Act, for the use and benefit of such trade union and the members thereof, and the real or personal estate of any branch of a trade union shall be vested in the trustees of such branch [or the trustees of the trade union if the rules of the trade union so provide], and be under the control of such trustees, their respective executors or administrators, according to their respective claims and interests, and upon the death or removal of any such trustees the same shall vest in the succeeding trustees for the same estate and interest as the former trustees had therein, and subject to the same trusts, without any conveyance or assignment whatsoever, save and except in the case of stocks and securities in the public funds of [. . .] Ireland, which shall be transferred into the names of such new trustees; and in all actions, or suits, or indictments, or summary proceedings before any court of summary jurisdiction, touching or concerning any such property, the same shall be stated to be the property of the person or persons for the time being holding the said office of trustee, in their proper names, as trustees of such trade union, without any further description.

COMMENTARY

The words in square brackets were inserted by section 3 of the Trade Union Act Amendment Act 1876. Reference to Great Britain has been deleted.

Actions, etc. by or against trustees, etc.

9. The trustees of any trade union registered under this Act, or any other officer of such trade union who may be authorised so to do by the rules thereof, are hereby empowered to bring or defend, or cause to be brought or defended, any action, suit, prosecution, or complaint in any court of law or equity, touching or concerning the property, right, or claim to property of the trade union; and shall and may, in all cases concerning the real or personal property of such trade union, sue and be sued, plead and be impleaded, in any court of law or equity, in their proper names, without other description than the title of their office; and no such action, suit, prosecution, or complaint shall be discontinued or shall abate by the death or removal from office of such persons or any of them, but the same shall and may be proceeded in by their successor or successors as if such death, resignation, or removal had not taken place; and such successors shall pay or receive the like costs as if the action, suit, prosecution, or complaint had been commenced in their names for the benefit of or to be reimbursed from the funds of such trade union, and the summons to be issued to such trustee or other officer may be served by leaving the same at the registered office of the trade union.

COMMENTARY

Conflicting decisions have been given as to the interpretation of this section. In *Linaker* v. *Pilcher* (1901) 17 T.L.R. 256, Mathew J. interpreted it as meaning that trustees could be made party to any action which endangered the funds of the union. In *Drennan* v. *Beechey* [1935] N.I. 74, however, the Northern Ireland Court of Appeal said that trustees could only be sued if the cause of action arose out of the use of, or claim to, some specific property of the trade union.

Trade Union Act 1871

Limitation of responsibility of trustees

10. A trustee of any trade union registered under this Act shall not be liable to make good any deficiency which may arise or happen in the funds of such trade union, but shall be liable only for the moneys which shall be actually received by him on account of such trade union.

Treasurers, etc. to account

11. Every treasurer or other officer of a trade union registered under this Act, at such times as by the rules of such trade union he should render such account as herein-after mentioned, or upon being required so to do, shall render to the trustees of the trade union, or to the members of such trade union, at a meeting of the trade union, a just and true account of all moneys received and paid by him since he last rendered the like account, and of the balance then remaining in his hands, and of all bonds or securities of such trade union, which account the said trustees shall cause to be audited by some fit and proper person or persons by them to be appointed; and such treasurer, if thereunto required, upon the said account being audited, shall forthwith hand over to the said trustees the balance which on such audit appears to be due from him, and shall also, if required, hand over to such trustees all securities and effects, books, papers, and property of the said trade union in his hands or custody; and if he fail to do so the trustees of the said trade union may sue such treasurer in any competent court for the balance appearing to have been due from him upon the account last rendered by him, and for all the moneys since received by him on account of the said trade union, and for the securities and effects, books, papers, and property in his hands or custody, leaving him to set off in such action the sums, if any, which he may have since paid on account of the said trade union; and in such action the said trustees shall be entitled to recover their full costs of suit, to be taxed as between attorney and client.

COMMENTARY

The Registrar of Friendly Societies is of the opinion that the effect of this section is to require of trade union accounts a standard of not less than the "true and fair view" standard under the Companies Acts 1963–1990. Accordingly, the Registrar has recommended that all trade unions should submit their accounts for audit to a qualified accountant: see paragraph 3.10 of the *Report of the Registrar of Friendly Societies 1985–86*.

Punishment for withholding money, etc.

12. If any officer, member, or other person being or representing himself to be a member of a trade union registered under this

Trade Union Act 1871

Act, or the nominee, executor, administrator, or assignee of a member thereof, or any person whatsoever, by false representation or imposition obtain possession of any moneys, securities, books, papers, or other effects of such trade union, or, having the same in his possession, wilfully withhold or fraudulently misapply the same, or wilfully apply any part of the same to purposes other than those expressed or directed in the rules of such trade union, or any part thereof, the court of summary jurisdiction for the place in which the registered office of the trade union is situate, upon a complaint made by any person on behalf of such trade union, or by the registrar, [...] or of the trade union, with his concurrence, may, by summary order, order such officer, member, or other person to deliver up all such moneys, securities, books, papers, or other effects to the trade union, or to repay the amount of money applied improperly, and to pay, if the court think fit, a further sum of money not exceeding twenty pounds, together with costs not exceeding [one pound]; and, in default of such delivery of effects, or repayment of such amount of money, or payment of such penalty and costs aforesaid, the said court may order the said person so convicted to be imprisoned, with or without hard labour, for any time not exceeding three months: Provided, that nothing herein contained shall prevent the said trade union [...] from proceeding by indictment against the said party; provided also, that no person shall be proceeded against by indictment if a conviction shall have been previously obtained for the same offence under the provisions of this Act.

COMMENTARY

Section 5 of the Trade Union Act Amendment Act 1876 provides that the jurisdiction conferred by this section upon the court of summary jurisdiction for the place in which the registered office of a trade union is situate may be exercised either by that court or by the court of summary jurisdiction for the place where the offence has been committed.

The sum in square brackets was substituted by virtue of the Decimal Currency Acts 1969 and 1979.

References exclusive to Scotland have been deleted.

Registry of Trade Union

Regulations for registry

13. With respect to the registry, under this Act, of a trade union, and of the rules thereof, the following provisions shall have effect:

(1) An application to register the trade union and printed copies of the rules, together with a list of the titles and names of the officers, shall be sent to the registrar under this Act:

Trade Union Act 1871

(2) The registrar, upon being satisfied that the trade union has complied with the regulations respecting registry in force under this Act, shall register such trade union and such rules:

(3) No trade union shall be registered under a name identical with that by which any other existing trade union has been registered, or so nearly resembling such name as to be likely to deceive the members or the public:

(4) Where a trade union applying to be registered has been in operation for more than a year before the date of such application, there shall be delivered to the registrar before the registry thereof a general statement of the receipts, funds, effects, and expenditure of such trade union in the same form, and showing the same particulars as if it were the annual general statement required as herein-after mentioned to be transmitted annually to the registrar:

(5) The registrar upon registering such trade union shall issue a certificate of registry, which certificate, unless proved to have been withdrawn or cancelled, shall be conclusive evidence that the regulations of this Act with respect to registry have been complied with:

(6) [The Minister for Labour] may from time to time make regulations respecting registry under this Act, and respecting the seal (if any) to be used for the purpose of such registry, and the forms to be used for such registry, and the inspection of documents kept by the registrar under this Act, and respecting the fees, if any, to be paid on registry, not exceeding the fees specified in the second schedule to this Act, and generally for carrying this Act into effect.

COMMENTARY

As adapted by section 2 of the Registry of Friendly Societies Act 1936 and the Labour (Transfer of Departmental Administration and Ministerial Functions) Order 1966 (S.I. No. 164 of 1966) the powers, duties and functions in subsection (6) are vested solely in, and administered solely by, the Minister for Labour. Note, however, that section 13 of the Trade Union Act 1975 confers power to make regulations under that Act on the Minister for Industry and Commerce. The fees currently payable in respect of matters to be transacted or for the inspection of documents are specified in Part I of the Schedule to the Trade Union (Fees) Regulations 1983 (S.I. No. 292 of 1983), reproduced *infra* at p. 115.

Rules of registered trade unions

14. With respect to the rules of a trade union registered under this Act, the following provisions shall have effect:

(1) The rules of every such trade union shall contain provisions in respect of the several matters mentioned in the first schedule to this Act:

Trade Union Act 1871

(2) A copy of the rules shall be delivered by the trade union to every person on demand on payment of a sum not exceeding [£0.05].

COMMENTARY

The sum in square brackets was substituted by virtue of the Decimal Currency Acts 1969 and 1970.

Registered office of trade unions

15. Every trade union registered under this Act shall have a registered office to which all communications and notices may be addressed; if any trade union under this Act is in operation for seven days without having such an office, such trade union and every officer thereof shall each incur a penalty not exceeding [two hundred] pounds for every day during which it is so in operation.

Notice of the situation of such registered office, and of any change therein, shall be given to the registrar and recorded by him: until such notice is given the trade union shall not be deemed to have complied with the provisions of this Act.

COMMENTARY

The figure in square brackets was substituted by section 4 of the Industrial Relations Act 1990.

Annual returns to be prepared as registrar may direct

16. A general statement of the receipts, funds, effects, and expenditure of every trade union registered under this Act shall be transmitted to the registrar before the first day of June in every year, and shall show fully the assets and liabilities at the date, and the receipts and expenditure during the year preceding the date to which it is made out, of the trade union; and shall show separately the expenditure in respect of the several objects of the trade union, and shall be prepared and made out up to such date, in such form, and shall comprise such particulars, as the registrar may from time to time require; and every member of, and depositor in, any such trade union shall be entitled to receive, on application to the treasurer or secretary of that trade union, a copy of such general statement, without making any payment for the same.

Together with such general statement there shall be sent to the registrar a copy of all alterations of rules and new rules and changes of officers made by the trade union during the year preceding the date up to which the general statement is made out, and a copy of the rules of the trade union as they exist at that date.

Every trade union which fails to comply with or acts in contravention of this section, and also every officer of the trade union so failing, shall each be liable to a penalty not exceeding [five hundred] pounds for each offence.

Every person who wilfully makes or orders to be made any false entry in or any omission from any such general statement, or in or from the return of such copies of rules or alterations of rules, shall be liable to a penalty not exceeding [one thousand] pounds for each offence.

COMMENTARY

The figures in square brackets were substituted by section 4 of the Industrial Relations Act 1990.

Registrars

17. The [Registrar of Friendly Societies] shall be the [registrar] under this Act.

The [registrar] shall lay before [each House of the Oireachtas] annual reports with respect to the matters transacted by [the registrar] in pursuance of this Act.

COMMENTARY

The words in square brackets have been substituted by virtue of the Adaptation of Enactments Act 1922 and Orders made thereunder. See commentary to section 7 of the Trade Union Act 1913, *infra* at p. 57.

Circulating false copies of rules, etc. a misdemeanour

18. If any person with intent to mislead or defraud gives to any member of a trade union registered under this Act, or to any person intending or applying to become a member of such trade union, a copy of any rules or of any alterations or amendments of the same other than those respectively which exist for the time being, on the pretence that the same are the existing rules of such trade union, or that there are no other rules of such trade union, or if any person with the intent aforesaid gives a copy of any rules to any person on the pretence that such rules are the rules of a trade union registered under this Act which is not so registered, every person so offending shall be deemed guilty of a misdemeanour.

LEGAL PROCEEDINGS

Summary proceedings for offences, penalties, etc.

19. [All] offences and penalties under this Act may be prosecuted and recovered in manner directed by The Summary Jurisdiction Acts.

[Summary] orders under this Act may be made and enforced on complaint before a court of summary jurisdiction in manner provided by The Summary Jurisdiction Acts.

Provided as follows:

1. The "Court of Summary Jurisdiction," when hearing and determining an information or complaint, shall be constituted in some one of the following manners; that is to say,

(A) [...]
(B) In Ireland,
   [of a District Justice].

[...]
Provided that [...]—

2. The description of any offence under this Act in the words of such Act shall be sufficient in law.

3. Any exception, exemption, proviso, excuse, or qualification, whether it does or does not accompany the description of the offence in this Act, may be proved by the defendant, but need not be specified or negatived in the information, and if so specified or negatived, no proof in relation to the matters so specified or negatived shall be required on the part of the informant or prosecutor.

COMMENTARY

References to England and Scotland have been deleted and the reference to a District Justice has been substituted by virtue of sections 77 and 78 of the Courts of Justice Act 1924.

Appeal to quarter sessions

20. [If] any party feels aggrieved by any order or conviction made by a court of summary jurisdiction on determining any complaint or information under this Act, the party so aggrieved may appeal therefrom, subject to the conditions and regulations following:

(1) The appeal shall be made to [the Circuit Court] for the county or place in which the cause of appeal has arisen, holden not less than 15 days and not more than four months after the decision of the court from which the appeal is made:
(2) The appellant shall, within seven days after the cause of appeal has arisen, give notice to the other party and to the court of summary jurisdiction of his intention to appeal, and of the ground thereof:
(3) The appellant shall immediately after such notice enter into

a recognizance before a [District Justice or a Peace Commissioner] in the sum of 10 pounds, with two sufficient sureties in the sum of 10 pounds, conditioned personally to try such appeal, and to abide the judgment of the court thereon, and to pay such costs as may be awarded by the court:
(4) Where the appellant is in custody the [District Justice] may, if he think fit, on the appellant entering into such recognizance as aforesaid, release him from custody:
(5) The court of appeal may adjourn the appeal, and upon the hearing thereof they may confirm, reverse, or modify the decision of the court of summary jurisdiction, or remit the matter to the court of summary jurisdiction with the opinion of the court of appeal thereon, or make such other order in the matter as the court thinks just, and if the matter be remitted to the court of summary jurisdiction the said last-mentioned court shall thereupon re-hear and decide the information or complaint in accordance with the opinion of the said court of appeal. The court of appeal may also make such order as to costs to be paid by either party as the court thinks just.

COMMENTARY

Reference to England has been deleted. The reference to the Circuit Court in paragraph (1) has been substituted by virtue of section 51 of the Courts of Justice Act 1924. The reference to a District Justice or Peace Commissioner in paragraph (3) has been substituted by virtue of sections 77 and 88 of the Courts of Justice Act 1924. The reference to a District Justice in paragraph (4) has been substituted by virtue of section 77 of the Courts of Justice Act 1924, no substituted reference having been made to a Peace Commissioner in this paragraph for obvious reasons.

Appeal in Scotland as prescribed by 20 Geo. 2. c. 43

21. [...]

COMMENTARY

This section, which has since been repealed in the United Kingdom, was only applicable to Scotland.

Interested person not to act as a member of a court of appeal

22. A person who is a master, or father, son, or brother of a master, in the particular manufacture, trade, or business in or in connexion with which any offence under this Act is charged to have been committed shall not act as or as a member of a court of summary jurisdiction or appeal for the purposes of this Act.

Trade Union Act 1871

Definitions

Definitions. As to the term "Summary Jurisdiction Acts" and as to "trade union"

23. In this Act—

The term Summary Jurisdiction Acts means as follows:
[...].

As to Ireland, within the police district of Dublin metropolis, the Acts regulating the powers and duties of justices of the peace for such district, or of the police of such district, and elsewhere in Ireland, "The Petty Sessions (Ireland) Act, 1851," and any Act amending the same.
[...].

[The term "trade union" means such combination, whether temporary or permanent, for regulating the relations between workmen and masters, or between workmen and workmen, or between masters and masters, or for imposing restrictive conditions on the conduct of any trade or business, whether such combination would or would not, if the principal Act had not been passed, have been deemed to have been an unlawful combination by reason of some one or more of its purposes being in restraint of trade]: Provided that this Act shall not affect—

1. Any agreement between partners as to their own business;
2. Any agreement between an employer and those employed by him as to such employment;
3. Any agreement in consideration of the sale of the goodwill of a business or of instruction in any profession, trade, or handicraft.

COMMENTARY

References to England and Scotland have been deleted. The relevant Acts for "the police district of Dublin metropolis" are the Dublin Police Acts 1836, 1837, 1842 and 1859, as to which see Chapter 2 of the Law Reform Commission's Report on *Offences under the Dublin Police Acts and Related Offences* (LRC 14–1985). The Dublin metropolitan police district was eventually defined by the District Court (Areas) Order 1926 (S.R. & O. No. 52 of 1926) and was then enlarged by the District Court Districts (Dublin) Order 1945 (S.R. & O. No. 279 of 1945), the District Court Districts (Dublin) (Amendment) Order 1970 (S.I. No. 300 of 1970) and the District Court Districts (Dublin) (Amendment) Order 1982 (S.I. No. 88 of 1982).

The words in square brackets were substituted by section 16 of the Trade Union Act Amendment Act 1876. See also section 1(1) of the Trade Union Act 1913 which provides that the fact that a combination has under its constitution objects or powers other than statutory objects (which are defined in section 1(2) of the 1913 Act) shall not prevent the combination being a trade union for the purpose of the Trade Union Acts. In effect, therefore, the definition of trade union in section 2(1) of the 1913 Act supersedes the definition in this section.

Trade Union Act 1871

Repeal

Repeal of Trades Unions Funds Protection Act, 1869, as herein stated

24. The Trades Unions Funds Protection Act, 1869, is hereby repealed.

Provided that this repeal shall not affect—

(1) Anything duly done or suffered under the said Act:
(2) Any right or privilege acquired or any liability incurred under the said Act:
(3) Any penalty, forfeiture, or other punishment incurred in respect of any offence against the said Act:
(4) The institution of any investigation or legal proceeding or any other remedy for ascertaining, enforcing, recovering, or imposing any such liability, penalty, forfeiture, or punishment as aforesaid.

Schedules

First Schedule

Of Matters to be provided for by the Rules of Trade Unions Registered under this Act

See 18 & 19 Vict. c. 63. s. 25

1. The name of the trade union and place of meeting for the business of the trade union.

2. The whole of the objects for which the trade union is to be established, the purposes for which the funds thereof shall be applicable, and the conditions under which any member may become entitled to any benefit assured thereby, and the fines and forfeitures to be imposed on any member of such trade union.

3. The manner of making, altering, amending, and rescinding rules.

4. A provision for the appointment and removal of a general committee of management, of a trustee or trustees, treasurer, and other officers.

5. A provision for the investment of the funds, and for an annual or periodical audit of accounts.

6. The inspection of the books and names of members of the trade union by every person having an interest in the funds of the trade union.

Trade Union Act 1871

COMMENTARY

See also section 14(5) of the Industrial Relations Act 1990, which extends this Schedule to include the requirement that the rules of every trade union must contain certain provisions relating to balloting in respect of strikes and other industrial action. Authorised trade unions are further required by section 12(1)(a) of the Trade Union Act 1941 to include in their rules "provisions specifying the conditions of entry into and cessor of membership."

Second Schedule

Maximum Fees

	£	s.	d.
For registering trade union	1	0	0
For registering alterations in rules	0	10	0
For inspection of documents	0	2	6

COMMENTARY

By virtue of the Decimal Currency Acts 1969 and 1970, the maximum fee for registering alterations in rules should be read as £0.50p and that for inspection of documents should be read as £0.12p. The current fees in respect of these and other matters are set out in Part 1 of the Schedule to the Trade Union (Fees) Regulations 1983 (S.I. No. 292 of 1983), reproduced *infra*, at p. 115.

CONSPIRACY AND PROTECTION OF PROPERTY ACT 1875

(*38 & 39 Vict. c. 86*)

An Act for amending the Law relating to Conspiracy, and to the Protection of Property, and for other purposes.

[*13 August 1875*]

Short title

1. This Act may be cited as "The Conspiracy and Protection of Property Act 1875."

2. [...]

COMMENTARY

This section was repealed by the Statute Law Revision Act 1894.

CONSPIRACY, AND PROTECTION OF PROPERTY

Amendment of law as to conspiracy in trade disputes

3. [...]

Nothing in this section shall exempt from punishment any persons guilty of a conspiracy for which a punishment is awarded by any Act of Parliament.

Nothing in this section shall affect the law relating to riot, unlawful assembly, breach of the peace, or sedition, or any offence against the State [...].

A crime for the purposes of this section means an offence punishable on indictment, or an offence which is punishable on summary conviction, and for the commission of which the offender is liable under the statute making the offence punishable to be imprisoned either absolutely or at the discretion of the court as an alternative for some other punishment.

Where a person is convicted of any such agreement or combination as aforesaid to do or procure to be done an act which is punishable only on summary conviction, and is sentenced to imprisonment, the imprisonment shall not exceed three months, or such longer time, if any, as may have been prescribed by the statute for the punishment of the said act when committed by one person.

CONSPIRACY AND PROTECTION OF PROPERTY ACT 1875

COMMENTARY

Section 10(3) of the Industrial Relations Act 1990 provides that this section and subsections (1) and (2) of section 10 of the 1990 Act shall be construed together as one section.

The words in square brackets before paragraph 1 were repealed by section 7 of the Industrial Relations Act 1990. The words in square brackets in paragraph 2, namely "or the Sovereign" have been deleted as surplusage. By virtue of section 5(4) of the Adaptation of Enactments Act 1922 the reference to "Act of Parliament" in this section, and in sections 4 and 21 of this Act, shall be taken as meaning and including either "Act of the British Parliament" or "Act of the Oireachtas" as the case may require.

Breach of contract by persons employed in supply of gas or water

4. Where a person employed by a municipal authority or by any company or contractor upon whom is imposed by Act of Parliament the duty, or who have otherwise assumed the duty of supplying any city, borough, town, or place, or any part thereof, with gas or water, wilfully and maliciously breaks a contract of service with that authority or company or contractor, knowing or having reasonable cause to believe that the probable consequences of his so doing, either alone or in combination with others, will be to deprive the inhabitants of that city, borough, town, place, or part, wholly or to a great extent of their supply of gas or water, he shall on conviction thereof by a court of summary jurisdiction, or on indictment as herein-after mentioned, be liable either to pay a penalty not exceeding twenty pounds or to be imprisoned for a term not exceeding three months, with or without hard labour.

Every such municipal authority, company, or contractor as is mentioned in this section shall cause to be posted up, at the gasworks or waterworks, as the case may be, belonging to such authority or company or contractor, a printed copy of this section in some conspicuous place where the same may be conveniently read by the persons employed, and as often as such copy becomes defaced, obliterated, or destroyed, shall cause it to be renewed with all reasonable despatch.

If any municipal authority or company or contractor make default in complying with the provisions of this section in relation to such notice as aforesaid, they or he shall incur on summary conviction a penalty not exceeding five pounds for every day during which such default continues, and every person who unlawfully injures, defaces, or covers up any notice so posted up as aforesaid in pursuance of this Act, shall be liable on summary conviction to a penalty not exceeding [two pounds].

COMMENTARY

Section 110 of the Electricity Supply Act 1927 extends this section to persons employed by the Electricity Supply Board or by any authorised undertaker or permitted undertaker in like manner as it applies to persons in this section, with the substitution of references to electricity for the references to gas or water.

The sum in square brackets was substituted by virtue of the Decimal Currency Acts 1969 and 1970.

Breach of contract involving injury to persons or property

5. Where any person wilfully and maliciously breaks a contract of service or of hiring, knowing or having reasonable cause to believe that the probable consequences of his so doing, either alone or in combination with others, will be to endanger human life, or cause serious bodily injury, or to expose valuable property whether real or personal to destruction or serious injury, he shall on conviction thereof by a court of summary jurisdiction, or on indictment as herein-after mentioned, be liable either to pay a penalty not exceeding twenty pounds, or to be imprisoned for a term not exceeding three months, with or without hard labour.

MISCELLANEOUS

Penalty for neglect by master to provide food, clothing, etc. for servant or apprentice

6. Where a master, being legally liable to provide for his servant or apprentice necessary food, clothing, medical aid, or lodging, wilfully and without lawful excuse refuses or neglects to provide the same, whereby the health of the servant or apprentice is or is likely to be seriously or permanently injured, he shall on summary conviction be liable either to pay a penalty not exceeding twenty pounds, or to be imprisoned for a term not exceeding six months, with or without hard labour.

Penalty for intimidation or annoyance by violence or otherwise

7. Every person who, with a view to compel any other person to abstain from doing or to do any act which such other person has a legal right to do or abstain from doing, wrongfully and without legal authority,—

1. Uses violence to or intimidates such other person or his wife or children, or injures his property; or
2. Persistently follows such other person about from place to place; or
3. Hides any tools, clothes, or other property owned or used

by such other person, or deprives him of or hinders him in the use thereof; or,
4. Watches or besets the house or other place where such other person resides, or works, or carries on business, or happens to be, or the approach to such house or place; or,
5. Follows such other person with two or more other persons in a disorderly manner in or through any street or road,

shall, on conviction thereof by a court of summary jurisdiction, or on indictment as herein-after mentioned, be liable either to pay a penalty not exceeding twenty pounds, or to be imprisoned for a term not exceeding three months, with or without hard labour. [...].

COMMENTARY

In *Ward Lock & Co.* v. *Operative Printers Assistants' Society* (1906) 22 T.L.R. 327, the Court of Appeal held that this section "legalises nothing, and it renders nothing wrongful that was not so before." Its object, *per* Fletcher Moulton L.J. at 329, was "solely to visit certain selected classes of acts which were previously wrongful, *i.e.* were at least civil torts, with penal consequences capable of being summarily inflicted." See, however, the contrasting view of Lindley L.J. in *J. Lyons & Sons* v. *Wilkins* [1899] 1 Ch. 255, 267. Section 7 is analysed in detail in Kerr and Whyte, *Irish Trade Union Law* (1985) pp. 289–293. The sentence limit of three months has been described by His Honour Judge Roe as "absurd": see *Irish Times*, May 13, 1988.

In *Attorney General* v. *O'Brien* (1936) 70 I.L.T.R. 101 it was held that the section created only one offence, the five subheadings merely indicating various methods of committing the offence. In *R.* v. *Jones* [1974] I.C.R. 310, 318, James L.J., whilst not seeking to define "intimidation" in subheading 1 exhaustively, said that it included "putting persons in fear by the exhibition of force or violence, or the threat of force or violence, and there is no limitation restricting the meaning to cases of violence or threats of violence to the person." In *Attorney General* v. *O'Brien*, Kennedy C.J. said that "watching" in subheading 4 "did not necessarily connote or involve long duration, or, in fact, any specific duration of time." In *Galt* v. *Philp* [1984] I.R.L.R. 156, it was held that "watching or besetting" was not confined to the maintenance of an external watch. A "sit-in" could thus constitute an offence under the section.

By virtue of the Offences Against the State (Scheduled Offences) (No. 2) Order 1972 (S.I. No. 282 of 1972), offences under section 7 are "scheduled offences" under section 36 of the Offences Against the State Act 1939.

For all practical purposes, there is no difference now in the treatment between persons who have been sentenced to imprisonment where hard labour is included in the sentence. See Minister for Justice at 196 *Dáil Debates* Col. 3217 (July 25, 1962).

The words in square brackets were repealed by section 2(2) of the Trade Disputes Act 1906.

Reduction of penalties

8. Where in any Act relating to employers or workmen a pecuniary penalty is imposed in respect of any offence under such Act, and no power is given to reduce such penalty, the justices or court having jurisdiction in respect of such offence may, if they think it just so to do, impose by way of penalty in respect of such offence any sum not less than one fourth of the penalty imposed by such Act.

Legal Proceedings

Power for offender under this Act to be tried on indictment and not by court of summary jurisdiction

9. Where a person is accused before a court of summary jurisdiction of any offence made punishable by this Act, and for which a penalty amounting to twenty pounds, or imprisonment, is imposed, the accused may, on appearing before the court of summary jurisdiction, declare that he objects to being tried for such offence by a court of summary jurisdiction, and thereupon the court of summary jurisdiction may deal with the case in all respects as if the accused were charged with an indictable offence and not an offence punishable on summary conviction, and the offence may be prosecuted on indictment accordingly.

Proceedings before court of summary jurisdiction

10. Every offence under this Act which is made punishable on conviction by a court of summary jurisdiction or on summary conviction, and every penalty under this Act recoverable on summary conviction, may be prosecuted and recovered in manner provided by the Summary Jurisdiction Act.

Regulations as to evidence

11. Provided, that upon the hearing and determining of any indictment or information under sections four, five and six of this Act, the respective parties to the contract of service, their husbands or wives shall be deemed and considered as competent witnesses.

COMMENTARY

Although sections 4, 5 and 6 of the Act are not listed in the Schedule to the Criminal Justice (Evidence) Act 1924, the effect of the decision of the Supreme Court in *McGonagle v. McGonagle* [1951] I.R. 12 is to preserve the spousal competency created by this section. As to whether the spouse is a compellable witness, see the discussion of the Law Reform Commission's Report on the *Competence and Compellability of Spouses as Witnesses* (LRC 13–1985) by Jackson, (1986) 8 *D.U.L.J.* (n.s.) 46 and see also Jackson, (1989) 11 *D.U.L.J.* (n.s.) 149.

Appeal to quarter sessions

12. [If] any party feels aggrieved by any conviction made by a court of summary jurisdiction on determining any information under this Act, the party so aggrieved may appeal therefrom, subject to the conditions and regulations following:

(1) The appeal shall be made to [the Circuit Court] for the county or place in which the cause of appeal has arisen, holden not less than fifteen days and not more than four months after the decision of the court from which the appeal is made:

(2) The appellant shall, within seven days after the cause of appeal has arisen, give notice to the other party and to the court of summary jurisdiction of his intention to appeal, and of the ground thereof:

(3) The appellant shall immediately after such notice enter into a recognizance before a [District Justice or a Peace Commissioner], with or without sureties, conditioned personally to try such appeal, and to abide the judgment of the court thereon, and to pay such costs as may be awarded by the court:

(4) Where the appellant is in custody the [District Justice] may, if he think fit, on the appellant entering into such recognizance as aforesaid, release him from custody:

(5) The court of appeal may adjourn the appeal, and upon the hearing thereof they may confirm, reverse, or modify the decision of the court of summary jurisdiction, or remit the matter to the court of summary jurisdiction with the opinion of the court of appeal thereon, or make such other order in the matter as the court thinks just, and if the matter be remitted to the court of summary jurisdiction the said last mentioned court shall thereupon re-hear and decide the information in accordance with the opinion of the said court of appeal. The court of appeal may also make such order as to costs to be paid by either party as the court thinks just.

COMMENTARY

Reference to England has been deleted and the references to the Circuit Court, a District Justice and a Peace Commissioner have been substituted by virtue of sections 51, 77, 78 and 88 of the Courts of Justice Act 1924.

Definitions

General definitions: "The Summary Jurisdiction Act." "Court of summary jurisdiction"

13. [...]

COMMENTARY

These definitions have been omitted, as applicable only to England.

Definitions of "municipal authority" and "public company"

14. [...]

COMMENTARY

These definitions have been omitted, as applicable only to England.

"Maliciously" in this Act construed as in Malicious Injuries to Property Act

15. The word "maliciously" used in reference to any offence under this Act shall be construed in the same manner as it is required by the fifty-eighth section of the Act relating to malicious injuries to property, that is to say, the Act of the session of the twenty-fourth and twenty-fifth years of the reign of Her present Majesty, chapter ninety-seven, to be construed in reference to any offence committed under such last-mentioned Act.

COMMENTARY

The statute referred to in this section is the Malicious Injuries Act 1861 under which "maliciously" was defined in terms of an act which is "intentional, illegal and wrongful": see *McDowell v. Dublin Corporation* [1903] 2 I.R. 541. The fact that there was no personal animosity or spite was irrelevant. See generally Greer and Mitchell, *Compensation for Criminal Damage to Property* (1982) pp. 47–52.

SAVING CLAUSE

Saving as to sea service

16. Nothing in this Act shall apply to seamen or to apprentices to the sea service.

COMMENTARY

"Seamen" was defined in *R. v. Lynch* [1898] 1 Q.B. 61 as meaning persons employed or engaged on board ship, so that the section does not exempt persons whose calling or occupation is the sea but who are not actually so employed or engaged. In *Kennedy v. Cowie* [1891] 1 Q.B. 771 it was held that this section meant only that the punishments prescribed by the Act were not to fall on seamen. The case of an offence against a seaman by a person who was not a seaman was therefore not excluded.

REPEAL

Repeal of Acts

17. On and after the commencement of this Act, there shall be repealed:—

CONSPIRACY AND PROTECTION OF PROPERTY ACT 1875

I. The Act of the session of the thirty-fourth and thirty-fifth years of the reign of Her present Majesty, chapter thirty-two, intituled "An Act to amend the Criminal Law relating to violence, threats, and molestation"; and

II. "The Master and Servant Act, 1867," and the enactments specified in the First Schedule to that Act, with the exceptions following as to the enactments in such Schedule; (that is to say,)

(1) Except so much of sections one and two of the Act passed in the thirty-third year of the reign of King George the Third, chapter fifty-five, intituled "An Act to authorise justices of the peace to impose fines upon constables, overseers, and other peace or parish officers for neglect of duty, and on masters of apprentices for ill-usage of such their apprentice; and also to make provision for the execution of warrants of distress granted by magistrates," as relates to constables, overseers, and other peace or parish officers; and

(2) Except so much of sections five and six of an Act passed in the fifty-ninth year of the reign of King George the Third, chapter ninety-two, intituled "An Act to enable justices of the peace in Ireland to act as such, in certain cases, out of the limits of the counties in which they actually are; to make provision for the execution of warrants of distress granted by them; and to authorise them to impose fines upon constables and other officers for neglect of duty, and on masters for ill-usage of their apprentices," as relates to constables and other peace or parish officers; and

(3) Except the Act of the session of the fifth and sixth years of the reign of Her present Majesty, chapter seven, intituled "An Act to explain the Acts for the better regulation of certain apprentices;" and

(4) Except sub-sections one, two, three, and five of section sixteen of "The Summary Jurisdiction (Ireland) Act, 1851," relating to certain disputes between employers and the persons employed by them; and

III. Also there shall be repealed the following enactments making breaches of contract criminal, and relating to the recovery of wages by summary procedure; (that is to say,)

(a) An Act passed in the fifth year of the reign of Queen Elizabeth, chapter four, and intituled "An Act touching dyvers orders for artificers, labourers, servantes of husbandrye, and apprentices"; and

(b) So much of section two of an Act passed in the twelfth

year of King George the First, chapter thirty-four, and intituled "An Act to prevent unlawful combination of workmen employed in the woollen manufactures, and for better payment of their wages," as relates to departing from service and quitting or returning work before it is finished; and

(c) Section twenty of an Act passed in the fifth year of King George the Third, chapter fifty-one, the title of which begins with the words "An Act for repealing several Laws relating to the manufacture of woollen cloth in the county of York," and ends with the words "for preserving the credit of the said manufacture at the foreign market"; and

(d) An Act passed in the nineteenth year of King George the Third, chapter forty-nine, and intituled "An Act to prevent abuses in the payment of wages to persons employed in the bone and thread lace manufactory"; and

(e) Sections eighteen and twenty-three of an Act passed in the session of the third and fourth years of Her present Majesty, chapter ninety-one, intituled "An Act for the more effectual prevention of frauds and abuses committed by weavers, sewers, and other persons employed in the linen, hempen, union, cotton, silk, and woollen manufactures in Ireland, and for the better payment of their wages, for one year, and from thence to the end of the next session of Parliament"; and

(f) Section seventeen of an Act passed in the session of the sixth and seventh years of Her present Majesty, chapter forty, the title of which begins with the words "An Act to amend the Laws," and ends with the words "workmen engaged therein"; and

(g) Section seven of an Act passed in the session of the eighth and ninth years of Her present Majesty, chapter one hundred and twenty-eight, and intituled "An Act to make further regulations respecting the tickets of work to be delivered to silk weavers in certain cases."

Provided that,—

(1) Any order for wages or further sum of compensation in addition to wages made in pursuance of section sixteen of "The Summary Jurisdiction (Ireland) Act, 1851," may be enforced in like manner as if it were an order made by a court of summary jurisdiction in pursuance of the Employers and Workmen Act, 1875, and not otherwise; and

(2) The repeal enacted by this section shall not affect—
- (a) Anything duly done or suffered, or any right or liability acquired or incurred under any enactment hereby repealed; or
- (b) Any penalty, forfeiture, or punishment incurred in respect of any offence committed against any enactment hereby repealed; or
- (c) Any investigation, legal proceeding, or remedy in respect of any such right, liability, penalty, forfeiture, or punishment as aforesaid; and any such investigation, legal proceeding, and remedy may be carried on as if this Act had not passed.

COMMENTARY

Paragraph III(e)

Section 30 of this Act (the Textile Manufactures (Ireland) Act 1840) was repealed by the Statute Law Revision Act 1983 and section 32 was repealed by the Statute Law Revision Act 1894.

Paragraph III(g)

The remainder of this Act was repealed by the Statute Law Revision Act 1983.

APPLICATION OF ACT TO SCOTLAND

Application to Scotland: Definitions
18. [...]

COMMENTARY

This section has been omitted as applicable only to Scotland.

Recovery of penalties, etc. in Scotland
19. [...]

COMMENTARY

This section has been omitted as applicable only to Scotland.

Appeal in Scotland as prescribed by 20 Geo. 2. c. 43
20. [...]

COMMENTARY

This section has been omitted as applicable only to Scotland.

APPLICATION OF ACT TO IRELAND

Application to Ireland
21. This Act shall extend to Ireland, with the modifications following; that is to say,

Conspiracy and Protection of Property Act 1875

The expression "The Summary Jurisdiction Act" shall be construed to mean, as regards the police district of Dublin metropolis, the Acts regulating the powers and duties of justices of the peace for such district; and elsewhere in Ireland, the Petty Sessions (Ireland) Act, 1851, and any Acts amending the same:

The expression "court of summary jurisdiction" shall be construed to mean [a District Justice]:

The expression "municipal authority" shall be construed to mean the town council of any borough for the time being subject to the Act of the session of the third and fourth years of the reign of Her present Majesty, chapter one hundred and eight, entitled "An Act for the Regulation of Municipal Corporations in Ireland," and any commissioners invested by any general or local Act of Parliament, with power of improving, cleansing, lighting, or paving any town or township.

COMMENTARY

The relevant Acts for "the police district of Dublin metropolis" are the Dublin Police Acts 1836, 1837, 1842 and 1859. See further the commentary to section 23 of the Trade Union Act 1871, *supra* at p. 13.

The short title of the Act referred to here is the Municipal Corporations (Ireland) Act 1840 which is still in force, although it has been considerably amended.

TRADE UNION ACT AMENDMENT ACT 1876

(39 & 40 Vict, c. 22)

An Act to amend the Trade Union Act 1871.

[30 June 1876]

Construction and short title

1. This Act and the Trade Union Act, 1871, herein-after termed the principal Act, shall be construed as one Act, and may be cited together as the "Trade Union Acts, 1871 and 1876," and this Act may be cited separately as the "Trade Union Act Amendment Act, 1876."

Trade unions to be within [ss.62–67] of Friendly Societies Act, [1896]

2. Notwithstanding anything in section five of the principal Act contained, a trade union, whether registered or unregistered, which insures or pays money on the death of a child under ten years of age shall be deemed to be within the provisions of [sections 62–67 of the Friendly Societies Act 1896].

COMMENTARY

The words in square brackets have been substituted by virtue of the repeal of the Friendly Societies Act 1875 by the 1896 Act and the replacement of section 28 with sections 62–67.

Amendment of s.8 of principal Act

3. [...]

COMMENTARY

These amendments have been incorporated into the 1871 Act, *supra* at p. 3.

Provision in case of absence, etc. of trustee

4. When any person, being or having been a trustee of a trade union or of any branch of a trade union, and whether appointed before or after the legal establishment thereof, in whose name any stock belonging to such union or branch transferable at the [...] Bank of Ireland is standing, either jointly with another or others, or solely, is absent from [...] Ireland [...], or becomes bankrupt, or files any petition, or executes any deed for liquidation of his affairs by assignment or arrangement or for composition with his creditors, or becomes a lunatic, or is dead, or has been removed from his office of trustee, or if it be unknown whether such person is living or dead, the registrar, on application in writing from the secretary and three members of the union or branch, and on proof satisfactory to him, may direct the transfer of the stock into the names of any other persons as trustees for the union or branch; and such transfer shall be made by the surviving or continuing trustees, and if there be no such trustee, or if such trustees refuse or be unable to make such transfer, and the registrar so direct, then by the Accountant-General or Deputy or Assistant Accountant-General of the [...] Bank of Ireland, [...]; and [...] the [...] Bank of Ireland [is] hereby indemnified for anything done by [it] or any of [its] officers in pursuance of this provision against any claim or demand of any person injuriously affected thereby.

COMMENTARY

References to the Bank of England have been deleted. Certain words were also deleted by the Statute Law Revision Act 1894. By virtue of the Schedule to the Interpretation Act 1937 the expression "Bank of Ireland" means either, as the context requires, the Governor and Company of the Bank of Ireland or the bank of the said Governor and Company.

Jurisdiction in offences

5. The jurisdiction conferred in the case of certain offences by section twelve of the principal Act upon the court of summary jurisdiction for the place in which the registered office of a trade union is situate may be exercised either by that court or by the court of summary jurisdiction for the place where the offence has been committed.

Registry of unions doing business in more than one country

6. [...]

COMMENTARY

This section was held to be no longer applicable to Saorstat Éireann after the passing of the 1922 Constitution since the whole basis of the section (trade unions carrying on business in more than one country) was a legislative union between Britain and Ireland: *Irish Transport & General Workers' Union* v. *Green* [1936] I.R. 471, 478, *per* Meredith J.

TRADE UNION ACT AMENDMENT ACT 1876

Life Assurance Companies Acts not to apply to registered unions

7. [...]

COMMENTARY

This section was repealed by the Assurance Companies Act 1909.

Withdrawal or cancelling of certificate

8. No certificate of registration of a trade union shall be withdrawn or cancelled otherwise than be the [Registrar of Friendly Societies] and in the following cases:

(1) At the request of the trade union to be evidenced in such manner as [the registrar] shall from time to time direct:
(2) On proof to his satisfaction that a certificate of registration has been obtained by fraud or mistake, or that the registration of the trade union has become void under section six of the Trade Union Act, 1871, or that such trade union has wilfully and after notice from [the registrar], violated any of the provisions of the Trade Union Acts, or has ceased to exist.

Not less than two months previous notice in writing, specifying briefly the ground of any proposed withdrawal or cancelling of certificate (unless where the same is shown to have become void as aforesaid, in which case it shall be the duty of the [registrar] to cancel the same forthwith) shall be given by the [registrar] to a trade union before the certificate of registration of the same can be withdrawn or cancelled (except at its request).

A trade union whose certificate of registration has been withdrawn or cancelled shall, from the time of such withdrawal or cancelling, absolutely cease to enjoy as such the privileges of a registered trade union, but without prejudice to any liability actually incurred by such trade union, which may be enforced against the same as if such withdrawal or cancelling had not taken place.

COMMENTARY

The words in square brackets in this section have been deleted or substituted by virtue of the Registrar of Friendly Societies (Adaptation) Order 1926 made by the Executive Council under section 12 of the Adaptation of Enactments Act 1922 on October 4, 1926. See also the commentary to section 7 of the Trade Union Act 1913, *infra* at p. 57.

Membership of minors

9. A person under the age of [eighteen], but above the age of

sixteen, may be a member of a trade union, unless provision be made in the rules thereof to the contrary, and may, subject to the rules of the trade union, enjoy all the rights of a member except as herein provided, and execute all instruments and give all acquittances necessary to be executed or given under the rules, but shall not be a member of the committee of management, trustee, or treasurer of the trade union.

COMMENTARY

The figure in square brackets has been substituted by virtue of section 2(3) of the Age of Majority Act 1985.

Nomination

10. A member of a trade union not being under the age of sixteen years may, by writing under his hand, delivered at, or sent to, the registered office of the trade union, nominate any person not being an officer or servant of the trade union (unless such officer or servant is the husband, wife, father, mother, child, brother, sister, nephew, or niece of the nominator), to whom any moneys payable on the death of such member not exceeding [one hundred] pounds shall be paid at his decease, and may from time to time revoke or vary such nomination by a writing under his hand similarly delivered or sent; and on receiving satisfactory proof of the death of a nominator, the trade union shall pay to the nominee the amount due to the deceased member not exceeding the sum aforesaid.

COMMENTARY

The figure in square brackets was substituted by section 3 of the Provident Nominations and Small Intestacies Act 1883.

Change of name

11. [...]

COMMENTARY

This section was repealed by section 16 of the Trade Union Act 1975.

Amalgamation

12. [...]

COMMENTARY

This section was repealed by section 16 of the Trade Union Act 1975.

Registration of changes of names and amalgamations

13. [...]

Trade Union Act Amendment Act 1876

COMMENTARY

This section was repealed by section 16 of the Trade Union Act 1975.

Dissolution

14. The rules of every trade union shall provide for the manner of dissolving the same, and notice of every dissolution of a trade union under the hand of the secretary and seven members of the same, shall be sent within fourteen days thereafter to the [registrar] and shall be registered by [him]: Provided, that the rules of any trade union registered before the passing of this Act shall not be invalidated by the absence of a provision for dissolution.

COMMENTARY

The words in square brackets in this section have been deleted or substituted by virtue of the Registrar of Friendly Societies (Adaptation) Order 1926 made by the Executive Council under section 12 of the Adaptation of Enactments Act 1922 on October 4, 1926. See also the commentary to section 7 of the Trade Union Act 1913, *infra* at p. 57.

Penalty for failure to give notice

15. A trade union which fails to give any notice or send any document which it is required by this Act to give or send, and every officer or other person bound by the rules thereof to give or send the same, or if there be no such officer, then every member of the committee of management of the union, unless proved to have been ignorant of, or to have attempted to prevent the omission to give or send the same, is liable to a penalty of not less than one pound and not more than five pounds, recoverable at the suit of the [registrar], or of any person aggrieved, and to an additional penalty of the like amount for each week during which the omission continues.

COMMENTARY

The words in square brackets in this section have been deleted or substituted by virtue of the Registrar of Friendly Societies (Adaptation) Order 1926 made by the Executive Council under section 12 of the Adaptation of Enactments Act 1922 on October 4, 1926. See also the commentary to section 7 of the Trade Union Act 1913, *infra* at p. 57.

Definition of "trade union" altered

16. [...]

COMMENTARY

This section amends section 23 of the Trade Union Act 1871, *supra* at p. 12.

REGULATIONS AS TO THE REGISTRATION OF TRADE UNIONS DATED NOVEMBER 1, 1876

(1) In the following Regulations and Forms the [term "registrar" means the Registrar of Friendly Societies].

COMMENTARY

The words in square brackets have been substituted by virtue of the Registrar of Friendly Societies (Adaptation) Order 1926 made by the Executive Council under section 12 of the Adaptation of Enactments Act 1922 on October 4, 1926. The regulations and the forms subjoined thereto have been consequently amended throughout.

(2) The registrar shall not register a trade union under a name identical with that of any other existing trade union known to him, whether registered or not registered, or so nearly resembling such name as to be likely to deceive the members or the public.

(3) Upon an application for the registration of a trade union which is already in operation, the registrar, if he has reason to believe that the applicants have not been duly authorised by such trade union to make the same, may, for the purpose of ascertaining the fact, require from the applicants such evidence as may seem to him necessary.

(4) Application for registry of a trade union shall be made in Form A subjoined to these regulations, and shall be accompanied by two printed copies of the rules, marked and signed, as mentioned in the said form.

(5) The certificate of registry of a trade union shall be in Form B subjoined to these Regulations.

(6) An alteration of the rules of a trade union may be either—

(a) A partial alteration, consisting of the addition of a new rule or part of a rule or rules to the existing rules, or of the substitution of a new rule or part of a rule or rules for any of the existing rules, or of a rescission of any of the existing rules or any part thereof without any substitution or of more than one or all of those modes; or,

(b) A complete alteration consisting of the substitution of an entire set of rules for the existing set of rules.

COMMENTARY

The Registrar of Friendly Societies has recommended that, in the case of any major partial alteration of rules, Press Notices should appear in a national newspaper or newspapers prior to the ballot advising members of the same and that voting procedures should be fully supervised by an independent auditor (see paragraph 3.6 of the *Report of the Registrar of Friendly Societies 1985–86*).

(7) An application for the registration of a partial alteration of rules must be made by seven members of the trade union, and must be made in the Form C annexed hereto, and must be accompanied by a statutory declaration in Form D hereto annexed, and by a printed copy of the existing rules, and by the following documents:—

(a) If the partial alteration consists of the addition or substitution of a new rule or part of a rule or rules, two copies of such rule or part of a rule or rules, each copy being marked O and signed by each of the applicants.

(b) If the partial alteration consists of the rescission of any of the rules without any substitution, two copies of the resolution for such rescission, each copy being marked O and signed by each of the applicants.

The registrar, before registering the partial alteration of rules, shall ascertain that the rules of the trade union, if altered in accordance with the proposed partial alteration, will provide for all the matters required by the above-mentioned Acts to be provided for by the rules of a registered trade union.

(8) The certificate of registry of a partial alteration shall be in Form E annexed hereto, and shall be delivered to the applicants, attached to one of the copies of the new rule or rules, or, when the alteration consists of rescission merely, attached to the old set of rules.

(9) An application for the registration of a complete alteration of rules shall be made by seven members of the trade union, and shall be in Form F annexed hereto, and must be accompanied by a statutory declaration in Form D annexed hereto, and by a printed copy of the existing rules and by two printed copies of the new rules, each copy being marked P and signed by each of the applicants; and the registrar before registering the new set of rules shall ascertain that it provides for all matters which, by the above-mentioned Acts, are to be provided for by the rules of a registered trade union.

(10) The certificate of registry of a complete alteration of rules shall be in Form G annexed hereto, and shall be delivered to the applicants attached to one of the copies of the new set of rules.

RECORDING OF RULES ALREADY REGISTERED

(11) [...]

Regulations Dated November 1, 1876

COMMENTARY

The words in square brackets have been deleted consequent upon the decision of Meredith J. in *Irish Transport & General Workers' Union* v. *Green* [1936] I.R. 471 that section 6 of the 1876 Act was not applicable to Saorstat Éireann. See commentary to section 6 of the 1876 Act, *supra* at p. 28. Forms H and I have consequently also been omitted.

Withdrawal or Cancelling of Certificate of Registration

(12) Every request by a trade union for withdrawal or cancelling of its certificate of registration shall be sent to the [registrar] in Form J annexed hereto.

(13) Notice before withdrawal or cancelling of certificate, where required, shall be in Form K annexed hereto.

(14) The withdrawal or cancelling of certificate shall be in Form L annexed hereto.

Registered Office

(15) Notice of the situation of the registered office of a trade union, and of any change therein, shall be given to the registrar in form M annexed hereto.
 [(15a)...]
 [(15b)...]

COMMENTARY

Regulations 15a and 15b were inserted by Regulations as to the Registration of Trade Unions dated April 29, 1890, but since they concern matters arising under section 6 of the Trade Union Act Amendment Act 1876 they have been omitted. See commentary to section 6 of the 1876 Act, *supra* at p. 28.

Change of Name

(16) The application for approval, and notice of change of name of a trade union shall be in Form N annexed hereto, and shall be sent in duplicate, accompanied by a statutory declaration in Form O annexed hereto, to the [registrar]. The [registrar], before approving the change of name, shall ascertain that the new name is not identical with that of any existing trade union known to him, or so nearly resembling the same as to be calculated to deceive; and if the change of name be approved, the word "approved" shall be written at the foot or end of each copy of the application, and the same shall be signed by the [registrar].

Regulations Dated November 1, 1876

Transfer of Stock

(17) Every application to the registrar to direct a transfer of stock shall follow, as near as may be, Form P annexed hereto, and shall be accompanied by a statutory declaration in Form Q annexed hereto, or as near thereto as the facts admit, and by the certificate of the stock in respect of which the application is made.

(18) Before making the application, the trade union shall submit to the registrar for examination a draft copy, on foolscap paper, written on one side only, of the proposed application and declaration.

(19) The registrar, before directing the transfer, may require further proof of any statement in the application.

(20) The registrar shall give a direction in Form R annexed hereto, so framed in each case as to suit the particular circumstances, and shall register the same and deliver the same to the applicants endorsed with the word "registered," and duly authenticated.

Dissolution

(21) When a trade union is dissolved, notice of the dissolution shall be given to the [registrar] in duplicate in Form S annexed hereto, and the [registrar] shall return one copy to the trade union, endorsed with the word "registered," and duly authenticated.

Amalgamation

(22) [...]

COMMENTARY

The words in square brackets have been deleted by virtue of the repeal of sections 11 to 13 of the Trade Union Act Amendment Act 1876 by section 16 of the Trade Union Act 1975. Forms T and U have consequently also been omitted.

Nominations

(23) Every registered trade union shall keep a record or register of all nominations made by the members, and of all revocations and variations of the same, and for the recording or registering of every such nomination, revocation, or variation the rules of the trade union may require the member nominating to pay a sum not exceeding threepence.

Regulations Dated November 1, 1876

Fees

(24) [...].

COMMENTARY

The words in square brackets were revoked by the Trade Union (Fees) Regulations 1978 (S.I. No. 86 of 1978).

Authentication of Documents by Registrar

(25) Every document under the Trade Union Acts 1871 and 1876, bearing the [signature of the registrar] shall be deemed to be duly authenticated for the purposes of the said Acts and the regulations made thereunder.

Form A—Reg. 4

Trade Union Acts, 1871 and 1876, 34 & 35 Vict. c. 31 and 39 & 40 Vict. c. 22.

APPLICATION FOR REGISTRY OF TRADE UNION

1. This application is made by the seven persons whose names are subscribed at the foot hereof.

2. The name under which it is proposed that the trade union on behalf of which this application is made shall be registered is _____ , as set forth in Rule No. _____ .
To the best of our belief there is no other existing trade union, whether registered or not registered, the name of which is identical with the proposed name or so nearly resembles the same as to cause confusion.

3. The place of meeting for the business of the [*Name of Trade Union*], and the office to which all communications and notices may be addressed, is at _____ , as set forth in Rule No. _____ .

4. The [*Name of Trade Union*] was established on the _____ day of _____ .

5. The whole of the objects for which the [*Name of Trade Union*] is established and the purposes for which the funds thereof are applicable are set forth in Rule No. _____ .

6. The conditions under which members may become entitled to benefits assured are set forth in Rule No. _____ .

7. The fines and forfeitures to be imposed on members are set forth in Rule No. _____ .

Regulations Dated November 1, 1876

8. The manner of making, altering, amending, and rescinding rules is set forth in Rule No. _____ .

9. The provision for the appointment and removal of a general committee of management, of trustee or trustees, treasurer, and other officers, is set forth in Rule No. _____ .

10. The provision for the investment of funds and for the periodical audit of accounts is set forth in Rule No. _____ .

11. The provision for the inspection of the books and names of the members by every person having an interest in the funds is set forth in Rule No. _____ .

12. The provision for the manner of dissolving the trade union is set forth in Rule No. _____ .

13. Accompanying this application are sent—
   1. Two printed copies, each marked A, of the rules.
   2. A list, marked B, of the titles and names of the officers.
   3. A general statement, marked C [*this will only be necessary in cases where the trade union has been in operation more than a year previous to the date of the application*] showing—
      (a) The assets and liabilities of the [*Name of Trade Union*] at the date up to which the statement is made out.
      (b) The receipts and expenditure of [*Name of Trade Union*] during the year preceding the date [*this date will be fixed by the registrar*] up to which the statement is made out, such expenditure being set forth under separate heads corresponding to the several objects of the Trade Union.

14. We have been duly authorised by the trade union to make this application on its behalf, such authorisation consisting of _____

(Signed)   1.
           2.
           3.
           4.
           5.
           6.
           7.

_____ day of _____ 19 _____ .

[*This will only be necessary where the Trade Union has been in operation before the date of the application.*]

In paragraph 14 must be stated whether the authority to make this application was given by a "resolution of a general meeting of the trade union," or, if not, in what other way it was given.

REGULATIONS DATED NOVEMBER 1, 1876

The two copies of rules must be signed by the seven members signing this application.

The application should be *dated*, and forwarded to The Registrar of Friendly Societies, 13 Hume Street, Dublin 2.

FORM B—REG. 5

TRADE UNION ACTS, 1871 AND 1876

CERTIFICATE OF REGISTRY OF TRADE UNION

It is hereby certified that the _____ has been registered under the Trade Union Acts 1871 and 1876, this _____ day of _____ 19 ____ .

[Signature of registrar]

FORM C—REG. 7

TRADE UNION ACTS, 1871 AND 1876

APPLICATION FOR REGISTRY OF PARTIAL ALTERATION OF RULES

_____ Trade Union.   Register No. _____

1. This application for the registry of a partial alteration of the rules of the _____ trade union, is made by the seven persons whose names are subscribed at the foot hereof.

With this application are sent—

(a) A printed copy of the registered rules marked to show where and in what way they are altered:
(b) Two printed [*or* written] copies of the alteration, each marked O, signed by each of the applicants:
(c) A statutory declaration of an officer of this trade union, that in making the alteration of rules now submitted for registry the rules of the _____ Trade Union were duly complied with.

2. We have been duly authorised by the _____ Trade Union to make this application on its behalf, such authorisation consisting of a resolution passed at a general meeting on the [*here insert the date, or, if there was no such resolution, state in what other way the authorisation was given*] _____ day of _____ 19 ____ .

REGULATIONS DATED NOVEMBER 1, 1876

(Signed)   1.
            2.
            3.
            4.
            5.
            6.
            7.

_____ day of _____ 19 ____ .

To the Registrar of Friendly Societies,
13 Hume Street, Dublin 2.

FORM D—REG. 7, 9

TRADE UNION ACTS, 1871 AND 1876

DECLARATION ACCOMPANYING ALTERATION OF RULES

_____ Trade Union.   Register No. _____

I,_____ of _____ , an officer of the above-named trade union, do solemnly and sincerely declare that in making the alteration of the rules of the trade union, the application for the registry of which is appended to this declaration, the rules of the said trade union have been duly complied with.

And I make this solemn declaration, conscientiously believing the same to be true, and by virtue of the provisions of the Statutory Declarations Act [1938].

[Declared before me by A.B. who is personally known to me (or who is identified to me by C.D. who is personally known to me) at _____ this _____ day of _____ 19 ____].

COMMENTARY

Section 1(1) of the Statutory Declarations Act 1938 provides that it shall be lawful for any of the following persons to take and receive such a declaration: a notary public; a commissioner for oaths; a peace commissioner; and a person authorised by law to take and receive statutory declarations. The meaning of this last-mentioned category of persons is defined in section 1(3). Forms D, O and Q have been altered in accordance with section 4 of the Statutory Declarations Act 1938.

FORM E—REG. 8

TRADE UNION ACTS, 1871 AND 1876

CERTIFICATE OF REGISTRY OF PARTIAL ALTERATION OF RULES

_____ Trade Union.   Register No. _____

Regulations Dated November 1, 1876

It is hereby certified that the foregoing partial alteration has been registered under the above-mentioned Acts this _____ day of _____ 19____ .

[Signature of registrar]

Form F—Reg. 9

Trade Union Acts, 1871 and 1876

FORM OF APPLICATION FOR REGISTRY OF COMPLETE ALTERATION OF RULES

_____ Trade Union.   Register No. _____

1. This application for the registry of a complete alteration of the registered rules of the _____ Trade Union is made by the seven persons whose names are subscribed at the foot hereof.

2. The complete alteration submitted for registry is the substitution of the set of rules, two printed copies of which (each copy marked P, and signed by the applicants) accompany this application, for the set of rules already registered.

3. The name under which it is proposed that the trade union on behalf of which this application is made shall be registered is _____ as set forth in Rule No. _____ .

To the best of our belief there is no other existing trade union, whether registered or not registered, the name of which is identical with the proposed name, or so nearly resembles the same as to cause confusion.

4. The place of meeting for the business of the [*Name of Trade Union*], and the office to which all communications and notices may be addressed, is at _____, as set forth in Rule No. _____ .

5. The [*Name of Trade Union*] was established on the _____ day of _____ .

6. The whole of the objects for which the [*Name of Trade Union*] is established, and the purposes for which the funds thereof are applicable, are set forth in Rule No. _____ .

7. The conditions under which members may become entitled to benefits assured are set forth in Rule No. _____ .

8. The fines and forfeitures to be imposed on members are set forth in Rule No. _____ .

9. The manner of making, altering, amending, and rescinding rules is set forth in Rule No. _____ .

10. The provision for the appointment and removal of a general committee of management, of trustee or trustees, treasurer, and other officers, is set forth in Rule No. _____ .

REGULATIONS DATED NOVEMBER 1, 1876

11. The provision for the investment of funds and for the periodical audit of accounts is set forth in Rule No. _____ .

12. The provision for the inspection of the books and names of the members by every person having an interest in the funds is set forth in Rule No. _____ .

13. The provision for the manner of dissolving the trade union is set forth in Rule No. _____ .

14. This application is accompanied by a statutory declaration of _____ , an officer of the said trade union, to the effect that in making the alteration of rules now submitted for registry the rules of the trade union were duly complied with.

15. We have been duly authorised by the [*Name of Trade Union*] to make this application on its behalf, such authorisation consisting of a resolution passed at a general meeting held on the [*here insert the date, or, if there was no such resolution, state in what other way authorisation was given*].

(Signed)
1.
2.
3.
4.
5.
6.
7.

_____ day of _____ 19 ____ .

The Registrar of Friendly Societies,
13 Hume Street, Dublin 2.

FORM G—REG. 10

TRADE UNION ACTS, 1871 AND 1876

CERTIFICATE OF REGISTRY OF COMPLETE ALTERATION OF RULES

_____ Trade Union.   Register No. _____

It is hereby certified that the set of rules, copy whereof is appended hereto, has been registered under the above-mentioned Acts in substitution for the set of rules already registered for the _____ Trade Union this _____ day of _____ 19 ____ .

[Signature of registrar]

Regulations Dated November 1, 1876

COMMENTARY

Forms H and I have been omitted consequent upon the deletion of regulation 11. See commentary to regulation 11, *supra.* at p. 35.

Form J—Reg. 12

Trade Union Acts, 1871 and 1876

REQUEST TO WITHDRAW OR CANCEL CERTIFICATE OF REGISTRY

_____ Trade Union.
Register No. _____ .
To the registrar.

1. The above-mentioned trade union desires that its certificate of registry under the Trade Union Acts may be withdrawn [or cancelled] on the following ground, *viz.*, [*state reason for desiring withdrawal or cancelling of certificate of registry*] and at a general meeting [*if not at a general meeting, state in what manner the request has been determined upon*] duly held on the _____ day of _____ 19 ____ , it was resolved as follows:—

"That the trustees be authorised to request the registrar to withdraw [*or* cancel] the certificate of registry of this trade union."

2. This request is made by the trustees accordingly.

_____
_____ } Trustees.
_____

Registered Office _____
Date _____ 19 ____ .

Form K—Reg. 13

Trade Union Acts, 1871 and 1876

NOTICE BEFORE WITHDRAWAL OR CANCELLING OF CERTIFICATE OF REGISTRY

_____ Trade Union.
Register No. _____ .

Notice is hereby given to the above-mentioned trade union that it is the intention of the registrar to proceed on the _____ day

Regulations Dated November 1, 1876

of _____ 19 ____ , [*this will be not less than two months after the date of the notice*] to cancel [*or* to withdraw] the registry of the trade union, unless cause be shown to the contrary in the meantime.

The ground of such proposed cancelling [*or* withdrawal] is that the certificate of registry has been obtained by fraud [*or* mistake], *or* that the registry of the trade union has become void under s.6 of the Trade Union Act 1871, *or* that the trade union has wilfully and after notice from me violated the provisions of the above-mentioned Acts *or* has ceased to exist. [*The facts should be briefly specified where practicable.*]

(Signature) _____

Registrar

Date _____ 19 ____ .

Form L—Reg. 14

Trade Union Acts, 1871 and 1876

WITHDRAWAL OR CANCELLING OF CERTIFICATE OF REGISTRY

_____ Trade Union.

Register No. _____ .

The certificate of registry of the above-mentioned trade union is hereby withdrawn *or* cancelled at its request [*or as the case may be. The registrar may, if he thinks fit, add a statement, as in Form K, of the ground of the cancelling*].

(Signed) _____

Registrar

Date _____ .

Form M—Reg. 15

Trade Union Acts, 1871 and 1876

NOTICE OF CHANGE OF REGISTERED OFFICE

_____ Trade Union.

Register No. _____ .

To the Registrar of Friendly Societies.

Notice is hereby given that the registered office of the above-mentioned trade union is removed from _____ in the parish of

REGULATIONS DATED NOVEMBER 1, 1876

_____ , and is now situated at _____ in the parish of _____ in the county of _____ .
Dated this _____ day of _____ 19 ____ .

$\left.\begin{array}{c}\text{_____}\\ \text{_____}\end{array}\right\}$ Trustees.

NOTE.—Until this notice has been given, the trade union will not have complied with the provisions of the Act.

Received this _____ day of _____ notice of removal of the registered office of the _____ , Register No. _____ , to _____ in the county of _____ .

[Signature of registrar]

[*This part to be detached by the registrar when the notice is registered, and returned to the trade union.*]

FORM N—REG. 16

TRADE UNION ACTS, 1871 AND 1876

APPLICATION FOR APPROVAL, AND NOTICE OF CHANGE OF NAME

Name already registered _____ .
Registered No. _____ .
To the registrar.

Application for approval of a change of name of the above-mentioned trade union is made by the three persons whose names are subscribed at the foot hereof.

The following is a copy of a resolution passed by the consent of two thirds of the total number of members of the trade union:—

[*The resolution to be copied at length.*]

And notice of the said change is hereby given to the registrar for registry.

_____ Secretary.

Registered Office _____ .
Date _____ 19 ____ .

$\left.\begin{array}{l}1 \text{ _____}\\ 2 \text{ _____}\\ 3 \text{ _____}\\ 4 \text{ _____}\\ 5 \text{ _____}\\ 6 \text{ _____}\\ 7 \text{ _____}\end{array}\right\}$ Members.

REGULATIONS DATED NOVEMBER 1, 1876

FORM O—REG. 16

TRADE UNION ACTS, 1871 AND 1876

DECLARATION TO ACCOMPANY APPLICATION FOR APPROVAL OF CHANGE OF NAME

County of _____ to wit.
Name of trade union _____ .
Register No. _____ .
I, _____ of _____ , the secretary of the above-named trade union, do solemnly and sincerely declare that in making the change of name, notice of which is appended to this declaration, the provisions of the 39 & 40 Vict. c. 22., in respect of change of name, having been complied with.

And I make this solemn declaration, conscientiously believing the same to be true, and by virtue of the provisions of the Statutory Declarations Act [1938].

[Declared before me by A.B. who is personally known to me (or who is identified to me by C.D. who is personally known to me at _____ this _____ day of _____ 19 ____ .]

FORM P—REG. 17

TRADE UNION ACTS, 1871 AND 1876

APPLICATION FOR DIRECTION TO TRANSFER STOCK

[*This form applies (with the necessary modifications) to a branch of a trade union.*]

_____ Trade Union.
Register No. _____ .
Application for a direction to transfer stock is made by the four persons whose names are subscribed at the foot hereof, being the secretary and three members of the above-mentioned trade union.

1. The trade union on the _____ day of _____ , duly appointed _____ , of _____ in the county of _____ [*here name and describe all the trustees then appointed*] to be trustees.

2. On the _____ day of _____ the sum of _____ was invested in the purchase of _____ stock transferable at the Bank of Ireland in the names of the said trustees, and the same is still standing in their names, as follows [*state exactly in what names the stock stands*]:—

REGULATIONS DATED NOVEMBER 1, 1876

3. The said _____ is absent from Ireland [*or* became bankrupt on the _____ day _____ , *or* filed a petition (*or* executed a deed) for liquidation of his affairs by assignment or arrangement *or* for composition with his creditors, on the _____ day of _____ , *or* has become a lunatic, *or* died on the _____ day of _____ , *or* has not been heard of for _____ years, and it is not known whether he is living or dead.] [*This clause will not be necessary where the application is in consequence of the mere removal of a trustee.*]

4. On the _____ day of _____ the trade union duly removed the said _____ from his office of trustee, and appointed _____ [*give full name and description*] in his place.

5. Since such removal application has been made in writing to the said [*removed trustee*] to join in the transfer of the said stock into the names of the said [*here give the names of the other trustees, and of the new trustees appointed in the place of the one removed*] as trustees for the said trade union, but he has refused to comply [*or* has not complied] with such application. [*This paragraph may be omitted, or varied, as the facts require.*]

6. This application to the registrar is made pursuant to 39 & 40 Vict. c. 22. s.4, that he may direct the said stock to be transferred into the names of the said _____ as trustees for the trade union by _____

[1]

_____ Secretary.
_____ Member.
_____ Member.
_____ Member.

Registered Office _____ .
Date _____ day of _____ 19 ____ .
To the Registrar.

[1] [*This blank should be filled by the names of the surviving or continuing trustees (if any), and if they be willing and able to make the transfer; but if there be no such trustee, or if any such trustee refuse or be unable to make the transfer, then by the words* the Accountant General, or Deputy, or Assistant Accountant General of the said Bank; *and a full statement of the facts and of the grounds of such refusal or inability should be made.*]

FORM Q—REG. 17

TRADE UNION ACTS, 1871 AND 1876

DECLARATION VERIFYING STATEMENTS IN AN APPLICATION FOR DIRECTION TO TRANSFER STOCK

[*This form applies (with the necessary modifications) to a branch of a trade union.*]

REGULATIONS DATED NOVEMBER 1, 1876

County of _____ to wit.
_____ Trade Union.
Register No. _____ .
I, _____ , of _____ in the county of _____ , do solemnly and sincerely declare that I am the secretary of the above-mentioned trade union.

That _____ and _____ , whose names are subscribed at the foot of the application hereto annexed, are members of the said trade union.

That on the _____ day of _____ 19 ____ , _____ and _____ therein mentioned, were appointed trustees of the said trade union.

That on the _____ day of _____ 19 ____ , the sum of _____ was invested in the purchase of _____ stock, transferable at the Bank of Ireland in the names of the said trustees, and the declarant believes that it is still standing in their names, as follows [*state as in Form P*]:—

That the said _____ is absent from Ireland [*or*, became bankrupt, &c., *as in Form P*].

That on the _____ day of _____ 19 ____ , the said _____ was removed from his office of trustee, and _____ was appointed in his place.

That since such removal application has been made in writing to the said _____ to join in the transfer of the said stock into the names of the said _____ as trustees for the said Trade Union, but he has refused to comply [*or* has not complied] with such application. [*This paragraph may be omitted or varied as the facts require.*]

And I make this solemn declaration, conscientiously believing the same to be true, and by virtue of the provisions of the Statutory Declaration Act [1938].

[Declared before me by A.B. who is personally known by me (or who is identified to me by C.D. who is personally known to me) at _____ this _____ day of _____ 19 ____ .]

FORM R—REG. 20

TRADE UNION ACTS, 1871 AND 1876

DIRECTION BY THE REGISTRAR TO TRANSFER STOCK

[*This form applies, with the necessary modifications, to a branch of a trade union.*]

Whereas it has been made to appear to the Registrar that _____ stock, transferable at the Bank of Ireland is now stand-

Regulations Dated November 1, 1876

ing in the names of _____ and _____ as trustees of _____ Trade Union registered under the above-mentioned Acts.

And that the said _____ is absent from Ireland, [*or* became bankrupt, &c., *as in Form P.*]

And that _____ has been appointed trustee of the said Trade Union in place of the said _____ .

(a) The Registrar under the said Acts hereby directs, pursuant to section 4 of the 39 & 40 Vict. c. 22, that the said sum of _____ standing in the books of the Bank of Ireland in the names of the said _____ be transferred in the said books by the said _____ into the names of the said _____ .

(b) And that there is no surviving or continuing trustee of the said trade union, or that the surviving or continuing trustee or trustees refuse or are unable to transfer the said stock. [*The paragraphs marked (a) or (b) will be used as the case requires.*]

The Registrar under the said Acts hereby directs, pursuant to section 4 of the 39 & 40 Vict. c. 22, that the said sum of _____ , so standing in the books of the Bank of Ireland be transferred in the said books by the Accountant-General, or Deputy or Assistant Accountant-General, of the said Bank into the names of the said _____ .

Address _____ .
Date _____ 19 ____ .

[Signature of registrar]

Form S—Reg. 21

Trade Union Acts, 1871 and 1876

NOTICE OF DISSOLUTION

_____ Trade Union.
Register No. _____ .
To the Registrar, 13 Hume Street, Dublin 2.

Notice is hereby given that the above-mentioned trade union was dissolved in pursuance of the rules thereof on the _____ day of _____ .

1.	_____	Secretary.
2.	_____	Member.
3.	_____	Member.
4.	_____	Member.

Regulations Dated November 1, 1876

     5. _____ Member.
     6. _____ Member.
     7. _____ Member.
     8. _____ Member.

Name and address to which registered copy is to be returned. _____
  Date _____ 19 _____ .

COMMENTARY

Forms T and U have been omitted consequent upon the deletion of regulation 22. See commentary to regulation 22, *supra* at p. 36.

TRADE UNION ACT 1913

(2 & 3 Geo. 5, c. 30)

An Act to amend the Law with respect to the objects and powers of Trade Unions. [*7 March 1913*]

COMMENTARY

This Act was the legislative response to the House of Lords decision in *Amalgamated Society of Railway Servants* v. *Osborne* [1910] A.C. 87. On the Act generally see Ewing, *Trade Unions, The Labour Party and the Law* (1982); Kidner "Trade Union Political Fund Rules" (1980) 31 *N.I.L.Q.* 3; Kerr and Whyte, *Irish Trade Union Law* (1985) pp. 89–95; Drake, *The Trade Union Acts* (1985) pp. 30–47.

Amendment of law as to objects and powers of trade unions

1.—(1) The fact that a combination has under its constitution objects or powers other than statutory objects within the meaning of this Act shall not prevent the combination being a trade union for the purposes of the Trade Union Acts, 1871 to 1906, so long as the combination is a trade union as defined by this Act, and, subject to the provisions of this Act as to the furtherance of political objects, any such trade union shall have power to apply the funds of the union for any lawful objects or purposes for the time being authorised under its constitution.

(2) For the purposes of this Act, the expression "statutory objects" means the objects mentioned in section sixteen of the Trade Union Act Amendment Act, 1876 [39 & 40 Vict. c. 22], namely, the regulation of the relations between workmen and masters, or between workmen and workmen, or between masters and masters, or the imposing of restrictive conditions on the conduct of any trade or business, and also the provision of benefits to members.

Definition of trade union

2.—(1) The expression "trade union" for the purpose of the Trade Union Acts, 1871 to 1906, and this Act, means any combination, whether temporary or permanent, the principal objects of which are under its constitution statutory objects: Provided that any combination which is for the time being registered as a trade

Trade Union Act 1913

union shall be deemed to be a trade union as defined by this Act so long as it continues to be so registered.

(2) The Registrar of Friendly Societies shall not register any combination as a trade union unless in his opinion, having regard to the constitution of the combination, the principal objects of the combination are statutory objects, and may withdraw the certificate of registration of any such registered trade union if the constitution of the union has been altered in such a manner that, in his opinion, the principal objects of the union are no longer statutory objects, or if in his opinion the principal objects for which the union is actually carried on are not statutory objects.

(3) Any unregistered trade union may, if they think fit, at any time without registering the union apply to the Registrar of Friendly Societies for a certificate that the union is a trade union within the meaning of this Act, and the Registrar, if satisfied, having regard to the constitution of the union and the mode in which the union is being carried on, that the principal objects of the union are statutory objects, and that the union is actually carried on for those objects, shall grant such a certificate, but the Registrar may, on an application made by any person to him for the purpose, withdraw any such certificate if satisfied, after giving the union an opportunity of being heard, that the certificate is no longer justified.

(4) Any person aggrieved by any refusal of the Registrar to register a combination as a trade union, or to give a certificate that an unregistered trade union is a trade union within the meaning of this Act, or by the withdrawal under this section of a certificate of registration, or of a certificate that an unregistered union is a trade union within the meaning of this Act, may appeal to the High Court [...] within the time and in the manner and on the conditions directed by rules of court.

(5) A certificate of the Registrar that a trade union is a trade union within the meaning of this Act shall, so long as it is in force, be conclusive for all purposes.

COMMENTARY

Subsection (3)

According to paragraph 3.7 of the *Report of the Registrar of Friendly Societies 1985–86* two unregistered trade unions hold certificates under this subsection: the Electricity Supply Board Staff Association (granted 1935) and the Irish Nurses Union (granted 1936).

Subsection (4)

Since there are no such rules in the Rules of the Superior Courts 1986, appeals are possibly still governed by the Trade Union Act Rules 1913 (S.R. & O. 1913 No. 1274) under which the procedure was by originating notice of motion in the Chancery Division of the High Court within two months of the registrar's decision or such further time as he or the court allows. Presumably any such appeal would now be brought by way of special summons: see R.S.C. 1986, 0.3(21).

References to Scotland have been deleted.

Subsection (5)

See, however, *Maher v. Attorney General* [1973] I.R. 110 where a similar provision in the Road Traffic Act 1968 was held to be an invalid legislative infringement on the judicial power.

Restriction on application of funds for certain political purposes

3.—(1) The funds of a trade union shall not be applied, either directly or in conjunction with any other trade union, association, or body, or otherwise indirectly, in the furtherance of the political objects to which this section applies (without prejudice to the furtherance of any other political objects), unless the furtherance of those objects has been approved as an object of the union by a resolution for the time being in force passed on a ballot of the members of the union taken in accordance with this Act for the purpose by a majority of the members voting; and where such a resolution is in force, unless rules, to be approved, whether the union is registered or not, by the Registrar of Friendly Societies, are in force providing—

(a) That any payments in the furtherance of those objects are to be made out of a separate fund (in this Act referred to as the political fund of the union), and for the exemption in accordance with this Act of any member of the union from any obligation to contribute to such a fund if he gives notice in accordance with this Act that he objects to contribute; and

(b) That a member who is exempt from the obligation to contribute to the political fund of the union shall not be excluded from any benefits of the union, or placed in any respect either directly or indirectly under any disability or at any disadvantage as compared with other members of the union (except in relation to the control or management of the political fund) by reason of his being so exempt, and that contribution to the political fund of the union shall not be made a condition for admission to the union.

(2) If any member of a trade union alleges that he is aggrieved by a breach of any rule made in pursuance of this section, he may complain to the Registrar of Friendly Societies, and the Registrar of Friendly Societies, after giving the complainant and any representative of the union an opportunity of being heard, may, if he considers that such a breach has been committed, make such order for remedying the breach as he thinks just under the circumstances; and any such order of the Registrar shall be binding and

conclusive on all parties without appeal and shall not be removable into any court of law or restrainable by injunction, and on being recorded in the [Circuit Court], may be enforced as if it had been an order of the [Circuit Court]. [...]

(3) The political objects to which this section applies are the expenditure of money—

- (a) on the payment of any expenses incurred either directly or indirectly by a candidate or prospective candidate for election to [the Oireachtas] or to any public office, before, during, or after the election in connection with his candidature or election; or
- (b) on the holding of any meeting or the distribution of any literature or documents in support of any such candidate or prospective candidate; or
- (c) on the maintenance of any person who is a member of [the Oireachtas] or who holds a public office; or
- (d) in connection with the registration of electors or the selection of a candidate for [the Oireachtas] or any public office; or
- (e) on the holding of political meetings of any kind, or on the distribution of political literature or political documents of any kind, unless the main purpose of the meetings or of the distribution of the literature or documents is the furtherance of statutory objects within the meaning of this Act.

The expression "public office" in this section means the office of member of any county, county borough, district, or parish council, or board of guardians, or of any public body who have power to raise money, either directly or indirectly, by means of a rate.

(4) A resolution under this section approving political objects as an object of the union shall take effect as if it were a rule of the union and may be rescinded in the same manner and subject to the same provisions as such a rule.

(5) The provisions of this Act as to the application of the funds of a union for political purposes shall apply to a union which is in whole or in part an association or combination of other unions as if the individual members of the component unions were the members of that union and not the unions; but nothing in this Act shall prevent any such component union from collecting from any of their members who are not exempt on behalf of the association or combination any contributions to the political fund of the association or combination.

COMMENTARY

Subsection (1)

The wording of the parenthesis is curious as read literally it would appear to legitimise the furtherance of any political objects not enumerated in subsection (3) for, unless it had that meaning, the sense would be the same if the parenthesis were omitted. *Quaere* whether the words are a shortened form of "without prejudice to any question as to the application of the funds of a trade union to the furtherance of any other political objects."

In subsection (1)(*b*), the disadvantage suffered by a member who is exempt must be "material ... a disadvantage of substance": *per* Slynn J. in *Reeves v. Transport and General Workers' Union* [1980] I.C.R. 728, 741.

Subsection (2)

The words in square brackets were substituted by virtue of section 51 of the Courts of Justice Act 1924. References exclusive to Scotland have been deleted. The one recorded instance of a complaint being made in this jurisdiction pursuant to this subsection was *McCafferty v. Irish Transport and General Workers' Union*, on which see the *Report of the Registrar of Friendly Societies 1952* at pp. 37–40. See also *Birch v. National Union of Railwaymen* [1950] Ch. 602.

Although the Registrar's decision is stated to be binding and conclusive on all parties without appeal and that it cannot be removed into a court of law or be restrained by injunction, it is clear that Article 34.3.1^0 of the Constitution bars any legislative attempt to oust the jurisdiction of the High Court. See Casey, *Constitutional Law in Ireland* (1987) pp. 228–229 and Hogan and Morgan, *Administrative Law* (1986) pp. 200–201, (1991, 2nd ed.) pp. 374–378.

Subsection (3)

In subsection (3)(*b*), although the "distribution" of political literature must be financed out of the political fund, the paragraph is silent on the costs of preparing and printing such literature.

Persons who hold positions within a political party do not come within subsection (3)(*c*). *Quaere* whether a union official given paid leave of absence as a T.D. or Senator must be paid out of the political fund.

In Britain the Registrar, since 1925, has limited the scope of the phrase "political" in subsection (3)(*e*) by construing it as "party-political," *i.e.* as relating to literature or meetings held by a party which has or seeks to have members in Parliament: see *Coleman v. Post Office Employees Union* [1981] I.R.L.R. 427 and *A.S.T.M.S. v. Parkin* [1984] I.C.R. 127. Consequently, a trade union campaign opposing Government cuts in public spending is not "political" for the purposes of the Act.

The expression "public office" does not cover membership of the European Parliament.

The words in square brackets have been substituted for the word "Parliament" by virtue of section 5(1) of the Adaptation of Enactments Act 1922.

Approval of rules

4.—(1) A ballot for the purposes of this Act shall be taken in accordance with rules of the union to be approved for the purpose, whether the union is registered or not, by the Registrar of Friendly Societies, but the Registrar of Friendly Societies shall not approve any such rules unless he is satisfied that every member has an equal right, and, if reasonably possible, a fair opportunity of voting, and that the secrecy of the ballot is properly secured.

(2) If the Registrar of Friendly Societies is satisfied, and certifies, that rules for the purpose of a ballot under this Act or rules made

for other purposes of this Act which require approval by the Registrar, have been approved by a majority of members of a trade union, whether registered or not, voting for the purpose, or by a majority of delegates of such a trade union voting at a meeting called for the purpose, those rules shall have effect as rules of the union, notwithstanding that the provisions of the rules of the union as to the alteration of rules or the making of new rules have not been complied with.

COMMENTARY

The following trade unions operate a political fund: Services Industrial Professional Technical Union; Irish Print Union; Bakery and Food Workers' Amalgamated Union; Irish Distributive and Administrative Trade Union; Irish Municipal Employees' Trade Union; Irish National Teachers' Organisation. The Operative Plasterers' Allied Trades Society of Ireland maintains a political fund but no members currently contribute to it. The SIPTU ballot, which took place between December 11 and December 17, 1990, resulted in a majority of 13,112 to 5,780 in favour of establishing a political fund. The ballot was required because the Trade Union Act 1975 makes no provision for the continuance of political funds following the amalgamation of two or more trade unions.

Notice of objection to contribute towards political objects

5.—(1) A member of a trade union may at any time give notice, in the form set out in the Schedule to this Act or in a form to the like effect, that he objects to contribute to the political fund of the union, and, on the adoption of a resolution of the union approving the furtherance of political objects as an object of the union, notice shall be given to the members of the union acquainting them that each member has a right to be exempt from contributing to the political fund of the union, and that a form of exemption notice can be obtained by or on behalf of a member either by application at or by post from the head office or any branch office of the union or the office of the Registrar of Friendly Societies.

Any such notice to members of the union shall be given in accordance with rules of the union approved for the purpose by the Registrar of Friendly Societies, having regard in each case to the existing practice and to the character of the union.

(2) On giving notice in accordance with this Act of his objection to contribute, a member of the union shall be exempt, so long as his notice is not withdrawn, from contributing to the political fund of the union as from the first day of January next after the notice is given, or, in the case of a notice given within one month after the notice given to members under this section on the adoption of a resolution approving the furtherance of political objects, as from the date on which the member's notice is given.

Trade Union Act 1913

COMMENTARY

Members are deemed to have agreed to contribute unless they "contract out". Note that the position in Northern Ireland is different in that, as a result of amendments made by the Trade Disputes and Trade Unions Act (Northern Ireland) 1927, members must "contract in".

Mode of giving effect to exemption from contributions to political fund

6. Effect may be given to the exemption of members to contribute to the political fund of a union either by a separate levy of contributions to that fund from the members of the union who are not exempt, and in that case the rules shall provide that no moneys of the union other than the amount raised by such separate levy shall be carried to that fund, or by relieving any members who are exempt from the payment of the whole or any part of any periodical contributions required from the members of the union towards the expenses of the union, and in that case the rules shall provide that the relief shall be given as far as possible to all members who are exempt on the occasion of the same periodical payment and for enabling each member of the union to know as respects any such periodical contribution, what portion, if any, of the sum payable by him is a contribution to the political fund of the union.

Definition of Registrar of Friendly Societies

7. [...]

COMMENTARY

Deleted by virtue of the Registrar of Friendly Societies (Adaptation) Order 1926 made by the Executive Council under section 12 of the Adaptation of Enactments Act 1922 on October 4, 1926. Doubts as to the validity of the appointment of the first Registrar of Friendly Societies in Saorstat Éireann were removed by section 4 of the Registry of Friendly Societies Act 1936.

Short title and construction

8. This Act may be cited as the Trade Union Act, 1913, and shall be construed as one with the Trade Union Acts, 1871 and 1876; and this Act and the Trade Union Acts, 1871 to 1906, may be cited together as the Trade Union Acts, 1871 to 1913.

Trade Union Act 1913

Schedule

Form of Exemption Notice

Name of Trade Union

Political Fund (Exemption Notice)

I hereby give notice that I object to contribute to the Political Fund of the _____
_____ Union, and am in consequence exempt, in manner provided by the Trade Union Act, 1913, from contributing to that fund.

A.B. _____

Address _____

_____ day of _____ 19 ___ .

TRADE UNION ACT 1941

(*Number 22 of 1941*)

An Act to provide for the licensing of bodies carrying on negotiations for fixing wages or other conditions of employment, to provide for the establishment of a tribunal having power to restrict the rights of organisation of trade unions, and for other matters connected with the matters aforesaid.

[*23 September 1941*]

Be it enacted by the Oireachtas as follows:—

PART I

PRELIMINARY AND GENERAL

Short title and collective citation

1.—(1) This Act may be cited as the Trade Union Act, 1941.

(2) This Act and the Trade Union Acts, 1871 to 1935, may be cited together as the Trade Union Acts, 1871 to 1941.

Definitions

2.—In this Act—
the expression "the Minister" means the Minister for [Labour],
the word "prescribed" means prescribed by regulations made by the Minister under this Act.

COMMENTARY

The word in square brackets was substituted by virtue of the Labour (Transfer of Departmental Administration and Ministerial Functions) Order 1966 (S.I. No. 164 of 1966).

Regulation

3.—The Minister may make regulations in respect of any matter or thing referred to in this Act as prescribed or to be prescribed, but no such regulation shall be made in relation to any fee without the consent of the Minister for Finance.

COMMENTARY

See the Trade Union Act 1941 (Application for Negotiation Licence) Regulations

Trade Union Act 1941

1942 (S.R. & O. No. 106 of 1942), reproduced *infra* at p. 71; the Trade Union (Inspection of Register of Members) Regulations 1942 (S.R. & O. No. 156 of 1942), reproduced *infra* at p. 73; and the Trade Union Act 1971 (Notice of Intention to Apply for Negotiation Licence) Regulations 1972 (S.I. No. 158 of 1972), reproduced *infra* at p. 93.

Expenses

4.—The expenses incurred by the Minister in the administration of this Act shall, to such extent as may be sanctioned by the Minister for Finance, be paid out of moneys provided by the Oireachtas.

Part II

Licensing of Bodies Carrying on Negotiations for Fixing Wages or Other Conditions of Employment

Definitions for purposes of Part II

5.—(1) In this Part of this Act the expression "negotiation licence" means a licence issued by the Minister under this Part of this Act and authorising its holder to carry on negotiations for the fixing of wages or other conditions of employment.

(2) In this Part of this Act and the Schedule to this Act, the word "members," where applicable in respect of a body not registered under the Trade Union Acts, 1871 to 1935, means members of such body resident within the State.

Restrictions on carrying on of negotiations for fixing of wages, etc.

6.—(1) It shall not be lawful for any body of persons, not being an excepted body, to carry on negotiations for the fixing of wages or other conditions of employment unless such body is the holder of a negotiation licence.

(2) Where any body of persons acts in contravention of this section, the members of the committee of management or other controlling authority of such body and such of the officers of such body as consent to or facilitate such act shall each be guilty of an offence under this section and shall each be liable on summary conviction thereof to a fine not exceeding [one thousand] pounds, together with, in the case of a continuing offence, a further fine not exceeding [two hundred pounds] for every day during which the offence is continued.

(3) In this section the expression "excepted body" means any of the following bodies, that is to say:—

Trade Union Act 1941

(a) a body which carries on negotiations for the fixing of the wages or other conditions of employment of its own (but no other) employees,

(b) [...],

(c) a civil service staff association recognised by the Minister for Finance,

(d) an organisation of teachers recognised by the Minister for Education,

(e) [...],

(f) [a joint labour committee],

(g) a body in respect of which an order under sub-section (6) of this section is for the time being in force, and

[(h) a body all the members of which are employed by the same employer and which carries on negotiations for the fixing of the wages or other conditions of employment of its own members (but of no other employees).]

(4) [...].

(5) [...].

(6) The Minister may by order declare that this section shall not apply in respect of any particular body of persons.

(7) The Minister may by order (which shall come into operation on a specified date not earlier than one month after it is made) revoke any order under the next preceding sub-section of this section.

(8) [...].

(9) This section shall come into operation on such date not earlier than six months after the passing of this Act as the Minister by order appoints for that purpose.

COMMENTARY

Subsection (1)

See, however, section 3 of the Trade Union Act 1942 *infra* pp. 81–82.

Subsection (2)

The words in square brackets were substituted by section 4 of the Industrial Relations Act 1990.

Subsection (3)

Paragraph (b) was repealed by section 6 of the Trade Union Act 1942. The deletion of the words in square brackets in paragraph (e) was necessitated by the Industrial Relations Act 1976.

The words in square brackets in paragraph (f) were substituted by section 56 of the Industrial Relations Act 1946.

The words in square brackets in paragraph (h) were inserted by section 2 of the Trade Union Act 1942.

Subsections (4) and (5)

These subsections were repealed by section 6 of the Trade Union Act 1942.

Subsection (6)

It was initially felt that exemption could be effected by simple Ministerial Order. Subsequently, this policy was abandoned in favour of the use of Statutory Instruments. The bodies which have been exempted under this section are: Irish Nurses Organisation (Ministerial Order dated May 7, 1942); Banks Staffs Relations Committee (Ministerial Order dated November 24, 1942); Institute of Clerks of Works in Ireland (S.I. No. 221 of 1957); County and City Managers' Association (S.I. No. 17 of 1960); Association of Hospital and Public Pharmacists (S.I. No. 233 of 1960); Irish Dental Association (S.I. No. 63 of 1963); Incorporated Law Society of Ireland (S.I. No. 54 of 1965); Royal Institute of Architects of Ireland (S.I. No. 55 of 1965); Veterinary Medical Association of Ireland (S.I. No. 56 of 1965); Chartered Society of Physiotherapy (S.I. No. 227 of 1969); Irish Association of Chiropodists (S.I. No. 228 of 1969); Association of Occupational Therapists of Ireland (S.I. No. 229 of 1969); Association of Clinical Biochemists in Ireland (S.I. No. 230 of 1969); Institute of Chemistry in Ireland (S.I. No. 231 of 1969); Agricultural Science Association (S.I. No. 232 of 1969); Irish Association of Speech Therapists (S.I. No. 296 of 1971); Irish Hospital Consultants Association (S.I. No. 101 of 1990). During 1990 applications for excepted body status from the Association of General Practitioners and the Local Authority Medical Specialists were refused by the Minister (see Department of Labour *Annual Report 1990*, p. 55).

Subsection (8)

This subsection was repealed by section 6 of the Trade Union Act 1942.

Subsection (9)

The Trade Union Act 1941 (Commencement of Section 6) Order 1941 (S.R. & O. No. 590 of 1941) fixed this date as May 1, 1942.

Restrictions on grant and holding of negotiation licence

7.—(1) No body of persons shall be granted or hold a negotiation licence unless it is a body (in this Act referred to as an authorised trade union) which fulfils the following conditions, that is to say:—

(a) that either it is registered under the Trade Union Acts, 1871 to 1935, or, if not so registered, it is a trade union under the law of another country and its headquarters control is situated in that country, and
(b) that it has deposited and, subject to the provisions of this Act, keeps deposited with the High Court the appropriate sum.

(2) In this section the expression "the appropriate sum" means the sum appropriate to the number of members of the relevant body in accordance with the Schedule to this Act.

COMMENTARY

See also section 2 of the Trade Union Act 1971, *infra* pp. 89–90. In addition

Trade Union Act 1941

section 16(3) of the Industrial Relations Act 1990 provides that no body of persons shall be granted a negotiation licence unless it also complies with section 14(2) of the 1990 Act. This subsection requires that a trade union's rules contain certain provisions in relation to strikes and other industrial action. Note also that the Minister is empowered by section 2 of the Trade Union Act 1947 (as amended) to reduce the "appropriate sum": see *infra* pp. 85–86.

Variation of Schedule to this Act

8. [. . .]

COMMENTARY

This section was repealed by section 3(1) of the Trade Union Act 1947.

Application for negotiation licence

9.—(1) Any authorised trade union may apply to the Minister for a negotiation licence.

(2) Every application for a negotiation licence shall be made in the prescribed form, shall contain the prescribed particulars, and shall be accompanied by the prescribed documents and by a fee of one pound.

(3) All fees under this section shall be collected and taken in such manner as the Minister for Finance directs, and shall be paid into or disposed of for the benefit of the Exchequer in accordance with the directions of the said Minister.

(4) The Public Offices Fees Act, 1879, shall not apply in respect of any fee under this section.

COMMENTARY

The prescribed form is set out in the Trade Union Act 1941 (Application for Negotiation Licence) Regulations 1942 (S.R. & O. No. 106 of 1942), reproduced *infra* at p. 71.

Grant of negotiation licence

10.—Where application is duly made for a negotiation licence and the applicant is shown to the satisfaction of the Minister to be an authorised trade union, the Minister shall grant such licence.

COMMENTARY

In "Industrial Relations: Some Strategies for Change" (1979) 27 *Administration* 294, Professor McCarthy referred to this section as embodying the principle of "automaticity." See also 84 *Dáil Debates* Col. 157 (June 24, 1941).

Restriction on application of certain enactments

11. [. . .]

COMMENTARY

This section was repealed by section 7 of the Industrial Relations Act 1990.

Obligations of holder of negotiation licence where holder is a registered trade union

12.—(1) Whenever and so long as any authorised trade union registered under the Trade Union Acts, 1871 to 1935, is the holder of a negotiation licence, the following provisions shall have effect, that is to say:—

- (a) such trade union shall include in its rules provisions specifying the conditions of entry into and cesser of membership of such trade union,
- (b) such trade union shall maintain at its office a register of its members (including former members other than those dead and those who have been non-members for more than five years or since before the grant of such negotiation licence) and such register shall, as regards each member, show—
  - (i) his name and address,
  - (ii) the date of commencement of his membership,
  - (iii) where his membership has ceased, the date of the cesser and whether it was caused by resignation, suspension, expulsion, or otherwise, and
  - (iv) where his membership has ceased by suspension or expulsion, the date of the order directing and a reference to the rule or other provision authorising such suspension or expulsion,
- (c) such trade union shall, in accordance with regulations to be prescribed by the Minister, keep at its office such register of members open for inspection by any interested person who pays such fee, not exceeding five shillings in respect of each day (or part of a day) during which the inspection continues, as such trade union determines, and
- (d) a person who ceases, otherwise than by death, to be a member of such trade union shall, for the purposes of this Act, be deemed to continue to be a member thereof for one month after such cesser.

(2) If any authorised trade union in respect of which this section applies fails to comply with any requirement of this section, such trade union and such of the officers thereof as consent to or facilitate such failure shall each be guilty of an offence under this section and shall each be liable on summary conviction thereof to a fine not exceeding [one hundred] pounds together with, in the

case of a continuing offence, a further fine not exceeding [ten pounds] for every day during which the offence is continued.

(3) Any person may apply to the Minister for an authorisation in writing to inspect any register of members of a trade union kept in pursuance of this section and the Minister, if satisfied that the applicant has a *bona fide* interest in inspecting such register, shall issue to the applicant an authorisation such as aforesaid in respect of such period as the Minister thinks proper.

(4) In this section—
the word "office" means, in relation to a trade union, the office which for the time being is the registered office of such trade union for the purposes of the Trade Union Acts, 1871 to 1935;
the expression "interested person" means, in relation to a register of members of a trade union—

(a) any person having an interest in the funds of such trade union, or
(b) any officer of the Minister authorised by the Minister in writing to inspect such register, or
(c) during the period in respect of which an authorisation under sub-section (3) of this section is issued in relation to such register, the person specified in the authorisation.

COMMENTARY

Subsection (1)

In *Tierney* v. *Amalgamated Society of Woodworkers* [1959] I.R. 254 it was held that the provision in paragraph (a) did not confer any right to join a trade union on persons satisfying the specified conditions.

Section 4(1) of the Trade Union Act 1942 provides that paragraph (c) shall have effect as if it provided that a register of members of a trade union kept in pursuance of section 12 shall, in the case of an inspection thereof by an officer of the Minister authorised in writing to inspect such register, be kept open for inspection free of charge. See also the Trade Union (Inspection of Register of Members) Regulations 1942 (S.R. & O. No. 156 of 1942), reproduced *infra* at p. 73.

Subsection (2)

The words in square brackets were substituted by section 4 of the Industrial Relations Act 1990.

Obligations of holder of negotiation licence where holder is not a registered trade union

13.—(1) Whenever and so long as any authorised trade union not registered under the Trade Union Acts, 1871 to 1935, is the holder of a negotiation licence, the following provisions shall have effect, that is to say:—

(a) such trade union shall include in its rules or constitution

provisions specifying the conditions of entry into and cesser of membership of such trade union by persons resident within the State,
(b) such trade union shall have and maintain an office within the State for the purposes of this Act and shall give notice in writing to the Minister of the situation of such office and of every change thereof,
(c) such trade union shall maintain at the said office a register of its members (including former members other than those dead and those who have been non-members for more than five years or since before the grant of such negotiation licence) and such register shall, as regards each such member, show—
  (i) his name and address,
  (ii) the date of commencement of his membership,
  (iii) where his membership has ceased, the date of the cesser and whether it was caused by resignation, suspension, expulsion or otherwise, and
  (iv) where his membership has ceased by suspension or expulsion, the date of the order directing and a reference to the rule or other provision authorising such suspension or expulsion,
(d) such trade union shall, in accordance with regulations to be prescribed by the Minister, keep at the said office such register of members open for inspection by any interested person who pays such fee, not exceeding [£0.25] in respect of each day (or part of a day) during which the inspection continues, as such trade union determines,
(e) such trade union shall from time to time as occasion requires give notice in writing to the Minister of the name of a person ordinarily resident in the State whom it considers suitable for accepting service of documents on its behalf and any document whatsoever (whether for the purposes of this Act or for any other purposes) may be served on such trade union by enclosing it in an envelope addressed to such person at the said office and by delivering such envelope at the said office or by sending it thereto by registered post, and such document shall thereupon be deemed for all purposes to have been properly served on such trade union,
(f) such trade union shall give notice in writing to the Minister of every of the following changes not later than twenty-one days after the making thereof, that is to say:—
  (i) every change in its rules or constitution,
  (ii) every change in its committee of management or other controlling authority,

(iii) every change in its trustees, and
(iv) every change of its secretary or other principal officer, and

(g) a person who ceases, otherwise than by death, to be a member of such trade union shall, for the purposes of this Act, be deemed to continue to be a member thereof for one month after such cesser.

(2) If there is, in relation to any authorised trade union in respect of which this section applies, a failure to comply with any requirement of this section, such of the members and officers thereof as consent to or facilitate such failure shall each be guilty of an offence under this section and shall each be liable on summary conviction thereof to a fine not exceeding [one hundred] pounds together with, in the case of a continuing offence, a further fine not exceeding [ten pounds] for every day during which the offence is continued.

(3) Any person may apply to the Minister for an authorisation in writing to inspect any register of members of a trade union kept in pursuance of this section and the Minister, if satisfied that the applicant has a *bona fide* interest in inspecting such register, shall issue to the applicant an authorisation such as aforesaid in respect of such period as the Minister thinks proper.

(4) In this section the expression "interested person" means, in relation to a register of members of a trade union—

(a) any person having an interest in the funds of such trade union, or
(b) any officer of the Minister authorised by the Minister in writing to inspect such register, or
(c) during the period in respect of which an authorisation under sub-section (3) of this section is issued in relation to such register, the person specified in the authorisation.

COMMENTARY

Subsection (1)

Section 4(2) of the Trade Union Act 1942 provides that paragraph (d) shall have effect as if it provided that a register of members of a trade union kept in pursuance of section 13 shall, in the case of an inspection thereof by an officer of the Minister authorised in writing to inspect such register, be kept open for inspection free of charge.

The sum in square brackets was substituted by virtue of the Decimal Currency Acts 1969 and 1970.

Subsection (2)

The words in square brackets were substituted by section 4 of the Industrial Relations Act 1990.

General provisions in relation to deposits under this Part of this Act

14.—The following provisions shall apply and have effect in relation to deposits made with the High Court in pursuance of this part of this Act, that is to say:—

(a) every such deposit shall be made with the privity of the Accountant of the Courts of Justice and shall, when made, be under the control of the High Court;

(b) any such deposit may, in lieu of being made wholly in money, be made wholly or partly by the deposit of securities authorised by Rules of Court for the investment of moneys under the control of the High Court;

(c) where any such deposit is made wholly or partly in money, such money shall, at the request of the depositor, be invested in such securities so authorised as the depositor shall specify;

(d) the income derived from the securities in which such deposit is for the time being invested shall be paid to the depositor;

(e) the said securities or all or any of them shall, at the request and cost of the depositor, be varied into any other securities authorised as aforesaid and specified by the depositor;

(f) the depositor may at any time apply for the return, in whole or in part, of the deposit or so much thereof as has not been paid out in pursuance of an order of the High Court under this Part of this Act;

(g) where such application has been duly made, the deposit or so much thereof as has not been paid out as aforesaid shall be returned, in whole or in part, in accordance with such application upon or as soon as conveniently may be after the expiration of three months from the making of such application and, immediately after such return, the Minister shall be informed thereof;

(h) the following matters shall be governed by Rules of Court and no order of the High Court shall be required in connection with any of them, that is to say, payment of income from the securities in which the deposit is invested, the variation of such securities, and the return of the deposit.

COMMENTARY

The relevant Rules (R.S.C. 1986 O. 77, rr. 63–70) and the Forms therein mentioned are reproduced *infra* at pp. 75–80.

Change of deposit consequent on change of number of members

15. [. . .]

Trade Union Act 1941

COMMENTARY

This section was repealed by section 7 of the Industrial Relations Act 1990.

Payment of judgment debts out of deposits

16.—(1) Whenever a Court makes an order, decree, or judgment for the payment of money by a trade union which is the holder of a negotiation licence to any person, the High Court may, on the application in a summary manner of such person, order such money (with or without the costs of such application) to be paid to such person out of the deposit maintained by such trade union under this Part of this Act.

(2) Whenever, in pursuance of an order made by the High Court under this section, any money is paid out of a deposit maintained under this Part of this Act, the Accountant of the Courts of Justice shall forthwith determine the value of the balance remaining of such deposit (securities being calculated at their current market value) and, if such balance falls short of the full proper amount of such deposit, he shall give to the trade union concerned notice in writing of such deficiency and of the amount thereof.

(3) If, when a notice of deficiency of deposit is given in pursuance of the next preceding subsection of this section, the trade union concerned, not more than three months after receiving such notice, deposits with the High Court a sum equal to the amount of the deficiency stated in such notice, the sum so deposited shall be added to and treated as part of the said deposit and such trade union shall be deemed to have maintained such deposit at its full proper amount.

COMMENTARY

RSC 1986, O. 77, r. 70 provides that whenever any money is paid out of a deposit pursuant to this section the Accountant shall, as soon as may be, give notice to the trade union concerned of the deficiency (if any) mentioned in the section and of the amount thereof.

Revocation of negotiation licence

17.—The Minister may by order revoke any negotiation licence if he is satisfied that the holder thereof has ceased to be an authorised trade union.

COMMENTARY

See also section 16(5) of the Industrial Relations Act 1990 which empowers the Minister to revoke a licence where a trade union has persistently disregarded any requirement of the provisions on balloting in respect of strikes or other industrial action.

Trade Union Act 1941

Part III

Establishment and Functions of Trade Union Tribunal

[. . .]

COMMENTARY

The entire of Part III of the 1941 Act (*i.e.* sections 18–40, section 35 having already been repealed by the Trade Union Act 1942) was held by the Supreme Court to be invalid having regard to the provisions of the Constitution in *National Union of Railwaymen* v. *Sullivan* [1947] I.R. 77.

Schedule

Deposits

1. Where the number of members does not exceed 500 the deposit shall be £1,000.
2. Where the number of members exceeds 500 but does not exceed 2,000, the deposit shall be £1,000 together with £200 for each additional 300 members (or part of 300 members) in excess of 500 members.
3. Where the number of members exceeds 2,000 but does not exceed 5,000, the deposit shall be £2,000 together with £200 for each additional 300 members (or part of 300 members) in excess of 2,000 members.
4. Where the number of members exceeds 5,000 but does not exceed 10,000, the deposit shall be £4,000 together with £200 for each additional 500 members (or part of 500 members) in excess of 5,000 members.
5. Where the number of members exceeds 10,000 but does not exceed 20,000, the deposit shall be £6,000 together with £200 for each additional 1,000 members (or part of 1,000 members) in excess of 10,000 members.
6. Where the number of members exceeds 20,000 the deposit shall be £8,000 together with £200 for each additional 1,000 members (or part of 1,000 members) in excess of 20,000 members but subject to an overriding maximum of £10,000.

TRADE UNION ACT 1941 (APPLICATION FOR NEGOTIATION LICENCE) REGULATIONS 1942

(S.R. & O. No. 106 of 1942)

1. These Regulations may be cited as the Trade Union Act, 1941 (Application for Negotiation Licence) Regulations, 1942.

2. Every application under the Trade Union Act, 1941 (No. 22 of 1941), for a negotiation licence shall be made in the form contained in the Schedule to these Regulations and shall contain the particulars and be accompanied by the documents indicated in that form.

SCHEDULE

TRADE UNION ACT, 1941

Application for Negotiation Licence

1. Application is hereby made for a negotiation licence for [*Name of Trade Union*] (hereinafter referred to as the trade union).

2. The address of the trade union's head office is _____

3. The name of the general secretary or other principal officer of the trade union is _____

4. The date of the registration of the trade union under the Trade Union Acts, 1871 to 1935, was the _____ day of _____ , 19_____ , and the register number of the trade union is _____ . [*This paragraph need not be completed if the trade union is not registered in the State under the Trade Union Acts, 1871 to 1935.*]

5. The total number of the members of the trade union is _____ . [*This paragraph need not be completed if the trade union is not registered in the State under the Trade Union Acts, 1871 to 1935.*]

6. The total number of the members of the trade union resident within the State is _____ . [*This paragraph need not be completed if the trade union is not a trade union under the law of another country.*]

Negotiation Licence Regulations 1942

7. The trade union is a trade union under the law of _____ , and its headquarters control is situate in that country. [*This paragraph need not be completed if the trade union is not a trade union under the law of another country.*]

8. The date of the registration of the trade union under the law of _____ was the _____ day of _____ 19____ , and its register number is _____ . [*This paragraph need not be completed if the trade union is not registered under the law of another country.*]

9. On the _____ day of _____ 19____ , the trade union deposited the sum of £ _____ with the High Court and that sum remains deposited there.

10. The following documents accompany this application:

   (a) a true copy of the rules of the trade union,
   (b) a copy of the latest available annual report of the trade union,
   (c) a copy of the latest available statement of the accounts of the trade union.

11. A fee of £1 accompanies this application.

On behalf of [*Name of Trade Union*] we certify that to the best of our knowledge and belief the particulars given in this application are true.

Signed this _____ day of _____ 19 ____

      _____
      (_____)

      _____
      (_____)

      _____
      (_____)

[This application should be signed by the general Secretary or other principal officer of the trade union and by two members of the committee of management or other controlling authority of the trade union. The office held by each signatory should be stated within the brackets—(   ).]

TRADE UNION (INSPECTION OF REGISTER OF MEMBERS) REGULATIONS 1942

(S.R. & O. No. 156 of 1942)

1. These Regulations may be cited as the Trade Union (Inspection of Register of Members) Regulations, 1942.

2.—(1) The keeping by a trade union of a register of members open for inspection pursuant to paragraph (c) of sub-section (1) of section 12 of the Trade Union Act, 1941 (No. 22 of 1941), or paragraph (d) of subsection (1) of section 13 of that Act shall be in accordance with the following provisions:—

- (a) in the case of an inspection by an officer of the Minister for [Labour] authorised by that Minister in writing to inspect the register, the register shall be available on all week-days at any time while the office where it is kept is open.
- (b) in the case of any other inspection, the register shall be available between the hours of 10.30 a.m. and 12.30 p.m. on all week-days except Saturdays, provided that the person making the inspection gives at least two clear days' notice in writing of his intention to make the inspection.

(2) In this Article the word "week-day" does not include any—

- (a) 1st day of January,
- (b) 6th day of January,
- (c) 17th day of March,
- (d) 18th day of March in a year in which the 17th day of March falls on a Sunday,
- (e) Easter Monday,
- (f) Ascension Thursday,
- (g) Whit Monday,
- (h) Feast of Corpus Christi,
- (i) 29th day of June,
- (j) first Monday in August,
- (k) 15th day of August,
- (l) 8th day of December,
- (m) 25th day of December,
- (n) 26th day of December,
- (o) 27th day of December in a year in which the 25th or 26th day of December falls on a Sunday,

(p) bank holiday appointed under the Public Holidays Act, 1924 (No. 56 of 1924), instead of a day mentioned in any of the foregoing paragraphs.

COMMENTARY

Regulation 2(1)(a)

The word in square brackets was substituted by virtue of the Labour (Transfer of Departmental Administration and Ministerial Functions) Order 1966 (S.I. No. 164 of 1966).

Regulation 2(2)(p)

The bank holidays so appointed are Easter Monday, the Monday in Whitsun week, the first Monday in August and December 26 (if a weekday).

RULES OF THE SUPERIOR COURTS 1986

(S.I. No. 15 of 1986)

Order 77, Part VIII

63. In this Part of this Order—
"the Act" means the Trade Union Act, 1941 (No. 22 of 1941).

64. The Accountant may accept all or any part of a deposit in authorised securities.

65. (1) Pending or in default of any request by a depositor as to the investment of such part of a deposit made under the Act as is made in money, the Accountant may place such money on deposit receipt in the Bank.

(2) A request, signed by the secretary or treasurer of the depositor, shall, without any order, be a sufficient authority for the Accountant either as the case may be to invest such part of a deposit made under the Act as is made in money in the authorised securities specified in such request or to vary the authorised securities to which the request relates into the other authorised securities specified in such request. Such request shall be in the Forms Nos. 14 or 15 in Appendix P.

66. On the receipt of a request the Accountant shall pay the income from time to time as received from the securities in which such deposit or any part thereof is for the time being invested to the bankers of the depositor for the account of the depositor or in such other manner as may be indicated in the request. A request, signed by the secretary or treasurer of the depositor, shall, without any order be a sufficient authority for the Accountant to pay such income to such bankers or in such other manner, as the case may be, unless and until the Accountant receives a subsequent request for payment in a different manner. Any request under this rule shall be in the Form No. 16 in Appendix P, provided that, where payment is required in any manner other than by payment to the bankers of the depositor, such request shall be accompanied by a statutory declaration in the Form No. 17 in Appendix P.

67. A request, signed by the secretary and the treasurer of a depositor, shall without any order, be sufficient authority for the Accountant to pay or transfer to the depositor in accordance with such request all or any part of the deposit or so much thereof as has not already been paid out in pursuance of an order under Part II of the Act. Such request shall be in the Form No. 18 in Appendix P; provided that where payment of money is requested otherwise than to the bankers of a depositor or where a

transfer of securities is requested, such request shall be accompanied by a statutory declaration in the Form No. 19 in Appendix P.

68. In any case in which, under this Part of this Order, a request is required to be accompanied by a statutory declaration the Accountant may require such further evidence of verification of the matters stated in such declaration as he may think fit before complying with the request.

69. The Accountant shall, immediately after the return of a deposit or of part thereof, give notice to the Minister for Industry and Commerce of such return and of the amount returned.

70. Whenever any money is paid out of a deposit pursuant to section 16 of the Act, the Accountant shall, as soon as may be, give notice to the trade union concerned of the deficiency (if any) mentioned in the said section and of the amount thereof.

COMMENTARY

The Accountant is defined by RSC 1986, Ord. 125, r. 1 as meaning "the Accountant attached to the High Court or a deputy appointed by the Minister for Justice". Authorised securities are likewise defined as meaning "any investment in which money under the control or subject to the order of any court may be invested pursuant to the provisions of the Trustees (Authorised Investments) Act 1958, section 3".

Appendix P

No. 14

(O. 77, r. 65)

Request for Investment of Money Lodged Under the Trade Union Act, 1941

[Name and address of trade union]

The Accountant is hereby requested to invest the sum of £ _____ deposited by this Trade Union under the Trade Union Act, 1941, in the following security [or securities]:

Dated
(Signed)
Secretary or Treasurer.

ORDER 77, PART VIII

No. 15

(O. 77, r. 65)

REQUEST FOR VARIATION OF SECURITIES DEPOSITED UNDER THE TRADE UNION ACT, 1941

[Name and address of trade union]

The Accountant is hereby requested to sell the following security or securities comprised in this Trade Union's deposit, namely: —

and to invest the proceeds of said sale in the following security (or securities):—

Dated
(Signed)
    Secretary or Treasurer.

No. 16

(O. 77, r. 65)

REQUEST FOR PAYMENT TO A BANK OR OTHER PAYEE OF INCOME ON SECURITIES COMPRISED IN A DEPOSIT UNDER THE TRADE UNION ACT, 1941

[Name and address of trade union]

The Accountant is hereby requested and authorised to pay the income as received from the securities from time to time comprised in the deposit of this Trade Union to [name and address] whose receipt shall be a full and sufficient discharge.

Dated
(Signed)
    Secretary or Treasurer.

Rules of the Superior Courts 1986

No. 17

(O. 77, r. 66)

Statutory Declaration to be Made When Income to be Paid Otherwise Than to Bankers of Depositor

---

I, _____ of _____ do solemnly and sincerely declare that I am the Secretary [or Treasurer] of the _____ Trade Union, by which a deposit has been made pursuant to the Trade Union Act, 1941, and that I am authorised by the said Trade Union to request payment of the income or dividends on such deposit to be made to _____ . And I make this solemn declaration conscientiously believing the same to be true and by virtue of the Statutory Declarations Act, 1938.

(Signed)

Declared, &c.

No. 18

(O. 77, r. 67)

Request for Return of Deposit Made Under the Trade Union Act, 1941

[*Name and address of trade union*]

The Accountant is hereby requested to pay and/or transfer to:

Full name(s)
address(es)
and
description
of transferees

the following amounts of cash and/or securities all [*or* part of] the deposit made on behalf of the above-named Trade Union, namely:

Order 77, Part VIII

Cash: _____

Securities: _____

    (Signed)

                                   Secretary.

    (Signed)

                                     Treasurer.

No. 19

Statutory Declaration to be Made When Payment of Money Otherwise Than to Bankers or Transfer of Securities is Requested

I, _____ of _____ do solemnly and sincerely declare that I am the Secretary of the _____ Trade Union, by which a deposit has been made pursuant to the Trade Union Act, 1941.

I, _____ of _____ do solemnly and sincerely declare that I am the Treasurer of the said _____ Trade Union. And We, the said _____ and the said _____ do solemnly and sincerely declare that we are authorised by the said Trade Union to request the return of the said deposit [*or a specified portion thereof*] and that payment or transfer thereof be made to

                    [*set out manner*]

And we make this solemn declaration conscientiously believing the same to be true and by virtue of the Statutory Declaration Act, 1938.

    (Signed)

                                   Secretary.

    (Signed)

                                   Treasurer.

Declared, &c.

TRADE UNION ACT 1942

(*Number 23 of 1942*)

An Act to amend and extend the Trade Union Acts, 1871 to 1941.
[*9 December 1942*]

Be it enacted by the Oireachtas as follows:—

Definitions

1.—In this Act—
the expression "the Minister" means the Minister for [Labour];
the expression "the Act of 1941" means the Trade Union Act, 1941 (No. 22 of 1941).

COMMENTARY

The word in square brackets was substituted by virtue of the Labour (Transfer of Departmental Administration and Ministerial Functions) Order 1966 (S.I. No. 164 of 1966).

Extension of "excepted body" in section 6 of the Act of 1941

2.—In section 6 of the Act of 1941, the expression "excepted body" shall include a body all the members of which are employed by the same employer and which carries on negotiations for the fixing of the wages or other conditions of employment of its own members (but of no other employees).

Exemption in certain cases from requirement of holding negotiation licence

3.—(1) Notwithstanding anything contained in sub-section (1) of section 6 of the Act of 1941, a body which negotiates on a board in relation to which this section is applicable shall not, by reason only of so negotiating, be required to be the holder of a negotiation licence issued under Part II of the Act of 1941.

(2) In this section, the expression "board in relation to which this section is applicable" means any of the following bodies, that is to say:—

    (*a*) [a joint labour committee],

(b) [...]
(c) [...]
(d) an [industrial training] committee established under the [Industrial Training Act 1967],
(e) a joint industrial council recognised by the Minister, a joint conciliation or arbitration board so recognised, or any similar body so recognised.

(3) A certificate of the Minister that a body is or is not recognised for the purposes of this section by him shall be conclusive evidence in all proceedings of the matters which it certifies.

COMMENTARY

Subsection (2)(a)

The words in square brackets were substituted by section 56 of the Industrial Relations Act 1946.

Subsection (2)(b) and (c)

The deletion of the words in square brackets was necessitated by the Industrial Relations Act 1976.

Subsection (2)(d)

The Industrial Training Act 1967, which repealed the Apprenticeship Act 1959, which in turn had repealed the Apprenticeship Act 1931, has been amended by the Labour Services Act 1987.

Subsection (2)(e)

Section 65 of the Industrial Relations Act 1946 provides that a registered joint industrial council shall be a board in relation to which this section is applicable.

Subsection (3)

In *Maher v. Attorney General* [1973] I.R. 110 the Supreme Court held that section 44(2) of the Road Traffic Act 1968, which provided that an analyst's certificate as to the concentration of alcohol in a blood or urine specimen should be *conclusive* evidence as to the concentration of alcohol, was an invalid legislative infringement on the judicial power.

Inspection free of charge by officer of the Minister of register of members of trade union

4.—(1) Paragraph (c) of subsection (1) of section 12 of the Act of 1941 shall have effect as if it provided that a register of members of a trade union kept in pursuance of that section shall, in the case of an inspection thereof by an officer of the Minister authorised in writing to inspect such register, be kept open for inspection free of charge.

(2) Paragraph (d) of subsection (1) of section 13 of the Act of 1941 shall have effect as if it provided that a register of members of a trade union kept in pursuance of that section shall, in the case of

an inspection thereof by an officer of the Minister authorised in writing to inspect such register, be kept open for inspection free of charge.

Appeal from refusal of membership of trade union having exclusive right of organisation

5. [...]

COMMENTARY

Since Part III of the Trade Union Act 1941 was held to be invalid having regard to the provisions of the Constitution in *National Union of Railwaymen* v. *Sullivan* [1947] I.R. 77, this section (which was to be construed as one with Part III of the 1941 Act) has been deleted.

Repeal of certain provisions of the Act of 1941

6.—The following provisions of the Act of 1941 are hereby repealed: paragraph (b) of subsection (3) of section 6, subsections (4), (5), and (8) of section 6, and section 35.

Short title and collective citation

7.—(1) This Act may be cited as the Trade Union Act, 1942.

(2) This Act and the Trade Union Acts, 1871 to 1941, may be cited together as the Trade Union Acts, 1871 to 1942.

TRADE UNION ACT 1947

(*Number 17 of 1947*)

An Act to repeal and re-enact, with variations and for a limited period, the provisions of Section 8 of the Trade Union Act, 1941, and to provide for other matters connected therewith.

[*9 July 1947*]

Be it enacted by the Oireachtas as follows:—

Definitions

1.—In this Act—
the expression "the Act of 1941" means the Trade Union Act, 1941 (No. 22 of 1941);
the expression "the Minister" means the Minister for [Labour].

COMMENTARY

The word in square brackets was substituted by virtue of the Labour (Transfer of Departmental Administration and Ministerial Functions) Order 1966 (S.I. No. 164 of 1966).

Variation of Schedule to Act of 1941

2.—(1) Where, during the period of twelve months commencing on the passing of this Act, the Minister is satisfied that, as regards any particular trade union registered under the Trade Union Acts, 1871 to 1942, it would cause undue hardship if such trade union were compelled to make and keep with the High Court the full deposit specified by section 7 of the Act of 1941, the Minister may by order declare that every sum of money mentioned in the Schedule to the Act of 1941 shall, as regards such trade union, be deemed to be reduced to such extent not exceeding seventy-five per cent. as the Minister thinks proper.

(2) An order under subsection (1) of this section shall have effect in accordance with its terms for the period specified in that behalf therein, save that no such order shall have effect after the expiration of the period of twelve months commencing on the passing of this Act.

(3) The Minister may by order, made after six months' notice of the making thereof has been given to the trade union concerned, revoke any order previously made by him under subsection (1) of this section.

Trade Union Act 1947

COMMENTARY

Subsection (1)

19 orders have been made under this section and by the subsequent Acts listed below, reducing by 75 per cent. the sum which the trade unions named in the schedules are required to maintain or deposit with the High Court. They are S.I. Nos. 279 of 1948, 6 of 1950, 136 of 1950, 220 of 1950, 23 of 1952, 52 of 1952, 117 of 1952, 119 of 1954, 87 of 1955, 190 of 1955, 199 of 1956, 150 of 1956, 213 of 1956, 117 of 1957, 235 of 1957, 175 of 1959, 11 of 1960, 4 of 1961 and 32 of 1961. Most of the unions named, however, have had their negotiation licences revoked because they have ceased to exist.

The date of passing of this Act was July 9, 1947 and the twelve months limit was renewed annually by the Trade Union Acts 1948, 1949, 1950 and 1951 and then indefinitely by section 3 of the Trade Union Act 1952, *infra* at p. 87.

Repeal of section 8 of Act of 1941 and continuance of orders

3.—(1) Section 8 of the Act of 1941 is hereby repealed.

(2) Where an order under subsection (1) of section 8 of the Act of 1941 was in force immediately before the passing of this Act—

(a) the order shall continue to be in force, and
(b) the provisions of section 2 of this Act shall apply to the order as if it were an order under subsection (1) of that section.

Short title and collective citation

4.—(1) This Act may be cited as the Trade Union Act, 1947.

(2) This Act and the Trade Union Acts, 1871 to 1942, may be cited together as the Trade Union Acts, 1871 to 1947.

TRADE UNION ACT 1952

(*Number 13 of 1952*)

An Act to extend for an indefinite period the provisions of section 2 of the Trade Union Act, 1947, and to provide for other matters connected therewith. [*2 July 1952*]

Be it enacted by the Oireachtas as follows:—

Act of 1947

1.—In this Act the expression "the Act of 1947" means the Trade Union Act, 1947 (No. 17 of 1947).

Appointed day

2.—It shall be lawful for the Minister for [Labour] when he so thinks proper, by order to appoint a day (in this Act referred to as the appointed day) to be the appointed day for the purposes of this Act.

COMMENTARY

The word in square brackets was substituted by virtue of the Labour (Transfer of Departmental Administration and Ministerial Functions) Order 1966 (S.I. No. 164 of 1966). No such day has yet been appointed.

Extension of section 2 of the Act of 1947

3.—Section 2 of the Act of 1947 is hereby amended by the substitution for references to the period commencing on the passing of that Act and ending on the 8th day of July, 1952, inserted therein by the Trade Union Act, 1951 (No. 14 of 1951), of references to the period commencing on such passing and ending on the appointed day.

Continuance of existing orders

4.—Every order—

(a) made under subsection (1) of section 2, or continued in force by section 3, of the Act of 1947, and
(b) in force on the 8th day of July, 1952,

shall continue in force until the appointed day unless previously revoked.

Short title and collective citation

5.—(1) This Act may be cited as the Trade Union Act, 1952.

(2) The Trade Union Acts, 1871 to 1951 and this Act may be cited together as the Trade Union Acts, 1871 to 1952.

TRADE UNION ACT 1971

(*Number 33 of 1971*)

An Act to amend and extend the Trade Union Act, 1941.
[*10 December 1971*]

Be it enacted by the Oireachtas as follows:

Definitions

1.—In this Act—
"the Act of 1941" means the Trade Union Act, 1941;
"authorised trade union" has the meaning assigned to it by section 7 of the Act of 1941;
"the Congress" means the body known as the Irish Congress of Trade Unions;
"the Minister" means the Minister for Labour;
"trade union" has the same meaning as in the Trade Union Acts, 1871 to 1952.

Grant of negotiation licence

2.—(1) Notwithstanding Part II of the Act of 1941 but subject to section 3 of this Act, a body of persons shall not be granted a negotiation licence under that Part unless it is a body which, in addition to fulfilling a condition specified in section 7(1)(a) of the Act of 1941, fulfils the following conditions—

(a) that, not less than eighteen months before the date of the application for the negotiation licence it—
  (i) notifies the Minister, the Congress and any trade union, of which any members of the body are members, of its intention to make the application,
  (ii) causes to be published in at least one daily newspaper published in the State a notice in the prescribed form (within the meaning of the Act of 1941) of its intention to make the application, and
  (iii) deposited and kept deposited with the High Court the appropriate sum, and
(b) that it shows to the satisfaction of the Minister that, both at a date not less than eighteen months before the date of the

application for the negotiation licence and at the date of that application, it had not less than [1000] members resident in the State.

(2) Where after the passing of this Act a trade union is formed consisting wholly or mainly of two or more authorised trade unions which have amalgamated and each of which, immediately before the amalgamation, had been the holder of a negotiation licence, subsection (1) of this section shall not apply to the grant of a negotiation licence to the trade union so formed.

(3) [...].

(4) In this section "the appropriate sum" means the sum appropriate to the number of members of the relevant body in accordance with the Schedule to this Act.

COMMENTARY

Subsection (1)(a)(ii)

Every notice of intention to make an application for a negotiation licence shall be in the form contained in the Schedule to the Trade Union Act 1971 (Notice of Intention to Apply for Negotiation Licence) Regulations 1972 (S.I. No. 158 of 1972), reproduced *infra* at p. 93.

Subsection (1)(b)

The figure in square brackets was substituted by section 21(3) of the Industrial Relations Act 1990. Section 16(3) of the 1990 Act provides that a body of persons shall not be granted a negotiation licence unless, in addition to fulfilling the relevant conditions specified in section 7 of the Trade Union Act 1941 and section 2 of the Trade Union Act 1971 (as amended by section 21 of the 1990 Act), it complies with section 14(2) of the 1990 Act.

Subsection (2)

This subsection does not empower authorised trade unions to amalgamate. *Per* Keane J. in *National Union of Journalists* v. *Sisk* High Court, unreported, July 31, 1990, "it does no more than provide that, where they have amalgamated and where each held a negotiation licence, they do not have to comply with the new conditions set out in subsection (1) for the grant of a negotiation licence." While the subsection "certainly proceeds on the assumption that 'authorised trade unions' may amalgamate," they may only do so where both trade unions are registered in this jurisdiction (see commentary to sections 1, 2 and 9 of the 1975 Act, *infra* at pp. 95–96, 99–100).

Subsection (3)

This subsection was repealed by section 7 of the Industrial Relations Act 1990.

Subsection (4)

See section 21(3) of the Industrial Relations Act 1990 for the "appropriate sum", in respect of a body of persons applying for a negotiation licence after July 18, 1990.

Application to High Court

3.—(1) A body of persons (in this section referred to as the

Trade Union Act 1971

applicant) which fulfils a condition specified in section 7(1)(a) of the Act of 1941, and which has deposited and keeps deposited with the High Court the appropriate sum (within the meaning of section 2 of this Act), but otherwise does not fulfil a condition specified in section 2 of this Act, may apply to the High Court for a declaration under this section.

(2) The High Court, after hearing any evidence adduced by the applicant, the Minister, the Congress and any other trade union, may at its discretion declare that the granting of a negotiation licence to the applicant would not be against the public interest.

(3) On the making of a declaration under this section the applicant shall be deemed, for the purposes of section 10 of the Act of 1941, to have been shown to the satisfaction of the Minister to be an authorised trade union.

COMMENTARY

Subsection (1)

Order 107 of the Rules of the Superior Courts 1986 (S.I. No. 15 of 1986) provides that every application under this section shall be brought by special summons (rule 1); that the summons shall be entitled in the matter of the Trade Union Act 1971 and on the application of the person bringing the same (rule 2); and that the summons shall be served on the Minister for Labour (rule 3).

Subsection (2)

It has been held by Carroll J. that this machinery is to be relied on only as a last resort and that unions should explore all possible avenues compatible with the legislative policy of reducing the number of trade unions before applying to the Court: see *Irish Aviation Executive Staff Association* v. *Minister for Labour* [1981] I.L.R.M. 350. In order to ensure that the evidential requirements of this subsection are satisfied, the applicant union should apply to the High Court for directions in relation to the evidence to be adduced prior to the hearing: *Post Office Workers' Union* v. *Minister for Labour* [1981] I.L.R.M. 355.

Expenses

4.—The expenses incurred by the Minister in the administration of this Act shall, to such extent as may be sanctioned by the Minister for Finance, be paid out of moneys provided by the Oireachtas.

Short title and collective citation

5.—(1) This Act may be cited as the Trade Union Act, 1971.

(2) The Trade Union Acts, 1871 to 1952, and this Act may be cited together as the Trade Union Acts, 1871 to 1971.

TRADE UNION ACT 1971

SCHEDULE

(Section 2(4))

DEPOSITS

1. Where the number of members does not exceed 2,000, the deposit shall be £5,000.
2. Where the number of members exceeds 2,000 but does not exceed 5,000, the deposit shall be £5,000 together with £200 for each additional 300 members (or part of 300 members) in excess of 2,000 members.
3. Where the number of members exceeds 5,000 but does not exceed 10,000, the deposit shall be £7,000 together with £200 for each additional 500 members (or part of 500 members) in excess of 5,000 members.
4. Where the number of members exceeds 10,000 but does not exceed 20,000, the deposit shall be £9,000 together with £200 for each additional 1,000 members (or part of 1,000 members) in excess of 10,000 members.
5. Where the number of members exceeds 20,000 the deposit shall be £11,000 together with £200 for each additional 1,000 members (or part of 1,000 members) in excess of 20,000 members, but subject to an overriding maximum of £15,000.

TRADE UNION ACT, 1971 (NOTICE OF INTENTION TO APPLY FOR NEGOTIATION LICENCE) REGULATIONS, 1972

(*S.I. No. 158 of 1972*)

1. These regulations may be cited as the Trade Union Act, 1971 (Notice of Intention to apply for Negotiation Licence) Regulations, 1972.

2. Every notice under Section 2(1)(a)(ii) of the Trade Union Act, 1971 (No. 33 of 1971), of intention to make an application under Section 9 of the Trade Union Act, 1941 (No. 22 of 1941), for a negotiation licence under Part II of that Act, shall be in the form contained in the Schedule to these regulations.

Schedule

Trade Union Acts, 1871 to 1971

Notice is hereby given, pursuant to Section 2(1)(a)(ii) of the Trade Union Act, 1971, by the Trade Union referred to below, of its intention to make an application under Section 9 of the Trade Union Act, 1941, for a negotiation licence under that Act.

(Name of trade union)

(Address of head office of trade union)

TRADE UNION ACT 1975

(*Number 4 of 1975*)

An Act to amend the law relating to the amalgamation of Trade Unions and the alteration of the name of a Trade Union, to provide for transfer of engagements from one trade union to another, to amend and extend the Trade Union Acts, 1871 to 1971, and to provide for other matters connected with the aforesaid matters. [*22 April 1975*]

Be it enacted by the Oireachtas as follows:

Interpretation

1.—(1) In this Act—
"the amalgamating unions" and "the amalgamated union," in relation to a proposed amalgamation, mean respectively the trade unions proposing to amalgamate and the trade union which is to result from the proposed amalgamation;
"Minister" means the Minister for Labour;
"Registrar" means the Registrar of Friendly Societies;
"trade union," save where the context otherwise requires, has the same meaning as in the Trade Union Acts, 1871 to 1971;
"the transferor trade union" and "the transferee trade union," in relation to a proposed transfer of engagements, mean respectively the trade union proposing to transfer its engagements and the trade union proposing to accept them.

(2) For the purposes of sections 3 and 4 "member," in relation to a trade union, means a member for the time being entitled to any benefits provided out of the funds of the trade union but, where the rules of a trade union specify the persons (or class of persons) entitled to vote on a particular matter (or class of matter), "member" means those persons.

(3) In this Act—

(a) a reference to a section is to a section of this Act unless it is indicated that reference to some other enactment is intended,
(b) a reference to a subsection is to the subsection of the section in which the reference occurs, unless it is indicated that reference to some other section is intended.

Trade Union Act 1975

COMMENTARY

In *National Union of Journalists* v. *Sisk* High Court, unreported, July 31, 1990, Keane J. held that a body which is a trade union under the law of a foreign country, which carries on its principal activities in that country, which is not registered as a trade union pursuant to the Trade Union Acts 1871–1990 and which has not been granted a certificate pursuant to section 2(3) of the Trade Union Act 1913 (hereafter referred to as a foreign union) cannot be regarded as a "trade union" within the meaning of the Trade Union Acts. Consequently the Registrar of Friendly Societies had been "entirely correct" to refuse to sanction a transfer of engagements from the Irish Print Union to the National Union of Journalists. The decision has been appealed to the Supreme Court.

Amalgamations of, and transfers of engagements by, trade unions

2.—(1) Subject to this Act, two or more trade unions may amalgamate, whether with or without a division or dissolution of the funds of one or more amalgamating union.

(2) Two or more trade unions shall not amalgamate unless in the case of each amalgamating union a resolution, approving an instrument of amalgamation which has been approved by the Registrar, is passed on a vote taken in a manner satisfying the conditions specified in section 3(1).

(3) Subject to this Act, a trade union may transfer its engagements to another trade union.

(4) A trade union shall not transfer its engagements to another trade union unless—

(a) the other union has undertaken to fulfil the engagements, and
(b) in the case of the transferor union, a resolution, approving an instrument of transfer which has been approved by the Registrar, is passed on a vote taken in a manner satisfying the conditions specified in section 3(1).

COMMENTARY

The High Court has confirmed (*National Union of Journalists* v. *Sisk* High Court, unreported, July 31, 1990) that the 1975 Act does not have extra-territorial effect and that the jurisdiction of the Registrar of Friendly Societies under the Act is limited to trade unions registered in the State, except in the case of a body of persons expressly provided for under section 9. Keane J. was of the opinion that to construe the Act in any other manner would mean "imputing to the legislature an intention that trade unions in foreign jurisdictions, having no connection of any sort with the Republic of Ireland and not possessing a single member in this jurisdiction, could require the Registrar to process applications for their amalgamation." Thus the Registrar would be obliged in any case where two foreign unions "wished, for ulterior motives of their own, to obtain some form of official sanction to an amalgamation or transfer, to go through the solemn charade of perusing the documentation and issuing the necessary approval, in reliance on undertakings which would be wholly unenforceable and subject to stipulations as to the vesting of assets which could not be controlled from this jurisdiction." It follows that the Registrar has no jurisdiction not only in respect of transfers of engagements from Irish trade unions to foreign unions but also in respect of amalgamations between Irish unions and foreign unions and transfers of engagements from foreign unions to Irish unions. (See further, commentary to section 9, *infra.*)

Conditions for amalgamations or transfers

3.—(1) The conditions referred to in section 2 are the following:

(a) every member of the union shall be entitled to vote on the resolution and the voting shall be by secret ballot;

(b) every member of the union shall be allowed to vote without interference or constraint and, so far as is reasonably possible, shall be given a fair opportunity of voting;

(c) the method of voting shall consist of the marking of a voting paper by the person voting;

(d) the union shall take all reasonable steps to ensure that, not less than seven days before voting on the resolution begins, every member of the union has received a notice in writing complying with subsection (3);

(e) not less than seven days before voting on the resolution begins, the union shall cause to be published in at least one daily newspaper published in the State notice (in such form as may be prescribed by regulations made by the Minister for Industry and Commerce under section 13) of the holding of the vote.

(2) Before a resolution to approve an instrument of amalgamation or transfer is voted on by the members of a trade union, the trade union shall satisfy the Registrar that the steps it proposes to take comply with subsection (1)(d).

(3) The notice referred to in subsection (1)(d) shall—

(a) either set out in full the relevant instrument or give sufficient account of it to enable a recipient of the notice to form a reasonable judgment of the main effects of the proposed amalgamation or transfer,

(b) state, if it does not set out the instrument in full, where copies of the instrument may be inspected,

(c) comply with any regulations under this Act, and

(d) be approved by the Registrar on being satisfied that it complies with the foregoing requirements of this subsection.

(4) The relevant instrument shall comply with the requirements of any regulations under this Act for the time being in force and relating thereto.

COMMENTARY

See the Trade Union Amalgamations Regulations 1976 (S.I. No. 53 of 1976), reproduced *infra* at p. 109.

Approval of documents by Registrar

4.—Before a resolution to approve an instrument of amalgamation of transfer is voted on by the members of a trade union, the instrument and the notice referred to in section 3(1)(*d*) shall be submitted to the Registrar, who shall approve them on being satisfied that they comply with the requirements of section 3.

Voting on resolution to approve amalgamation or transfer

5.—Where a vote is taken by a trade union on a resolution to approve an instrument of amalgamation or transfer, a simple majority of the votes recorded shall be sufficient to pass the resolution notwithstanding anything in the rules of the union.

COMMENTARY

In *Dunne* v. *Marks* High Court, unreported, May 30, 1968, Teevan J. held that spoiled votes did not constitute recorded votes for the purposes of the Trade Union (Amalgamation) Act 1917.

Registration of instrument of amalgamation or transfer

6.—An instrument of amalgamation or transfer shall not take effect before it has been registered by the Registrar under this Act, and shall not be so registered before the expiration of a period of six weeks beginning with the date on which an application for its registration is lodged with the Registrar.

Application of sections 2 to 6

7.—Sections 2 to 6 shall apply to every amalgamation or transfer of engagements notwithstanding anything in the rules of a trade union concerned.

Power to alter rules for purpose of transfer of engagements

8.—(1) Where a trade union proposes to transfer its engagements to another trade union and an alteration of the rules of the transferee union is necessary to give effect to the instrument of transfer, the committee of management or other governing body of the transferee union shall, notwithstanding anything in the rules, have power by memorandum in writing to alter the rules so far as may be necessary to give effect to the instrument of transfer.

(2) An alteration of the rules of a trade union under this section shall not take effect unless or until the instrument of transfer takes effect.

(3) This section shall not apply in the case of a trade union the rules of which expressly exclude the application to that union of this section.

Amalgamations and transfers by members of certain trade unions

9.—Where, in the case of a body of persons which is a trade union under the law of another country and has its headquarters control situated in that country, a majority of the members of that body who are resident in the area comprising the State and Northern Ireland so decide, the members of that body who are so resident may, in accordance with this Act, amalgamate with or transfer their engagements to another trade union and shall, from the making of such a decision, be a trade union for the purpose of section 2.

COMMENTARY

Keane J. was of the opinion that this section applies to the converse of the *N.U.J.* case (see commentary to sections 1 and 2, *supra*) since it enabled a foreign trade union with members resident in the area comprising the State and Northern Ireland to effect a transfer of engagements to another trade union when a majority of these members wish this to happen. Section 9, however, does not address the situation that would have arisen had the National Union of Journalists (N.U.J.) decided to amalgamate with, or transfer its engagements to, the Irish Print Union (I.P.U.). It addresses the situation where the Irish members of the N.U.J. wish to amalgamate with or transfer their engagements to another union. Section 9 enables those members so to do, regardless of what their union's rules provide, without recourse to the approval or sanction of the foreign members of the union. *Pace* Keane J., it is not correct to say that section 9 would have been "wholly superfluous" if the N.U.J.'s argument that a foreign union was a trade union within the meaning of section 1(1) was correct. It is true that a foreign union could then amalgamate with or transfer its engagements to an Irish union but Keane J. was of the opinion that, if the N.U.J.'s submissions were well founded, "the Oireachtas would not have found it necessary expressly to empower the relevant members to effect the transfer: it would simply have provided that the existing power of the union to effect the transfer could only be exercised where a majority of the members resident in the Republic of Ireland and Northern Ireland so resolved." That, however, would have given the Irish members a veto on any such amalgamation or transfer. Section 9, as outlined above, addresses a different situation, namely that of the Irish members of the N.U.J. deciding to amalgamate with or transfer their engagements to the I.P.U., contrary to the wishes or the rules, perhaps, of the N.U.J. as a whole. Were the N.U.J. to seek to amalgamate with or transfer its engagements to the I.P.U., the only situation where it might be reasonable for the legislature to confer a veto on the Irish members would be where the N.U.J. (assuming it was either permitted or required so to do) sought to effect a transfer of its *Irish* engagements only, by balloting all its members, Irish and foreign. The effect of section 9, however, is that in such a situation only the Irish members need be balloted; likewise where the Irish members wish to secede from the N.U.J.

In respect of the union with which such members wish to merge, it is interesting to note that the Minister for Labour rejected suggestions that section 9 be restricted to amalgamations with or transfers of engagements to "another trade union based in the State or Northern Ireland" on the ground that the Constitution would not permit such a limitation of the right to association: see 79 *Seanad Debates* Cols 1067–1068 (March 25, 1975). It must follow, however, from Keane J.'s decision in the *N.U.J.* case, that if an Irish union cannot amalgamate with or transfer its engagements to a foreign union even where that union has an Irish branch, then neither can the Irish members of a foreign union. Even with the aid of section 9, the trade union with which such members wished to merge would not be a "trade union" within the meaning of the Act and thus the amalgamation or transfer would not be one in respect of which the Registrar had any jurisdiction. Keane J. said that the constitutional guarantee of the right to form associations and unions contained in Article 40.6.1°(iii) did not require him to read the Act so as to extend its benefits to unions in other countries.

Complaints to Registrar regarding resolutions

10.—(1) A members of a trade union which passes or purports to pass a resolution approving an instrument of amalgamation or transfer may complain to the Registrar on one or more than one of the following grounds—

(a) that the manner in which the vote on the resolution was taken did not satisfy the conditions specified in section 3(1).
(b) that the votes recorded in relation to the resolution did not have the effect of passing it.

(2) A complaint under this section lodged with the Registrar after the expiry of the period of six weeks beginning on the date on which an application for registration under section 6 is lodged with him shall not be entertained.

(3) Where a complaint under this section is made, the Registrar shall not register the relevant instrument under this Act until the complaint is finally determined under this Act.

(4) Where a complaint is made under this section, the Registrar may, after giving the complainant and the trade union concerned an opportunity of being heard, either dismiss the complaint or find it to be justified.

(5) Where the Registrar finds a complaint under this section to be justified, he shall make an order specifying what steps he requires to be taken before he will consider an application for registration under section 6, of the instrument concerned.

(6) The Registrar shall furnish to the complainant and the trade union concerned a statement of the reasons for a decision by him on a complaint under this section.

(7) The Registrar may from time to time by order vary an order under subsection (5), and after making an order under that subsection in relation to an instrument of amalgamation or transfer shall not entertain any application to register the instrument unless he is satisfied that the steps specified in the order (or, where it has been varied, in the order as varied) have been taken.

(8) The Schedule to this Act shall apply in relation to complaints under this section.

(9) Subject to subsection (10), the validity of a resolution approving an instrument of amalgamation or transfer shall not be questioned in any legal proceedings (except proceedings before the Registrar under this section or proceedings arising out of such proceedings) on any ground on which a complaint could be, or could have been, made to the Registrar under this section.

(10) In the course of proceedings on a complaint under this section the Registrar may, at the request of the complainant or of the trade union, state a case for the opinion of the High Court on a question of law arising in the proceedings, and the decision of the High Court on a case stated under this subsection shall be final.

(11) For the purposes of this section a complaint which is withdrawn shall be deemed to be finally determined at the time when it is withdrawn.

(12) An appeal shall lie to the High Court on a point of law against a decision of the Registrar under this section.

Disposal of property on amalgamation or transfer

11.—(1) Subject to this section, where an instrument of amalgamation or transfer takes effect, the property held for the benefit of an amalgamating union or of a branch of such a union by the trustees of the union or branch, or for the benefit of a transferor trade union or of a branch of such a trade union by the trustees of the union or branch, shall without any conveyance, assignment or assignation vest on the instrument taking effect or on the appointment of the appropriate trustees, whichever is the later, in the appropriate trustees.

(2) Where any land of which the ownership is registered under the Registration of Title Act, 1964, becomes vested by virtue of this section, the registering authority under that Act shall, upon payment of the appropriate fee, register the appropriate trustees in the appropriate register maintained under that Act as owner (within the meaning of that Act) of the land.

(3) Subsection (1) shall not apply to property excepted from the operation of this section by the instrument of amalgamation or transfer.

(4) In this section "the appropriate trustees" means—

(a) in the case of property to be held for the benefit of a branch of an amalgamated union or for the benefit of a branch of the transferee union, the trustees of that branch, unless the rules of the amalgamated union or transferee union provide that the property to be so held shall be held by the trustees of the union, and
(b) in any other case, the trustees of the amalgamated or transferee union.

Change of name of trade union

12.—(1) Subject to this section, a trade union may change its name by any method of doing so expressly provided for by its rules or, if its rules do not expressly provide for a method of doing so, by adopting in accordance with its rules an alteration of the provision in them which gives the union its name.

(2) A change of name by a trade union shall not take effect until it is registered by the Registrar under this Act, and the Registrar shall not register a change of name if it appears to him that registration of the union under the proposed new name would be contrary to section 13(3) of the Trade Union Act, 1871.

(3) Where a trade union changes its name the change of name shall not affect any right or obligation of the union or of any of its members, and, notwithstanding the change of name, any pending legal proceedings may be continued by or against the trustees of the union or any other officer of the union who can sue or be sued on its behalf.

COMMENTARY

Recent examples include the decision of the Irish Union of Distributive Workers and Clerks to change its name to the Irish Distributive and Administrative Trade Union; that of the Irish Creamery Managers' Association to change its name to the Dairy Executives' Association; that of the Federated Union of Employers to change its name to the Federation of Irish Employers; and that of the National Busworkers' Union to change its name to the National Rail and Busworkers' Union.

Regulations

13.—(1) The Minister for Industry and Commerce may, with the consent of the Minister, make regulations for carrying this Act into effect.

(2) Without prejudice to the generality of subsection (1), regulations under this section may provide for all or any of the following:—

(a) applications to the Registrar under this Act;
(b) the registration under this Act of any document;
(c) the inspection of documents kept by the Registrar under this Act;
(d) the charging of fees in respect of such matters and of such amounts as may with the approval of the Minister for Finance be prescribed by the regulations;
(e) requiring any application for the registration of an instrument of amalgamation or transfer or a change of name to be accompanied by such statutory declarations or other documents as may be specified in the regulations;
(f) making provision as to the form or content of any document required by this Act or by the regulations to be sent or submitted to the Registrar and the manner in which any such document shall be signed or authenticated;
(g) authorising the Registrar to require notice to be given or published in such manner as he may direct of the fact that an application for registration of an instrument of amalgamation or transfer has been or is to be made to him.

COMMENTARY

See the Trade Union Amalgamations Regulations 1976 (S.I. No. 53 of 1976), reproduced *infra* at p. 109.

Saver for pending amalgamations, etc.

14.—Where before the commencement of this Act—

(a) two or more trade unions have taken steps for the purpose of amalgamating and a ballot for that purpose has been taken by one of them,
(b) a trade union has taken steps for the purpose of transferring its engagements to another trade union and has passed a resolution for their transfer, or
(c) a trade union has taken steps for the purpose of changing its name and has obtained from its members the necessary consent.

the amalgamation, transfer of engagements or change of name, as the case may be, if not completed before such commencement may, notwithstanding this Act, be proceeded with and completed as if this Act had not been passed.

Grants towards exceptional expenses of amalgamation or transfer

15.—Whenever two or more trade unions amalgamate or whenever a trade union transfers its engagements to another trade union, the Minister may, with the consent of the Minister for Finance, make to one or more of those trade unions out of moneys to be provided by the Oireachtas a grant of such amount as the Minister thinks fit, towards such expenses as he is satisfied [. . .] were incurred by that trade union or those trade unions as a result of, in the course of, or in contemplation of such amalgamation or transfer.

COMMENTARY

The words in square brackets were deleted by section 22(1) of the Industrial Relations Act 1990. See also section 22(2) of the 1990 Act for the Minister's power to make a grant following an unsuccessful attempt to amalgamate or to effect a transfer of engagements.

Neither under this Act nor the 1990 Act is the Minister required to itemise the broad headings of the expenses in respect of which grants have been paid. Speaking during the Committee Stage of the Industrial Relations Bill 1989 the Minister said (399 *Dáil Debates* Col. 879) that each claim for expenses arising from a trade union merger was examined on its merits. Grants were generally paid in respect of postage, printing, advertising, meetings, conferences, pensions and legal fees and he emphasised that all moneys paid must be sanctioned by the Department of Finance and were subject to scrutiny by the Comptroller and Auditor General.

Repeals

16.—Sections 11 to 13 of the Trade Union Act Amendment Act, 1876, and the Trade Union (Amalgamation) Act, 1917, are hereby repealed.

Restriction on holding and grant of negotiation licence in case of certain trade unions

17.—(1) Notwithstanding Part II of the Act of 1941 and section 2 of the Act of 1971, a body of persons which is a trade union under the law of another country and has its headquarters control situated in that country shall not hold or be granted a negotiation licence under that Part unless, in addition to fulfilling the relevant conditions specified in section 7 of the Act of 1941 and section 2 of the Act of 1971, it fulfils the condition specified in subsection (2).

(2) The condition referred to in subsection (1) is that the trade union concerned has a committee of management or other controlling authority every member of which is resident in the State or Northern Ireland and which is empowered by the rules of that trade union to make decisions in matters of an industrial or political

nature which arise out of and are in connection with the economic or political condition of the State or Northern Ireland, are of direct concern to members of the trade union resident in the State or Northern Ireland and do not affect members not so resident.

(3) This section, so far as it applies to an existing holder of a negotiation licence, shall come into operation on such date as the Minister fixes for that purpose by order.

(4) In this section—
"the Act of 1941" means the Trade Union Act, 1941;
"the Act of 1971" means the Trade Union Act, 1971.

COMMENTARY

Subsection (1)

Section 16(4) of the Industrial Relations Act 1990 provides that such a body of persons shall not be granted a negotiation licence unless, in addition to fulfilling the conditions referred to in this section and section 16(3) of the 1990 Act, it forwards to the Registrar of Friendly Societies, at the time of application for a negotiation licence, a copy of its rules incorporating the provisions referred to in section 14(2) of the 1990 Act.

Subsection (3)

The Trade Union Act 1975 (Section 17) (Commencement) Order 1983 (S.I. No. 177 of 1983) fixed this date as July 1, 1983.

Expenses

18.—The expenses incurred in the administration of this Act shall, to such extent as may be sanctioned by the Minister for Finance, be paid out of moneys provided by the Oireachtas.

Short title and collective citation

19.—(1) This Act may be cited as the Trade Union Act, 1975.

(2) The Trade Union Acts, 1871 to 1971, and this Act may be cited together as the Trade Union Acts, 1871 to 1975.

SCHEDULE

(Section 10(8))

PROVISIONS SUPPLEMENTAL TO SECTION 10

1. On a complaint made under section 10 the Registrar may—

(a) require the attendance of the complainant or of any officer

of the trade union and may, on the application of the complainant or any such officer, require the attendance of any person as a witness;
(b) require the production of any documents relating to the matters complained of;
(c) administer oaths and take affirmations and require the complainant, any officer of the trade union or any person attending as a witness to be examined on oath or affirmation;
(d) grant to the complainant or to any officer of the trade union such discovery as to documents and otherwise, or such inspection of documents, as might be granted by the High Court;
(e) order the whole or any part of the expense of hearing the complaint, as certified by him, to be paid either out of the funds of the trade union or by the complainant; and
(f) order the trade union to pay to the complainant out of the funds of the union, or the complainant to pay to the union, either a specified sum in respect of the costs incurred by the complainant or the union (as the case may be) or the taxed amount of those costs.

2. A person who, on the application of any person, is required to attend before the Registrar as a witness in proceedings on a complaint under section 10 shall be entitled to be paid by the person on whose application he is so required—

(a) such sum in respect of loss of time and travelling expenses as he would be entitled to on being served with a summons to attend as a witness in the High Court, and
(b) if he duly attends, a sum equal to any further allowances to which he would be entitled if attending as a witness in proceedings in the High Court.

3. (1) Subject to subparagraph (2) of this paragraph, if any person without reasonable excuse fails or refuses to comply with a requisition of the Registrar under paragraph 1(a) to 1(c) of this Schedule or any order of the Registrar made in pursuance of paragraph 1(d) of this Schedule, he shall be liable on summary conviction to a fine not exceeding [two hundred] pounds or to imprisonment for a term not exceeding three months, or to both such fine and such imprisonment.

(2) A person shall not be convicted of an offence under this paragraph by reason of failure or refusal on his part to comply with a requisition to attend as a witness before the Registrar unless any sum to which he is entitled under paragraph 2(a) of this Schedule has been paid or tendered.

(3) Any costs required by an order under paragraph 1(f) of this Schedule to be taxed may be taxed in the High Court according to the scale prescribed by rules of that court for proceedings in that court as may be directed by the order or, if the order gives no direction, by that court.

(4) Any sum payable by virtue of an order under paragraph 1(e) or 1(f) of this Schedule shall, if the High Court so orders, be recoverable by execution issued from that court or otherwise as if payable under an order of that court.

COMMENTARY

The figure in square brackets in paragraph 3(1) was substituted by section 4 of the Industrial Relations Act 1990.

TRADE UNION AMALGAMATIONS REGULATIONS 1976

(S.I. No. 53 of 1976)

GENERAL

1. These Regulations may be cited as the Trade Union Amalgamations Regulations, 1976, and shall come into operation on the 21st day of February, 1976.

2. In these Regulations—
"the Act" means the Trade Union Act, 1975 (No. 4 of 1975);
"duly authenticated" means bearing the Registrar's signature and the date of signing;
"Schedule 1" means Schedule 1 to these Regulations;
"Schedule 2" means Schedule 2 to these Regulations;
"Schedule 3" means Schedule 3 to these Regulations.

Approval of proposed instruments and notices

3. (1) An application pursuant to section 4 of the Act for approval of a proposed instrument of amalgamation or transfer shall be submitted to the Registrar—

(a) in the case of a proposed amalgamation, by one of the amalgamating trade unions, or
(b) in the case of a proposed transfer of engagements, by the transferor trade union,

and shall in each case be accompanied by two copies of the proposed instrument each signed as required by paragraph 6 of Schedule 1 or paragraph 4 of Schedule 2 (as may be appropriate) and by a copy of the rules of each trade union which would be a party to the proposed instrument.

(2) Two copies of the notice referred to in section 3(1)(d) of the Act and required by section 4 of the Act to be submitted to the Registrar shall be so submitted.

(3) The Registrar shall indicate his approval under section 4 of the Act of such instrument or notice by returning one copy to the trade union which submitted it, marked with the word "Approved" or the word "Ceadaithe" and duly authenticated.

Contents of instrument of amalgamation or transfer

4. (1) The instrument of amalgamation shall contain the particulars and information specified in Schedule 1.

(2) An instrument of transfer shall contain the particulars and information specified in Schedule 2.

Contents of notice of vote

5. The notice required by section 3(1)(e) of the Act shall be in the form specified in Schedule 3 to these Regulations.

Application for registration of instruments

6. (1) A trade union proposing to have an instrument of amalgamation registered under section 6 of the Act shall apply to the Registrar on a form provided by him for that purpose, and the application shall be signed by three members of the committee of management or other governing body, and the secretary, of each of the amalgamating trade unions.

(2) An application under paragraph (1) shall be accompanied by two copies of the instrument, two copies of the proposed rules of the amalgamated trade union and a statutory declaration on a form provided by the Registrar for that purpose from each of the amalgamating unions.

(3) Each copy of proposed rules furnished under paragraph (2) shall be signed by the secretary of each of the amalgamating unions.

(4) An application for registration of an instrument of transfer under section 6 of the Act shall be signed by three members of the committee of management or other governing body, and the secretary, of each of the trade unions concerned and shall be submitted to the Registrar by the transferee trade union on a form provided by him for that purpose.

(5) An application under paragraph (4) shall be accompanied by two copies of the instrument, by statutory declarations, on forms provided by the Registrar for that purpose, by the secretaries of the transferor trade union and transferee trade union respectively and by two copies of any amendments to the rules of the transferee trade union since the date of the relevant submission under Regulation 3(1).

(6) Where in his opinion it is necessary to do so in order to ensure adequate publicity for the purpose of section 10(2) of the Act the Registrar may, not later than seven days after he receives the application for registration of the instrument, require notice to be given or published, in such manner and form and before such date as he may direct, of the fact that the application for registration has been or is to be made to him.

(7) Before registering under section 6 of the Act an instrument furnished under this Regulation, the Registrar shall satisfy himself that the proposed rules of the amalgamated trade union or transferee trade union (as may be appropriate) are in no way inconsistent with the terms of the instrument.

(8) Where he registers under section 6 of the Act an instrument furnished to him under this Regulation, the Registrar shall return one copy to the address specified for that purpose on the form referred to in paragraph (1) or to the transferee trade union (as may be appropriate), marked with the word "Registered" or the word "Cláraithe" and duly authenticated.

Registration of change of name

7. (1) A trade union proposing to have a change of name registered under Section 12 of the Act shall apply to the Registrar in duplicate on a form provided by him for that purpose, and the application shall be signed by three members of the committee of management or other governing body, and the secretary of the trade union.

(2) An application under paragraph (1) shall be accompanied by a statutory declaration on a form provided by the Registrar for that purpose by the secretary of the union as to the method in which the change of name was effected.

(3) Upon approving the change of name the Registrar shall return to the trade union one copy of the application under this Regulation, marked with the word "Registered" or the word "Cláraithe" and duly authenticated.

SCHEDULE 1

(Regulation 4 (I))

CONTENTS OF INSTRUMENT OF AMALGAMATION

1. The instrument shall state that it is an instrument of amalgamation between the trade unions named therein as the amalgamating trade unions, and that on the coming into operation of the instrument the members of the amalgamating trade unions will become members of the amalgamated trade union and be subject to that union's rules.

2. The instrument shall either set out the proposed rules of the amalgamated trade union or state who are the persons authorised to draw up those rules.

3. If the instrument does not set out the proposed rules it shall contain a summary of what those rules will provide with regard to the following matters:—

(i) the name and principal purposes of the amalgamated trade union;
(ii) the conditions of admission to membership;
(iii) the structure of the amalgamated trade union;
(iv) the method of appointing and removing its governing body and principal officials and of altering its rules;
(v) the contributions and benefits applicable to members of the amalgamating trade unions.

4. The instrument shall specify any property held for the benefit of any of the amalgamating trade unions or for the benefit of a branch of any of those unions which is not to be vested in the appropriate trustees and shall state the proposed disposition of any such property.

5. Without prejudice to section 6 of the Act, the instrument shall state the date on which it is to take effect.

6. The instrument shall be signed by three members of the committee of management or other governing body and the secretary of each of the amalgamating trade unions.

Schedule 2

(Regulation 4(2))

Contents of Instrument of Transfer

1. The instrument shall state that it is an instrument of transfer of the engagements of the trade union named therein as the transferor trade union to the trade union named therein as the transferee trade union and that on the coming into operation of the instrument the members of the transferor trade union will become members of the transferee trade union and be subject to that union's rules.

2. The instrument shall:—

(i) state what conditions and benefits will be applicable to members of the transferor trade union under the transferee trade union's rules;
(ii) if members of the transferor trade union are to be allocated to a branch or section or to branches or sections of the

Trade Union Amalgamations Regulations 1976

transferee trade union, give particulars of such allocation or the method by which it is to be decided;

(iii) state whether before registration of the instrument the transferee trade union's rules are to be altered in their application to members of the transferor trade union and, if so, the effect of any alterations;

(iv) without prejudice to section 6 of the Act, state the date on which the instrument is to take effect.

3. The instrument shall specify any property held for the benefit of the transferor trade union or for the benefit of a branch of the transferor trade union which is not to be vested in the appropriate trustees and shall state the proposed disposition of any such property.

4. The instrument shall be signed by three members of the committee of management or other governing body and the secretary of each of the trade unions.

Schedule 3

(Regulation 5)

Trade Union Acts, 1871 to 1975

Notice of Vote on Amalgamation/Transfer of Engagements*

The _____ (here insert name of trade union) hereby gives notice of the holding of a vote on the proposed amalgamation with/transfer of engagements to* _____ _____ (here insert name of other trade union(s) concerned).

*Strike out whichever is inapplicable.

TRADE UNION (FEES) REGULATIONS 1983

(S.I. No. 292 of 1983)

1. These Regulations may be cited as the Trade Union (Fees) Regulations, 1983.

2. These Regulations shall come into operation on the 17th day of October, 1983.

3. The Interpretation Act, 1937 (No. 38 of 1937), applies to these Regulations.

4. (1) The fees specified in Part I of the Schedule to these Regulations shall be payable in respect of matters to be transacted or for the inspection of documents under the Trade Union Acts, 1871 to 1975, other than matters to be transacted under the Trade Union Act, 1975 (No. 4 of 1975).

(2) The fees specified in Part II of the Schedule shall be payable in respect of matters to be transacted under the Trade Union Act, 1975.

(3) No fees shall be payable in respect of the services specified in Part III of the Schedule to these Regulations.

5. The Trade Union (Fee) Regulations, 1978 (S.I. No. 86 of 1978) are hereby revoked.

Trade Union (Fees) Regulations 1983

Schedule

Part I

Ref. No.	Service	Fee
1.	Certificate of registry of a trade union	£1.00
2.	Certificate of registry alteration of rules	£0.50
3.	Direction to transfer stock	£10.00
4.	Registry of notice of a dissolution	£2.00
5.	Authentication of a document required to be authenticated by the Registrar which is not chargeable with any other fee	£2.00
6.	Inspection of trade union file	£0.12 Provided that the Registrar may dispense with the fee in cases where he considers that it is in the public interest so to do.
7.	Copy of extract of any document (in addition to fee for Registrar's signature)	Ten pence per photostat copy of any page or extract of any document or portion of any page or extract thereof.

Part II

Ref. No.	Service	Fee
1.	Certificate of Registry of change of name of Trade Union	£5.00
2.	Registry of an instrument of amalgamation	£10.00
3.	Registry of an instrument of transfer of engagements	£10.00

Part III

1. Cancellation or withdrawal of certificate of registry of trade union.
2. Filing of notice of change of registered office.
3. Any document supplied to a public department.
4. Any document in respect of which a fee is already chargeable under the Trade Union Acts, 1871 to 1975, or under any other Act.

INDUSTRIAL RELATIONS LEGISLATION

INDUSTRIAL RELATIONS ACT 1946

(Number 26 of 1946)

An Act to make further and better provision for promoting harmonious relations between workers and their employers and for this purpose to establish machinery for regulating rates of remuneration and conditions of employment and for the prevention and settlement of trade disputes, and to provide for certain other matters connected with the matters aforesaid. [*27 August 1946*]

Be it enacted by the Oireachtas as follows:—

Part I

Preliminary and General

Short title

1.—This Act may be cited as the Industrial Relations Act, 1946.

Commencement

2.—This Act shall come into operation on the day appointed for the purpose by order of the Minister.

COMMENTARY

The Industrial Relations Act 1946 (Commencement) Order 1946 (S.R. & O. No. 304 of 1946) appointed September 23, 1946 as the day on which the Act came into operation.

Definitions generally

3.—In this Act—
the expression "the Court" means the Labour Court;
the expression "the Minister" means the Minister for [Labour];
the word "prescribed" means prescribed by regulations made by the Minister under this Act;
the expression "registered joint industrial council" has the meaning given to it by section 59 of this Act;
the expression "trade dispute" means any dispute or difference between employers and workers or between workers and workers connected with the employment or non-employment, or the terms

of the employment, or with the conditions of employment, of any person;

the expression "trade union" means a trade union which is the holder of a negotiation licence granted under the Trade Union Act, 1941 (No. 22 of 1941).

COMMENTARY

The word in brackets was substituted by virtue of the Labour (Transfer of Departmental Administration and Ministerial Functions) Order 1966 (S.I. No. 164 of 1966).

"Worker"

4. [...]

COMMENTARY

This section was repealed by section 7 of the Industrial Relations Act 1990.

Regulations

5.—The Minister may make regulations in relation to anything referred to in this Act as prescribed.

COMMENTARY

See the Industrial Relations Act 1946 Regulations 1950 (S.I. No. 258 of 1950), reproduced *infra* at p. 163.

Laying of regulations before Houses of the Oireachtas

6.—Every regulation made under this Act shall be laid before each House of the Oireachtas as soon as may be after it is made and, if a resolution annulling the regulation is passed by either House, within the next 21 days on which that House has sat after the regulation has been laid before it, the regulation shall be annulled accordingly, but without prejudice to the validity of anything previously done thereunder.

Prosecutions by the Minister

7.—An offence under any section or subsection contained in this Act may be prosecuted by the Minister.

Repeals

8.—The enactments specified in the second column of the First Schedule to this Act are hereby repealed to the extent specified in the third column of that Schedule.

Expenses

9.—The expenses incurred in the administration of this Act shall, to such extent as may be sanctioned by the Minister for Finance, be paid out of moneys provided by the Oireachtas.

PART II

THE LABOUR COURT

Establishment of the Labour Court

10.—(1) There shall be a body, to be known as the Labour Court, to fulfil the functions assigned to it by this Act.

(2) [...]

(3) The chairman shall be appointed by the Minister and shall hold office on such terms as shall be fixed by the Minister when appointing him.

(4) The Minister shall, in respect of each workers' member, designate an organisation representative of trade unions of workers to nominate a person for appointment, and, in respect of each employers' member, designate a trade union of employers to nominate a person for appointment and the Minister shall appoint the person so nominated.

(5) If, when a particular appointment of workers' members (or, in the event of a casual vacancy, a workers' member) is to be made—

(a) more than one organisation representative of trade unions of workers is in being, and
(b) the Minister is of opinion that it is undesirable that the appointment should be made under subsection (4) of this section.

he may, by regulations, declare that the appointment, instead of being made under the said subsection (4), shall be made under this subsection, and thereupon the following provisions shall have effect—

(i) the Minister shall invite trade unions of workers and organisations representative of trade unions of workers to nominate persons for appointment, and
(ii) he shall make the appointment from amongst the persons so nominated.

(6) The [Civil Service Commissioners Act 1956] shall not apply to the office of chairman or ordinary member of the Court.

(7) An ordinary member shall, unless he dies, resigns or is removed, hold office—

(a) if appointed under subsection (4) of this section, for such period, not exceeding five years, as shall be fixed by the Minister when appointing him,
(b) if appointed under subsection (5) of this section, for five years or, if the regulations, by virtue of which he was appointed, are sooner revoked or annulled, until such revocation or annulment.

(8) An ordinary member may be removed from office by the Minister for stated reasons but, if the organisation by which he was nominated is in being, only with the consent of that organisation.

(9) The chairman and the ordinary members shall be paid such remuneration and allowances as the Minister, with the consent of the Minister for Finance, determines.

(10) The Chairman shall devote the whole of his time to the work of the Court.

(11) An ordinary member shall not hold the office of trustee, treasurer, secretary or any other office in, or be a member of any committee of, a trade union, or hold any office or employment which would prevent him from being at all times available for the work of the Court.

(12) A person shall not be appointed to be chairman or a member of the court unless he is ordinarily resident in the State.

COMMENTARY

Subsection (2)

This subsection was repealed by section 23 of the Industrial Relations Act 1990.

For the composition of the Court see now section 2 (as amended) of the Industrial Relations Act 1969, *infra* at p. 165.

Subsection (4)

In *Murphy* v. *Minister for Social Welfare* [1987] I.R. 295, Blayney J. held that the employment of an ordinary member of the Labour Court was not employment under a contract of service but was employment in the Civil Service of the State and was insurable employment as such for the purposes of the Social Welfare (Consolidation) Act 1981, as amended.

Subsection (6)

By virtue of section 8(2)(b) of the 1956 Act, references to the Civil Service Regulation Acts 1924 and 1926 are to be construed as a reference to the 1956 Act.

Divisions of the Court

11. [...]

INDUSTRIAL RELATIONS ACT 1946

COMMENTARY

This section was repealed by section 23 of the Industrial Relations Act 1969.

Deputy chairman

12. [...]

COMMENTARY

This section was repealed by section 23 of the Industrial Relations Act 1969.

Registrar and officers and servants of the Court

13.—(1) (a) The Minister shall appoint to be registrar of the Court a practising barrister or practising solicitor of not less than 10 years' standing.

(b) For the purposes of paragraph (a) of this subsection, service in a situation in the Civil Service, for appointment to which only barristers and solicitors were eligible, shall be treated as practice as a barrister or solicitor.

(2) The Minister, after consultation with the Court and with the consent of the Minister for Finance, may appoint such officers and servants of the Court as he thinks necessary to assist the Court in the performance of its functions.

(3) The registrar, officers and servants of the Court shall hold office on such terms and receive such remuneration as the Minister for Finance determines.

Technical assessors

14.—(1) The Court may appoint technical assessors to assist it on any matter relating to proceedings before the Court.

(2) Technical assessors shall be paid such fees as the Minister, with the consent of the Minister for Finance, determines.

Places for sittings of the Court and lodgment of documents

15.—(1) The headquarters of the Court shall be at Dublin, but sittings of the Court may be held elsewhere in the State.

(2) The Court may designate suitable places at which documents for the Court may be lodged.

Conciliation officers

16. [...]

COMMENTARY

This section was repealed by section 23 of the Industrial Relations Act 1969.

Finality of decisions of the Court

17.—No appeal shall lie from the decision of the Court on any matter within its jurisdiction to a court of law.

COMMENTARY

See *Branigan* v. *Keady* [1959] I.R. 283 where the Supreme Court held that this section was confined in its operation to a decision given in the exercise of a jurisdiction conferred by the Act. See, however, section 10(5) of the Anti-Discrimination (Pay) Act 1974 and section 26(5) of the Employment Equality Act 1977.

Seal of the Court

18.—(1) The Court shall have an official seal which shall be judicially noticed.

(2) The seal of the Court shall, when affixed to any document, be authenticated by the signature of the chairman or the registrar of the Court or of a person authorised by the Court to authenticate it.

(3) Every document purporting to express an order, award or other decision of the Court and to be sealed with the seal of the Court authenticated in accordance with this section shall, unless the contrary is proved, be deemed to have been duly and lawfully so sealed and shall, unless as aforesaid, be received in evidence as such order, award or decision without further proof and, in particular, without proof of any signature affixed to such document for the purpose of such authentication and without proof of the office or authority of the person whose signature such signature purports to be.

COMMENTARY

Section 56(2) of the Industrial Relations Act 1990 provides that this section shall apply to a document to which section 56(1) of the 1990 Act relates.

Proof of orders of the Court

19.—(1) Section 4 of the Documentary Evidence Act, 1925 (No. 24 of 1925), shall apply to every order of the Court.

(2) Subsection (1) of section 6 of the Documentary Evidence Act, 1925, is hereby amended by adding to the official documents mentioned in that subsection orders of the Court, and the said section 6 shall have effect accordingly.

Procedure of the Court

20.—(1) Subject to section 11 of this Act and subsection (2) of this section, the quorum for a meeting or sitting of the Court shall be five.

(2) The chairman may direct that, for the consideration of a particular matter, the Court shall consist of the chairman and two ordinary members selected by him, namely, a workers' member and an employers' member, and, if the chairman so directs, no other member shall act as a member of the Court in respect of that matter.

(3) Where—

(a) any question arises under this Act at a meeting or sitting of the Court, and
(b) the members of the Court are unable to agree upon the determination of the question,

the following provisions shall have effect—

(i) if the majority of the ordinary members agree upon the determination of the question, the question shall be determined accordingly,
(ii) if a majority of the ordinary members do not agree, but a majority of all the members agree, the question shall be determined accordingly,
(iii) otherwise, the question shall be determined in accordance with the opinion of the chairman.

(4) The decision of the Court shall be pronounced by the chairman or such other member as the chairman shall authorise for the purpose, and no other opinion, whether assenting or dissenting, shall be pronounced nor shall the existence of any such other opinion be disclosed.

(5) Subject to this section, the Court may make rules for the regulation of its proceedings.

(6) Rules under this section may provide for the cases in which persons may appear before the Court by counsel or solicitor and, except as so provided, no person shall be entitled to appear by counsel or solicitor before the Court.

(7) The Court may hold any sitting or part of a sitting in private.

COMMENTARY

Subsection (5)

Three sets of Rules have been made by the Court, only two of which are still operative. The Labour Court Provisional (Part III) Rules 1946, which came into operation on October 24, 1946, are reproduced *infra* at p. 153. The Labour Court Provisional (Part VI) Rules 1946, which came into operation on October 10, 1946, are reproduced *infra* at p. 157. The third set, relating to Part VII of the Act, lapsed when that Part expired: see the commentary to Part VII, *infra*.

Subsection (6)

Rule 6(2) of both sets of Rules provides that a party may apply to the Court for leave to appear by counsel or solicitor and that the Court may grant such leave if it is of the opinion that the matter in issue is of such a nature that the applicant ought to be assisted by counsel or solicitor. The validity of this rule was unsuccessfully challenged in *McElroy* v. *Mortished* High Court, unreported, June 17, 1949. The full text of Gavan Duffy J.'s judgment is included as an appendix to the Court's *Third Annual Report* (1949).

Power of Court to summon witnesses, etc.

21.—(1) The Court may for the purposes of any proceedings before it under this Act do all or any of the following things—

(a) summon witnesses to attend before it,
(b) examine on oath (which a member or the registrar of the Court is hereby authorised to administer) the witnesses attending before it,
(c) require any such witness to produce to the Court any document in his power or control.

(2) A witness before the Court shall be entitled to the same immunities and privileges as if he were a witness before the High Court.

(3) If any person—

(a) on being duly summoned as a witness before the Court makes default in attending, or
(b) being in attendance as a witness refuses to take an oath legally required by the Court to be taken, or to produce any document in his power or control legally required by the Court to be produced by him, or to answer any question to which the Court may legally require an answer,

he shall be guilty of an offence under this section and shall be liable on summary conviction thereof to a fine not exceeding [two hundred] pounds.

(4) Where a witness attends before the Court in pursuance of a summons under this section, the Minister may, if he thinks fit, pay to him such sum in respect of expenses incurred by him in connection with his attendance as the Minister, with the sanction of the Minister for Finance, determines.

COMMENTARY

Subsection (1)

In *State (Casey)* v. *Labour Court* (1984) 3 *J.I.S.L.L.* 135, O'Hanlon J. said that since the section conferred a discretion on the Court to regulate its own procedures in respect of these matters, neither the parties nor the High Court could dictate to the Court as to the manner in which it should conduct its own procedures "once it exercises its powers in accordance with the statute from which it derives its authority to act." O'Hanlon J. did add (at p. 138) that he did not think the Court should allow itself to be deterred by considerations of difficulty or inconvenience from taking evidence on oath where it would otherwise be proper or desirable to do so.

Subsection (3)

The figure in square brackets was substituted by section 4 of the Industrial Relations Act 1990. See section 56 of the Industrial Relations Act 1990 as to what constitutes evidence of a failure by a person to attend the Labour Court as a witness.

Prohibition on disclosure of information

22.—The Court shall not include in any report any information obtained by it in the course of any proceedings before it under this Act as to any trade union or as to the business carried on by any person which is not available otherwise than through evidence given at the proceedings, without the consent of the trade union or persons concerned, nor shall any member of the Court or the registrar or any officer or servant of the Court or any person concerned in the proceedings, without such consent, disclose any such information.

Reports, etc., by Court

23.—(1) The Court shall, as soon as may be after the expiration of each year, make to the [Minister] a general report (in this section referred to as an annual report) of its proceedings under this Act during that year.

(2) [...]

(3) An annual report shall contain particulars of each registered joint industrial council together with the name of the secretary of the council and the address of its principal office.

(4) A copy of each annual report shall be laid before each House of the Oireachtas.

(5) The Court shall furnish to the Minister a copy of each order, recommendation and award made by the Court under this Act as soon as may be after it is made.

COMMENTARY

Subsection (1)

The word in square brackets was substituted by section 15 of the Industrial Relations Act 1969.

Subsection (2)

This subsection was repealed by section 7 of the Industrial Relations Act 1990.

INDUSTRIAL RELATIONS ACT 1946

Duty of Court to consider certain matters with regard to employment conditions referred to it by the Minister

24.—The Court shall consider any matter referred to it by the Minister concerning the employment conditions prevailing as regards the workers of any class and their employers and shall furnish a report thereon to the Minister together with such recommendations (if any) as it thinks proper, and the Minister shall consider any report and recommendation so made.

COMMENTARY

See also section 38 of the Industrial Relations Act 1990 which empowers the Minister to refer to the Court disputes which affect the public interest or which are of special importance.

PART III

AGREEMENTS RELATING TO WAGES AND CONDITIONS OF EMPLOYMENT

COMMENTARY

The rules applicable at a formal sitting of the Court for the transaction of business under this Part are rules 4–13 of the Labour Court Provisional (Part III) Rules 1946, reproduced *infra* at p. 153. The registration provisions in this Part of the Act replaced and improved those contained in section 50 of the Conditions of Employment Act 1936. At the end of 1987 there were 56 employment agreements on the Register, of which only seven are active: see Appendix V to the Labour Court's *Forty-First Annual Report* (1987). For an assessment of the registration system see Horgan "The Failure of Legal Enforcement—A Review of the Registration of Agreements in the Labour Court" (1985) 4 *J.I.S.L.L.* 28.

Definitions for purposes of Part III

25.—In this Part—

the expression "employment agreement" means an agreement relating to the remuneration or the conditions of employment of workers of any class, type or group made between a trade union of workers and an employer or trade union of employers or made, at a meeting of a registered joint industrial council, between members of the council representative of workers and members of the council representative of employers;

the expression "the register" means the Register of Employment Agreements;

the word "registered," in relation to an employment agreement, means for the time being registered in the register;

the expression "registered employment agreement" means an employment agreement for the time being registered in the register.

Register of Employment Agreements

26.—The Court shall maintain a register to be known as the Register of Employment Agreements.

COMMENTARY

Section 40(2) of the Industrial Training Act 1967 declares that nothing in an employment agreement registered in the Register maintained under section 26 shall affect the provisions of section 41 of the 1967 Act (which, as amended, confers power on FÁS to ensure the provision of a sufficient number of trained persons to meet the requirements of an activity of industry). Section 40(3)(a) of the 1967 Act provides that, upon the coming into force of any rules under section 27 of that Act, any provisions of an employment agreement then in force registered in the Register which relate to matters the subject of the rules shall cease to have effect. In addition, section 40(4) of the 1967 Act provides that where an employment agreement is registered in the Register, at a time when rules under that Act are in force, any provisions of the agreement which relate to matters the subject of the rules shall not have effect.

Registration of employment agreements

27.—(1) Any party to an employment agreement may apply to the Court to register the agreement in the register.

(2) Every application to register an employment agreement shall be accompanied by a copy of the agreement.

(3) Where an application is duly made to the Court to register in the register an employment agreement, the Court shall, subject to the provisions of this section, register the agreement in the register if it is satisfied—

(a) that, in the case of an agreement to which there are two parties only, both parties consent to its registration and, in the case of an agreement to which there are more than two parties, there is substantial agreement amongst the parties representing the interests of workers and employers, respectively, that it should be registered,

(b) that the agreement is expressed to apply to all workers of a particular class, type or group and their employers where the Court is satisfied that it is a normal and desirable practice or that it is expedient to have a separate agreement for that class, type or group,

(c) that the parties to the agreement are substantially representative of such workers and employers,

(d) that the agreement is not intended to restrict unduly employment generally or the employment of workers of a particular class, type or group or to ensure or protect the retention in use of inefficient or unduly costly machinery or methods of working,

(e) that the agreement provides that if a trade dispute occurs between workers to whom the agreement relates and their employers a strike or lock-out shall not take place until the dispute has been submitted for settlement by negotiation in the manner specified in the agreement, and

(f) that the agreement is in a form suitable for registration.

(4) Where an application is made to the Court to register an employment agreement, the Court shall direct such parties thereto as the Court shall specify to publish specified particulars of the agreement in such manner as, in the opinion of the Court, is best calculated to bring the application to the notice of all persons concerned.

(5) (a) The Court shall not register an employment agreement until the lapse of 14 days after publication of particulars of the agreement in accordance with subsection (4) of this section.

(b) If within that period the Court receives notice of an objection to the agreement being registered, the Court shall, unless it considers the objection frivolous, consider the objection and shall hear all parties appearing to the Court to be interested and desiring to be heard, and if, after such consideration, the Court is satisfied that the agreement does not comply with the requirements specified in subsection (3) of this section, the Court shall refuse to register the agreement.

(6) A registered employment agreement shall not prejudice any rights as to rates of remuneration or conditions of employment conferred on any worker by another Part of this Act or by any other Act.

COMMENTARY

See rules 14–17 of the Labour Court Provisional (Part III) Rules 1946.

Variation of registered employment agreement

28.—(1) If a registered employment agreement provides for the variation of the agreement in accordance with this section, any party to the agreement may apply to the Court to vary it in its application to any worker or workers to whom it applies.

(2) Where an application is made under this section to vary an agreement, the following provisions shall have effect:—

(a) the Court shall consider the application and shall hear all persons appearing to the Court to be interested and desiring to be heard;

(b) after such consideration, the Court may, as it thinks fit, refuse the application or make an order varying the agreement in such manner as it thinks proper;
(c) if the Court makes an order varying the agreement, the agreement shall, as from such date not being earlier than the date of the order as the Court specifies in the order, have effect as so varied.

COMMENTARY

See rules 18 and 19 of the Labour Court Provisional (Part III) Rules 1946.

Cancellation of registration

29.—(1) The registration of an employment agreement may be cancelled by the Court on the joint application of all parties thereto if the Court is satisfied that the consent of all such parties to its cancellation has been given voluntarily.

(2) The Court may cancel the registration of an employment agreement if satisfied that there has been such substantial change in the circumstances of the trade or business to which it relates since the registration of the agreement that it is undesirable to maintain registration.

(3) Where a registered employment agreement does not provide for its duration or termination, the Court may, after the lapse of 12 months from the date of registration, cancel the registration on the application, made after six months' notice to the Court, of all parties thereto representative of workers or of employers.

(4) (a) Where a registered employment agreement is expressed to be for a specified period, it shall, if in force at the end of that period, and notwithstanding any provision that it shall cease to have effect at the expiration of such period, continue in force until its registration is cancelled in accordance with this Part.
(b) The registration of an employment agreement continued in force under paragraph (a) of this subsection may be cancelled by the Court on the application of any party thereto, made after three months' notice to the Court, and consented to by all parties thereto representative of workers or of employers.

(5) Where a registered employment agreement is terminated by any party thereto in accordance with its terms, the Court shall, on receiving notice of the termination, cancel the registration.

COMMENTARY

See rule 20 of the Labour Court Provisional (Part III) Rules 1946.

Adaptation of contracts of service consequential upon registration of employment agreement

30.—(1) A registered employment agreement shall, so long as it continues to be registered, apply, for the purposes of this section, to every worker of the class, type or group to which it is expressed to apply, and his employer, notwithstanding that such worker or employer is not a party to the agreement or would not, apart from this subsection, be bound thereby.

(2) If a contract between a worker of a class, type or group to which a registered employment agreement applies and his employer provides for the payment of remuneration at a rate (in this subsection referred to as the contract rate) less than the rate (in this subsection referred to as the agreement rate) provided by such agreement and applicable to such worker, the contract shall, in respect of any period during which the agreement is registered, have effect as if the agreement rate were substituted for the contract rate.

(3) If a contract between a worker of a class, type or group to which a registered employment agreement applies and his employer provides for conditions of employment (in this subsection referred to as the contract conditions) less favourable than the conditions (in this subsection referred to as the agreement conditions) fixed by the agreement and applicable to such worker, the contract shall in respect of any period during which the agreement is registered, have effect as if the agreement conditions were substituted for the contract conditions.

Publication of particulars in relation to employment agreements and right to obtain copies thereof

31.—(1) When an employment agreement is registered the Court shall publish in such manner as it thinks fit notice of the registration together with such particulars of the agreement as the Court considers necessary.

(2) When a registered employment agreement is varied the Court shall publish in such manner as it thinks fit notice of the variation together with such particulars of the variation as the Court considers necessary.

(3) When the registration of an employment agreement is cancelled the Court shall publish in such manner as it thinks fit notice of the cancellation.

(4) The Court may from time to time publish in such manner as it thinks fit lists of registered employment agreements together with such particulars of the agreements as the Court considers necessary.

(5) The Court shall cause to be supplied to any person who applies therefor and pays the prescribed fee a copy of a registered employment agreement.

COMMENTARY

Subsection (4)

Section 53(3) of the Industrial Relations Act 1990 provides that a copy of *Iris Oifigiúil* purporting to contain a notice or list published by the Court under this section shall be prima facie evidence of the contents of the notice or list, including any particulars published therewith.

Subsection (5)

See regulation 11 of the Industrial Relations Act 1946 Regulations 1950 (S.I. No. 258 of 1950), reproduced *infra* at p. 163).

Breaches of registered employment agreements

32.—(1) If a trade union representative of workers affected by a registered employment agreement complains to the Court that any employer of any class to which the agreement relates has failed or neglected to comply with the agreement, the following provisions shall have effect—

(a) the Court shall consider the complaint, and shall hear all persons appearing to the Court to be interested and desiring to be heard;

(b) if, after such consideration, the Court is satisfied that the complaint is well-founded, the Court may by order direct the said employer to do such things (including the payment of any sum due to a worker for remuneration in accordance with the agreement) as will in the opinion of the Court result in the said agreement being complied with by the said employer.

(2) If an employer or a trade union representative of employers affected by a registered employment agreement complains to the Court that a trade union representative of workers affected by the agreement is promoting or assisting out of its funds in the maintenance of a strike which to the knowledge of the general committee of management of the trade union of workers is in contravention of the agreement and which has for its object the enforcement of a demand on an employer to grant to a worker remuneration or conditions other than those fixed by the agreement, the following provisions shall have effect—

(a) the Court shall consider the complaint and shall hear all persons appearing to the Court to be interested and desiring to be heard;

(b) if, after such consideration, the Court is satisfied that the complaint is well-founded—

   (i) the Court may, by order, direct the said trade union of workers to refrain from assisting out of its funds in the maintenance of the said strike;
   (ii) the Court may cancel the registration of the agreement.

(3) Where—

(a) a strike continues after the Court has made an order under subsection (2) of this section in respect of the strike, and
(b) members of a trade union of workers, whose rates of remuneration or conditions of employment are not the subject of the strike, are unable or decline to work while the strike continues,

then, the payment to those members of strike benefit in accordance with the rules of the trade union shall not be regarded, for the purposes of this section, as assisting in the maintenance of the strike.

(4) If, where an order is made by the Court under paragraph (b) of subsection (1) of this section or under subparagraph (i) of paragraph (b) of subsection (2) of this section, the direction contained in the order is not carried out, the person to whom the direction is given shall be guilty of an offence under this section and shall be liable on summary conviction thereof to a fine not exceeding one [thousand] pounds, and, in the case of a continuing offence, a further fine not exceeding [two hundred] pounds for every day during which the offence is continued.

COMMENTARY

Subsection (1)

See rules 21–25 of the Labour Court Provisional (Part III) Rules 1946. See also section 10 of the Industrial Relations Act 1969.

Subsection (4)

The figures in square brackets were substituted by section 4 of the Industrial Relations Act 1990. Section 52 of the Industrial Relations Act 1990 provides that the powers of inspection given to inspectors by section 12 of the Industrial Relations Act 1969 shall be exercisable for the purpose of enforcing the provisions of this section.

Interpretation of registered employment agreements

33.—(1) The Court may at any time, on the application of any person, give its decision on any question as to the interpretation of a registered employment agreement or its application to a particular person.

Industrial Relations Act 1946

(2) A court of law, in determining any question arising in proceedings before it as to the interpretation of a registered employment agreement or its application to a particular person, shall have regard to any decision of the Court on the said agreement referred to it in the course of the proceedings.

(3) If any question arises in proceedings before a court of law as to the interpretation of a registered employment agreement or its application to a particular person, the court of law may, if it thinks proper, refer the question to the Court for its decision, and the decision of the Court thereon shall be final.

COMMENTARY

As to the constitutionality of subsection (3), see Kerr and Whyte, *Irish Trade Union Law* (1985) pp. 45–48, 152–153.

Part IV

Regulation by the Court of Remuneration and Conditions of Employment of Certain Workers

Definitions

Definitions for purposes of Part IV

34.—In this Part—

the expression "employment regulation order" means an order made under section 43 of this Act;

the expression "establishment order" means an order made under section 35 of this Act;

the word "inspector" means a person appointed an inspector under section 51 of this Act;

the expression "joint labour committee" means a committee established under section 35 of this Act;

the expression "statutory conditions of employment" means, in relation to a worker to whom an employment regulation order, which fixes conditions of employment, applies, the conditions of employment fixed by the order in respect of that worker;

the expression "statutory minimum remuneration" means, in relation to a worker to whom an employment regulation order, which fixes remuneration, applies, the remuneration fixed by the order in respect of that worker.

COMMENTARY

Although section 4(2) of the Industrial Relations Act 1976 provides that sections

35–40 of the Industrial Relations Act 1946 shall not apply to the Agricultural Workers' Joint Labour Committee, such committee is deemed to be a joint labour committee within the meaning of this section.

Joint Labour Committees

Power of the Court to establish joint labour committees

35.—Subject to the provisions of this Part, the Court may by order establish a committee to perform, in relation to the class, type or group of workers described in the order and their employers, the functions assigned to it by this Part.

COMMENTARY

The most recently established Joint Labour Committee (J.L.C.) is that for Retail Grocery and Allied Trades, which came into operation on April 2, 1991 (see S.I. No. 58 of 1991). There are fourteen other J.L.C.s, six of which were originally trade boards: Aerated Waters and Wholesale Bottling; Brush and Broom; Handkerchief and Household Piece Goods; Shirtmaking; Tailoring; and Womens' Clothing and Millinery (see commentary to section 53, *infra* p. 147). The remaining eight J.L.C.s were all established by the Court: Agricultural Workers (S.I. 198 of 1976); Catering (S.I. No. 225 of 1977); Contract Cleaning (City and County of Dublin) (S.I. No. 105 of 1984); Hairdressing (Dublin) (S.I. No. 212 of 1964); Hairdressing (Cork) (S.I. No. 226 of 1977); Hotels (S.I. No. 81 of 1965); Law Clerks (S.I. No. 308 of 1947); and Provender Milling (S.I. No. 223 of 1960).

Applications for establishment orders

36.—An application for the establishment of a joint labour committee with respect to any workers and their employers may be made to the Court by—

(a) the Minister, or
(b) a trade union, or
(c) any organisation or group of persons claiming to be representative of such workers or of such employers.

COMMENTARY

Note that section 39 of the Industrial Relations Act 1990 requires the Labour Relations Commission to carry out a periodic review with a view to ascertaining whether, in the Commission's opinion, new joint labour committees should be established or, as regards existing committees, whether any establishment order requires amendment or whether any committee should be abolished. The section further requires the Commission to send a copy of any such review to the Court and to the Minister.

Restrictions on making establishment orders

37.—The Court shall not make an establishment order in respect of any workers and their employers unless the Court is satisfied—

(a) in case the application is made by an organisation or a group of persons claiming to be representative of such workers or such employers, that the claim is well-founded, and
(b) that either—
  (i) there is substantial agreement between such workers and their employers to the establishment of a joint labour committee, or
  (ii) the existing machinery for effective regulation of remuneration and other conditions of employment of such workers is inadequate or is likely to cease or to cease to be adequate, or
  (iii) having regard to the existing rates of remuneration or conditions of employment of such workers or any of them, it is expedient that a joint labour committee should be established.

Inquiry into application for an establishment order

38.—Where an application is duly made to the Court for an establishment order, the Court shall consider such application and, subject to section 37 of this Act, the following provisions shall have effect—

(a) the Court shall, after consultation with such parties as it thinks necessary, prepare a draft establishment order (in this section referred to as the draft),
(b) the Court shall publish in the prescribed manner a notice setting out—
  (i) that the Court proposes to hold an inquiry into the application,
  (ii) the day (which [shall be not less than 30 days from the date of publication of the notice or later than 60 days from the receipt of the application by the Court]) and time and place at which the inquiry will be held,
  (iii) the place where copies of the draft may be obtained,
(c) objections to the draft may, before the date for the holding of the inquiry, be submitted to the Court, and every such objection shall be in writing and state the grounds of objections and the omissions, additions or modifications asked for,
(d) the Court shall hold the inquiry on the day so specified in

the notice and consider any objections to the draft which have been submitted in accordance with paragraph (c) of this section.

COMMENTARY

The words in square brackets were substituted by section 45(1) of the Industrial Relations Act 1990.

Making of establishment orders

39.—(1) Where the Court has held, in pursuance of section 38 of this Act, an inquiry into an application for an establishment order, the Court may, subject to section 37 of this Act, if it thinks fit make the order either in terms of the draft prepared in accordance with the said section 38 or with such modifications of the said terms as it considers necessary.

(2) Where the Court makes an establishment order, it shall publish the order in the prescribed manner, and the order shall come into operation on the date on which it is so published or such later date (not being later than 14 days after the date on which it is so published) as is specified therein.

COMMENTARY

Section 45(2) of the Industrial Relations Act 1990 provides that the Court shall make an establishment order, or make known its decision not to do so, within 42 days of the completion of the enquiry held in accordance with section 38 of the 1946 Act. As to the prescribed manner for publishing the order, see regulation 4 of the Industrial Relations Act 1946 Regulations 1950 (S.I. No. 258 of 1950), reproduced *infra* at p. 159.

Revocation and variation of establishment orders

40.—Where an establishment order in respect of any workers and their employers is in force, the Court, on the application (which shall specify the grounds on which it is made) of—

(a) the Minister, or
(b) any trade union, or
(c) any organisation or group of persons which claims to be and is, in the opinion of the Court, representative of such workers or of such employers,

may by order abolish the joint labour committee established by such establishment order or amend such establishment order, and the provisions of section 38 and section 39 of this Act shall apply in relation to such application and to the order (if any) made under this section as if the application were an application under section 36 and the order were an establishment order.

Industrial Relations Act 1946

COMMENTARY

The three most recently abolished J.L.C.s are Boot and Shoe Repairing (S.I. No. 204 of 1988); General Waste Materials Reclamation (S.I. No. 205 of 1988); and Messengers (Dublin City and Dun Laoghaire) (S.I. No. 206 of 1988). The other J.L.C.s which have been abolished are Paper Box (S.I. No. 113 of 1963); Creameries (S.I. No. 340 of 1978); Hand Embroidery (S.I. No. 341 of 1978); Rope, Twine and Net (S.I. No. 342 of 1978); Tobacco (S.I. No. 343 of 1978); Sugar Confectionery (S.I. No. 344 of 1978); Packing (S.I. No. 186 of 1979); Button Making (S.I. No. 39 of 1984); Messengers (Cork City, Limerick City and Waterford City) (S.I. Nos. 40, 41 and 42, respectively, of 1984).

Constitution, officers and proceedings of joint labour committees

41. [...]

COMMENTARY

This section was repealed by section 7 of the Industrial Relations Act 1990. See now the Fifth Schedule to the Industrial Relations Act 1990.

Employment Regulation Orders

Proposals by joint labour committees in relation to remuneration and conditions of employment

42.—(1) Subject to the provisions of this section, a joint labour committee may submit to the Court proposals for fixing the minimum rates of remuneration to be paid either generally or for any particular work to all or any of the workers in relation to whom the committee operates, and such proposals may provide for a minimum weekly remuneration for all or any of such workers.

(2) Subject to the provisions of this section, a joint labour committee may submit to the Court proposals for regulating the conditions of employment of all or any of the workers in relation to whom the committee operates.

(3) A joint labour committee shall not submit proposals under this section for revoking or amending an employment regulation order unless the order has been in force for at least six months.

COMMENTARY

See section 48 of the Industrial Relations Act 1990, *infra* p. 220, for the procedure to be followed once a joint labour committee has formulated proposals for an employment regulation order.

Making of employment regulation orders

43.—(1) [...]

Industrial Relations Act 1946

(2) As soon as the Court makes an employment regulation order it shall publish notice of the making of the order and the contents thereof in the prescribed manner.

(3) An employment regulation order shall not prejudice any rights as to rates of remuneration or conditions of employment conferred on any worker by another Part of this Act or by any other Act.

(4) An employment regulation order may amend or revoke any previous employment regulation order.

(5) An employment regulation order may contain different provisions for different descriptions of workers.

COMMENTARY

Subsection (1)

This subsection was repealed by section 7 of the Industrial Relations Act 1990.

Subsection (2)

As to the prescribed manner see regulation 4 of the Industrial Relations Act 1946 Regulations 1950 (S.I. No. 258 of 1950), reproduced *infra* at p. 159.

Subsection (3)

Section 40(2) of the Industrial Training Act 1967 declares that nothing in an order made under this section shall affect the provisions of section 41 of the 1967 Act (which, as amended, confers power on FÁS to ensure the provision of a sufficient number of trained persons to meet the requirements of an activity of industry). Section 40(3)(b) of the 1967 Act provides that upon the coming into force of any rules under section 27 of that Act any provisions of an order then in force which relate to matters the subject of the rules shall cease to have effect. In addition Section 40(5) of the 1967 Act provides that where an order is made, at a time when rules under that Act are in force, any provisions of the order which relate to matters the subject of the rules shall not have effect.

Adaptation of contracts of service consequential upon employment regulation orders

44.—(1) The employer of a worker to whom an employment regulation order applies, shall—

(a) in case the order fixes remuneration, pay to such worker remuneration not less than the statutory minimum remuneration,

(b) in case the order fixes conditions of employment, grant to such worker conditions of employment not less favourable than the statutory conditions of employment.

(2) If a contract between a worker (being a worker to whom an employment regulation order, which fixes remuneration, applies) and his employer provides for the payment of less remuneration

than the statutory minimum remuneration, the contract shall have effect as if the statutory minimum remuneration were substituted for the less remuneration.

(3) If a contract between a worker (being a worker to whom an employment regulation order, which fixes conditions of employment, applies) and his employer provides for conditions of employment (in this subsection referred to as the contract conditions) less favourable than the statutory conditions of employment, the contract shall have effect as if the statutory conditions of employment were substituted for the contract conditions.

Enforcement of employment regulation orders

45.—(1) If an employer fails to pay to a worker (being a worker to whom an employment regulation order, which fixes remuneration, applies) remuneration not less than the statutory minimum remuneration, the employer shall be guilty of an offence under this subsection and shall be liable on summary conviction thereof to a fine not exceeding [seven hundred and] fifty pounds.

(2) Where the employer or any other person charged, in accordance with section 50 of this Act, as a person to whose act or default the offence was due has been found guilty of an offence under subsection (1) of this section consisting of a failure to pay to a worker remuneration not less than the statutory minimum remuneration, the court by which he is convicted may order the employer to pay to the worker such sum as is found by the said court to represent the difference between the statutory minimum remuneration and the remuneration actually paid.

(3) If, in respect of any worker (being a worker to whom an employment regulation order, which fixes conditions of employment, applies), the statutory conditions of employment are not complied with by the employer—

(a) the employer shall be guilty of an offence under this subsection and shall be liable on summary conviction thereof to a fine not exceeding [seven hundred and] fifty pounds,
(b) the court by which the employer is convicted may order the employer to pay to the worker such compensation as it considers fair and reasonable in respect of such non-compliance.

(4) Where proceedings are taken under subsection (1) of this section in respect of an offence consisting of a failure to pay to a worker remuneration not less than the statutory minimum remuneration, and notice of intention to avail of paragraph (a) of this subsection has been served with the summons, warrant or complaint—

(a) evidence may, if the employer or any other person charged, in accordance with section 50 of this Act, as a person to whose act or default the offence was due is found guilty of the offence, be given of any like contravention on the part of the employer in respect of any period during the three years immediately preceding the date of the offence, and

(b) on proof of such contravention, the court before which the proceedings are taken may order the employer to pay to the worker such sum as is found by the said court to represent the difference between the amount which ought to have been paid during that period to the worker by way of remuneration, if the worker were paid remuneration in accordance with the statutory minimum remuneration, and the amount actually so paid.

(5) In any proceedings against a person under subsection (1) of this section it shall lie with such person to prove that he has paid remuneration not less than the statutory minimum remuneration.

(6) In any proceedings against a person under subsection (3) of this section it shall lie with such person to prove that he has complied with the statutory conditions of employment.

(7) The powers given by this section for the recovery of sums due by an employer to a worker shall not be in derogation of any right of the worker to recover such sums in civil proceedings.

COMMENTARY

Subsection (1)

The words in square brackets were inserted by section 4 of the Industrial Relations Act 1990. Valuable guidance was given by O'Hanlon J. in *Minister for Labour* v. *Costello* [1988] I.R. 235 to District Justices as to how they should proceed when dealing with prosecutions brought by the Minister under this section.

Subsection (3)

The words in square brackets were inserted by section 4 of the Industrial Relations Act 1990.

Subsection (7)

Section 40 of the Industrial Training Act 1967 provides that this section, as respects a person to whom rules under section 27(1)(*f*) of the 1967 Act for the time being apply, shall cease to have effect. Note that section 49(1) of the Industrial Relations Act 1990 provides that an inspector may institute on behalf of a worker civil proceedings for the enforcement of any right of action of the worker against his employer in respect of the employer's failure to comply with a condition of employment of an employment regulation order.

Permits authorising employment of infirm and incapacitated persons at less than the statutory minimum remuneration

46.—(1) If, as respects any worker employed or desiring to be employed in such circumstances that an employment regulation order which fixes remuneration applies or will apply to him, the appropriate joint labour committee is satisfied, on application being made to it for a permit under this section either by the worker or the employer or a prospective employer, that the worker is affected by infirmity or physical incapacity which renders him incapable of earning the statutory minimum remuneration, the committee may, if it thinks fit, grant, subject to such conditions (if any) as it may determine, a permit authorising his employment at less than the statutory minimum remuneration, and while the permit is in force the remuneration authorised to be paid to him by the permit shall, if those conditions are complied with, be deemed, for the purposes of this Act, to be the statutory minimum remuneration.

(2) Where an employer employs any worker in reliance on any document purporting to be a permit granted under subsection (1) of this section authorising the employment of that worker at less than the statutory minimum remuneration, then, if the employer has notified the joint labour committee in question that, relying on that document, he is employing or proposing to employ that worker at a specified remuneration, the document shall, notwithstanding that it is not or is no longer a valid permit relating to that worker, be deemed, subject to the terms thereof and as respects only any period after the notification, to be such a permit until notice to the contrary is received by the employer from the committee.

Computation of remuneration

47.—(1) Subject to subsection (2) of this section, any reference in this Part to remuneration shall be construed as a reference to the amount obtained or to be obtained in cash by the worker from his employer clear of all deductions in respect of any matter whatsoever, except any deductions lawfully made under any enactment for the time being in force requiring or authorising deductions to be made from remuneration.

(2) Subject to any enactment for the time being in force, an employment regulation order may authorise specified benefits or advantages, provided for a worker by or on behalf of his employer, to be reckoned as payment of remuneration by the employer in lieu of payment in cash and such order shall define the monetary value at which every such benefit and advantage is to be reckoned.

Employers not to receive premiums from apprentices or learners

48.—(1) (a) Where a worker (being a worker to whom an

employment regulation order, which fixes remuneration, applies) is an apprentice or a learner, it shall not be lawful for his employer to receive directly or indirectly from him, or on his behalf or on his account, any payment by way of premium.

(b) Nothing in paragraph (a) of this subsection shall apply to any such payment as is referred to therein duly made in pursuance of any instrument of apprenticeship approved for the purpose of this subsection by a joint labour committee.

(2) If any employer receives any payment by way of premium in contravention of this section he shall be guilty of an offence under this section and shall be liable on summary conviction thereof to a fine not exceeding [seven hundred and fifty] pounds, and the court by which he is convicted may, in addition to the fine, order him to pay to the worker or other person by whom the payment was made the sum received by way of premium.

COMMENTARY

The figure in square brackets was substituted by section 4 of the Industrial Relations Act 1990.

Records and notices

49.—(1) The employer of any workers to whom an employment regulation order applies shall keep such records as are necessary to show whether or not the provisions of this Part are being complied with as respects them, and the records shall be retained by the employer for three years.

(2) The employer of any workers shall post in the prescribed manner such notices as may be prescribed for the purpose of informing them of any proposals under section 42 of this Act affecting such workers or any employment regulation order affecting such workers and shall give notice in any other manner which may be prescribed to the said workers of the said matters and of such other matters, if any, as may be prescribed.

(3) If an employer fails to comply with any of the requirements of this section, he shall be guilty of an offence under this section and shall be liable on summary conviction thereof to a fine not exceeding [five hundred] pounds.

COMMENTARY

Note that section 7 of the Industrial Relations Act 1976 provides that subsection (2) shall not apply to agricultural employers. The figure in square brackets was substituted by section 4 of the Industrial Relations Act 1990.

INDUSTRIAL RELATIONS ACT 1946

Criminal liability of agent and superior employer and special defence open to employer

50.—(1) Where the immediate employer of any worker is himself in the employment of some other person and the worker is employed on the premises of that other person, that other person shall for the purposes of this Part be deemed to be the employer of the worker jointly with the immediate employer.

(2) Where an employer is charged with an offence under any section or subsection contained in this Part, he shall be entitled, upon information duly laid by him and on giving to the prosecution not less than three days' notice of his intention, to have any other person to whose act or default he alleges that the offence was due brought before the court hearing the charge at the time appointed for the hearing of the charge, and thereupon the following provisions shall have effect—

- (a) if, after the commission of the offence has been proved, the employer proves that the offence was due to the act or the default of that other person, that other person may be convicted of the offence,
- (b) if the employer further proves that he has used all due diligence to secure that this Part and any relevant regulation or order made thereunder were complied with, he shall be acquitted of the offence.

(3) Where a defendant seeks to avail himself of subsection (2) of this section—

- (a) the prosecution, as well as the person whom the defendant charges with the offence, shall have the right to cross-examine him, if he gives evidence, and any witnesses called by him in support of his pleas and to call rebutting evidence,
- (b) the court hearing the charge may make such order as it thinks fit for the payment of costs by any party to the proceedings to any other party thereto.

(4) Where—

- (a) it appears to an inspector that an offence has been committed in respect of which proceedings might be taken under this Part against an employer, and
- (b) the inspector is reasonably satisfied that the offence of which complaint is made was due to an act or default of some other person, and that the employer could establish a defence under subsection (2) of this section,

the following provisions shall have effect—

(i) the inspector may cause proceedings to be taken against that other person without first causing proceedings to be taken against the employer,

(ii) if such proceedings are so taken, that other person may therein be charged with and, on proof that the offence was due to his act or default, be convicted of the offence with which the employer might have been charged.

Inspectors

51.—(1) The Minister may appoint such and so many persons as he thinks fit to be inspectors for the purposes of this Part.

(2) Every inspector shall be furnished by the Minister with a certificate of his appointment and when exercising any of the powers conferred on him by this Part shall, if so required by any person affected, produce such certificate to him.

Powers of inspectors

52.—(1) An inspector may, for the purpose of enforcing the provisions of this Part, do all or any of the following things, that is to say:—

(a) enter at all reasonable times any premises where he has reasonable grounds for believing that any workers to whom an employment regulation order applies are employed,

(b) require the production of wages sheets or other records of remuneration kept by an employer and any such records as are required by this Part to be kept by employers, and inspect and examine those sheets or records and copy any material part thereof,

(c) examine with respect to any matters under this Part any person whom he has reasonable grounds for believing to be or have been a worker to whom an employment regulation order applies or the employer of any such worker and require such person or employer to answer such questions (other than questions tending to incriminate such person) as such inspector may put touching such matters and to sign a declaration of the truth of the answers to such questions.

(2) If any person—

(a) obstructs or impedes an inspector in the exercise of any of the powers conferred on such inspector by this section, or

(b) refuses to produce any record which an inspector lawfully requires him to produce, or

Industrial Relations Act 1946

(c) prevents, or attempts to prevent any person from appearing before or being questioned by an inspector, or

(d) [...] fails or refuses to comply with any lawful requirement of an inspector under paragraph (b) of subsection (1) of this section,

such person shall be guilty of an offence under this subsection and shall be liable on summary conviction thereof to a fine not exceeding [five hundred] pounds.

(3) If any person required by this Part to keep records keeps or causes to be kept, or produces or causes to be produced or knowingly allows to be produced to an inspector, any record which is false in any material respect knowing it to be false, he shall be guilty of an offence under this subsection and shall be liable on summary conviction thereof to a fine not exceeding one [thousand] pounds or imprisonment for a period not exceeding three months or to both such fine and imprisonment.

(4) As inspector may institute proceedings for an offence under any section or subsection contained in this Part.

(5) (a) Any inspector may, if it appears to him that a sum is due from an employer to a worker (being a worker to whom an employment regulation order, which fixes remuneration, applies) on account of the payment to him of remuneration less than the statutory minimum remuneration, institute on behalf of and in the name of that worker civil proceedings for the recovery of that sum and in any such proceedings an order may be made for the payment of costs by the inspector as if he were a party to the proceedings.

(b) The power given by paragraph (a) of this subsection for the recovery of sums due by an employer to a worker shall not be in derogation of any right of the worker to recover such sums in civil proceedings.

COMMENTARY

Subsection (2)

The word in square brackets in paragraph (d) was deleted by section 50 of the Industrial Relations Act 1990.

The figure in square brackets was substituted by section 4 of the Industrial Relations Act 1990.

Subsection (3)

The word in square brackets was substituted by section 4 of the Industrial Relations Act 1990.

INDUSTRIAL RELATIONS ACT 1946

Provisions in relation to trade boards

Existing trade boards to become joint labour committees

53.—Any trade board which exists immediately before the commencement of this Act shall, upon such commencement, by virtue of this section be deemed to be a joint labour committee established under this Part by an establishment order (notwithstanding that its constitution is not in all respects in accordance with the provisions of this Act) and operating in relation to the workers and employers in relation to whom it operated immediately before such commencement.

COMMENTARY

Six of the fifteen joint labour committees were originally trade boards: Aerated Waters (S.R. & O. 1933 No. 45); Brush and Broom (S.R. & O. 1933 No. 47); Handkerchief and Household Piece Goods (S.R. & O. 1936 No. 9); Shirtmaking (S.R. & O. 1931 No. 21); Tailoring (S.R. & O. 1926 No. 26); Womens' Clothing and Millinery (S.R. & O. 1926 No. 27).

Existing orders under the Trade Boards Acts, 1909 and 1918

54.—Any order in force immediately before the commencement of this Act confirming, varying or cancelling any rate under the Trade Boards Acts, 1909 and 1918, shall continue in force and be deemed to be an employment regulation order.

Pending notices of proposals varying minimum rates of wages under the Trade Boards Acts, 1909 and 1918

55.—If any notice of proposals for varying minimum rates of wages under the Trade Boards Acts, 1909 and 1918, has been duly given by a trade board before the commencement of this Act, the like proceedings may be had on those proposals as might have been had thereon if the said Acts had not been repealed by this Act, and if an order is made confirming the proposals that order shall be deemed to be an employment regulation order.

Adaptation of references to trade boards

56.—References in any document (other than an enactment repealed by this Act) to a trade board shall be construed as references to a joint labour committee.

Determination of certain questions

Determination of certain questions

57.—(1) The Court may at any time, on the application of any person, give its decision on the question whether a particular joint labour committee operates as respects a particular person or whether a particular employment regulation order applies to a particular person.

(2) A court of law, in determining any question arising in proceedings before it whether a particular joint labour committee operates as respects a particular person or whether a particular employment regulation order applies to a particular person, shall have regard to any decision of the Court referred to it in the course of the proceedings.

(3) If any question arises in proceedings before a court of law whether a particular joint labour committee operates as respects a particular person or whether a particular employment regulation order applies to a particular person, the court of law may, if it thinks proper, refer the question to the Court for its decision, and the decision of the Court thereon shall be final.

Standard wages for areas

Standard wages for areas

58.—(1) The Court, after publication, in such manner as it thinks fit, of notice of its intention, may, on its own motion or on the application of any interested party, fix, in respect of any area selected by the Court, the wage (in this section referred to as the standard wage) which, in the opinion of the Court, should be paid to a male adult worker performing in that area unskilled work for a normal working week.

(2) In fixing the standard wage for any area the Court shall have regard to the prevailing level of wages for other workers in that area.

(3) Where the Court fixes a standard wage for any area it shall publish particulars thereof in such manner as it thinks fit.

(4) Nothing in this section shall be construed as imposing an obligation on employers in an area to pay the standard wage fixed under this section for that area.

PART V

REGISTERED JOINT INDUSTRIAL COUNCILS

Definitions for purposes of Part V

59.—In this Part—

INDUSTRIAL RELATIONS ACT 1946

the expression "qualified joint industrial council" means an association of persons which complies with the following conditions—

(a) that it is substantially representative of workers of a particular class, type or group and their employers,
(b) that its object is the promotion of harmonious relations between such employers and such workers,
(c) that its rules provide that, if a trade dispute arises between such workers and their employers a lock-out or strike will not be undertaken in support of the dispute until the dispute has been referred to the association and considered by it;

the expression "the register" means the Register of Joint Industrial Councils;
the word "registered" means registered in the register;
the expression "registered joint industrial council" means an association which is for the time being registered in the register.

Register of Joint Industrial Councils

60.—The Court shall maintain a register to be known as the Register of Joint Industrial Councils.

COMMENTARY

At present there are three councils on the register: the Joint Board of Conciliation and Arbitration for the Footwear Industry; the Joint Industrial Council for the Dublin Wholesale Fruit and Vegetable Trade; and the Joint Industrial Council for the Construction Industry. Unfortunately those for the last two mentioned industries have been suspended since July 1982 and October 1983 respectively. In addition, there are 13 other joint industrial councils which have not applied for registration: see the Labour Court's *Forty-First Annual Report* (1987) pp. 7–8.

Registration of joint industrial councils

61.—(1) Where an association claiming to be a qualified joint industrial council applies to the Court to be registered in the register, the Court shall, if satisfied that the claim is well-founded, register the association in the register.

(2) An application by an association for registration in the register shall be accompanied by copies of its rules and such other information with respect to the association as the Court may require.

(3) Where the Court registers an association in the register, it shall cause to be entered therein the name of the association, its principal office and the name of its secretary.

Cancellation of registration

62.—The Court shall cancel the registration in the register of any association if—

(a) the association applies to the Court to do so, or
(b) the Court is of opinion that the association has ceased to be a qualified joint industrial council, or has ceased to act.

Inspection of rules of registered joint industrial council

63.—The rules of a registered joint industrial council shall be open for public inspection at the offices of the Court at such times as may be fixed by the Court.

Appointment of chairman and secretary of a joint industrial council

64. [...]

COMMENTARY

This section was repealed by section 7 of the Industrial Relations Act 1990.

Registered joint industrial council to be a body in respect of which section 3 of the Trade Union Act, 1942, is applicable

65.—A registered joint industrial council shall be a board in relation to which section 3 of the Trade Union Act, 1942 (No. 23 of 1942), is applicable.

Part VI

Trade Disputes

COMMENTARY

The rules applicable to an investigation under this Part are contained in the Labour Court Provisional (Part VI) Rules 1946, reproduced *infra* at p. 157.

"Worker" for the purposes of Part VI

66. [...]

COMMENTARY

This section was repealed by section 3 of the Industrial Relations Act 1976.

Power of Court to investigate trade dispute

67. [...]

COMMENTARY

This section was repealed by section 7 of the Industrial Relations Act 1990.

Recommendation by Court on trade dispute

68.—(1) [The Court, having investigated a trade dispute, may make a recommendation setting forth its opinion on the merits of the dispute and the terms on which it should be settled.]

(2) The Court shall communicate a recommendation under this section to all the parties to the dispute and to such other persons as the Court thinks fit, and the Court may also publish the recommendation in such manner as it thinks fit.

COMMENTARY

The words in square brackets were substituted by section 19 of the Industrial Relations Act 1969.

Mediation in trade dispute by conciliation officer

69.—(1) The chairman of the Court may, before the Court undertakes the investigation of a trade dispute, appoint [an industrial relations] officer to act as mediator in the dispute for the purpose of effecting the permanent settlement thereof or such temporary settlement as will ensure that no stoppage of work shall occur pending the investigation of the dispute.

(2) The chairman of the Court may give a general authority to [an industrial relations] officer to act as mediator in relation to trade disputes generally or trade disputes of a particular character.

COMMENTARY

The words in square brackets were substituted by section 6(1) of the Industrial Relations Act 1969.

Reference of trade dispute to arbitration

70.—Where a trade dispute has occurred or is apprehended, the Court, with the consent of all the parties concerned in the dispute, may refer the dispute to the arbitration of one or more persons (who shall be paid such fees as the Minister, with the consent of the Minister for Finance, determines) or may itself arbitrate upon the dispute.

COMMENTARY

Section 5 of the Arbitration Act 1954 provides that the 1954 Act does not apply to an arbitration under this section.

Investigation by the Court of certain trade disputes resulting in stoppage of work and power to make awards in relation thereto

71. [. . .]

INDUSTRIAL RELATIONS ACT 1946

COMMENTARY

This section was repealed by section 7 of the Industrial Relations Act 1990.

Effect of awards under section 71
72. [. . .]

COMMENTARY

This section was repealed by section 7 of the Industrial Relations Act 1990.

PART VII

TRANSITORY PROVISIONS IN RELATION TO WAGES (STANDARD RATE) ORDERS AND BONUS ORDERS UNDER EMERGENCY POWERS (NO. 166) ORDER, 1942, AND EMERGENCY POWERS (NO. 260) ORDER, 1943

[. . .]

COMMENTARY

By virtue of section 74(1) this Part (*i.e.* sections 73–82) was to continue in force for one year from the commencement of the Act and then expire.

FIRST SCHEDULE

(Section 8)

ENACTMENTS REPEALED

Session and Chapter or Number and Year	Short title	Extent of Repeal
59 & 60 Vic., c. 30.	The Conciliation Act, 1896.	The whole Act.
9 Ed. VII, c. 22.	The Trade Boards Act, 1909.	The whole Act.
3 & 4 Geo. V, c. clxii.	The Trade Boards Provisional Orders Confirmation Act, 1913.	The whole Act.
8 & 9 Geo. V, c. 32.	The Trade Boards Act, 1918.	The whole Act.
9 & 10 Geo. V, c. 69.	The Industrial Courts Act, 1919.	The whole Act.
No. 2 of 1936.	The Conditions of Employment Act, 1936.	Section 50.
No. 4 of 1938.	The Shops (Conditions of Employment) Act, 1938.	Part V.

Industrial Relations Act 1946

Second Schedule

(Section 41)

[...]

COMMENTARY

This Schedule was repealed by section 7 of the Industrial Relations Act 1990.

LABOUR COURT PROVISIONAL (PART III) RULES 1946

PRELIMINARY

1. (1) These rules may be cited as "Labour Court Provisional (Part III) Rules 1946."

(2) These Rules shall come into operation on the 25th day of October, 1946.

2. (1) In these Rules—

the expression "the Act" means the Industrial Relations Act 1946 (No. 26 of 1946);

the expression "the Registrar" means the Registrar of the Court;

the expression "the Register" means the Register of Employment Agreements.

(2) The Interpretation Act 1937 (No. 38 of 1937) applies to these Rules.

A. Procedure at formal sittings

3. At a formal sitting of the Court for the transaction of business under Part III of the Act the following rules shall apply.

4. The Registrar shall make a public announcement of the place, date and time of the sitting and of the subject matter of the proceedings in such manner as the Chairman may direct.

5. The Registrar shall send notice of the sitting to all persons appearing to the Court to be concerned in the application or interested in the complaint the subject matter of the proceedings.

6. (1) At or before the sitting of the Court all persons appearing to the Court to be concerned in the application or interested in the complaint and desiring to be heard (hereinafter called the parties) shall inform the Registrar of the names of the person or persons appointed to act as spokesmen on their behalf. The Chairman may during the course of the proceedings permit the appointment of additional or substituted spokesmen.

(2) A party may apply to the Court for leave to appear by counsel or solicitor, and the Court may grant such leave if it is of opinion that in the circumstances the applicant ought to be assisted by counsel or solicitor.

7. Subject to the provisions of theses Rules the procedure to be observed at a sitting of the Court shall be regulated by the Chairman.

8. The appointed spokesmen shall address themselves to the Court.

9. (1) At any stage of the proceedings the Court may take evidence on oath.

(2) When the Court decides to examine a witness on oath, the witness shall be entitled to be represented by counsel or solicitor, and any party may apply to the Court for leave to be represented by counsel or solicitor and the Court may at its discretion grant or refuse such leave.

(3) The Court may permit counsel or solicitor, appearing as provided by this Rule, to examine, cross-examine and re-examine a witness placed on oath.

10. The Court may of its own motion or on the request of any party at any time decide to hold a sitting or part of a sitting in private.

11. The Court may suspend or adjourn a sitting, whether public or private, for the purpose of private consultation with any one, or more than one, of the parties, or to allow for private consultation between the parties.

12. Any person whose conduct is, in the opinion of the Court, frivolous, vexatious or obstructive may be required by the Chairman to withdraw from the sitting.

13. Subject to the provisions of the Act and of these Rules, the Court may announce its decision at a public or private sitting or otherwise as it thinks fit.

B. Registration of Employment Agreements (Section 27)

14. An application to the Court for the registration of an Employment Agreement shall be made in writing and shall state—

(i) the name and address of the applicant;
(ii) the names and addresses of the other parties to the Agreement;
(iii) the extent to which there is consent to registration by the parties to the Agreement;
(iv) the grounds on which it is claimed that the parties to the Agreement are substantially representative of the class, type or group of workers expressed to be affected by the Agreement and of their employers;

and shall be accompanied by a copy of the Agreement.

15. Before proceeding to consideration of the application the Court may request the applicant or any other party to the Agreement to furnish—

(i) such additional information;

(ii) such evidence in support of the statements made in the application, and
(iii) such evidence of the publication required by section 27(4) of the Act,

as the Court may desire.

16. When the Court orders the registration of an Employment Agreement, the Registrar shall—

(i) enter in the Register such particulars of the registration, and
(ii) publish in such manner notice of the registration together with such particulars of the Agreement

as the Court may direct.

17. If the Court refuses an application for registration of an Employment Agreement the Registrar shall inform all the parties to the Agreement of the refusal and of the reasons therefor.

C. Variation of registered Employment Agreement (Section 28)

18. An application to the Court, in accordance with the provisions of section 28 of the Act, for the variation of a registered Employment Agreement shall state—

(i) the name and address of the applicant, and
(ii) full details of the variation sought.

19. When the Court, in accordance with the provisions of section 28 of the Act, makes an Order varying an Employment Agreement, the Registrar shall—

(i) enter in the Register such particulars of the variation, and
(ii) publish notice of the variation in such manner

as the Court may direct.

D. Cancellation of registered Employment Agreement (Section 29)

20. When the Court, in accordance with the provisions of section 29 of the Act, orders cancellation of the registration of an Employment Agreement, the Registrar shall—

(i) enter in the Register such particulars of the cancellation, and
(ii) publish notice of the cancellation in such manner

as the Court may direct.

E. Complaints under section 32 of the Act

21. A complaint made under section 32 of the Act shall be made in writing and shall state—

(i) the full name and address of the complainant;
(ii) the name and address of the employer or of the trade union of workers concerning whom the complaint is made;
(iii) full details of the complaint.

22. The Court may request the complainant to furnish any further information which it considers relevant.

23. The Registrar shall send notice of the complaint to the employer or trade union of workers concerning whom the complaint is made and shall give such notice of the intention of the Court to proceed to consideration of the complaint as the Court may direct.

24. The complainant and the employer or the trade union of workers concerning whom the complaint is made shall be entitled to be represented by counsel or solicitor at a sitting of the Court for the consideration of a complaint.

25. When the Court has made an order after consideration of a complaint the Registrar shall—

(i) enter in a Register to be kept for that purpose such particulars of the Order, and
(ii) publish such notice, if any, of the making of the Order

as the Court may direct.

F. General

26. The Register of Employment Agreements and the Register referred to in Rule 24 shall be open to public inspection at the Office of the Court between the hours of 10 o'clock in the forenoon and 4 o'clock in the afternoon (Saturdays, Sundays and Public Holidays excepted).

27. Non-compliance with any of these Rules or with any practice for the time being in force in the Court shall not render the proceedings void, unless the Court shall so direct.

LABOUR COURT PROVISIONAL (PART VI) RULES 1946

PRELIMINARY

1. (1) These rules may be cited as "Labour Court Provisional (Part VI) Rules, 1946."
(2) These Rules shall come into operation on the 10th day of October, 1946.

2. (1) In these rules—
the expression "the Act" means the Industrial Relations Act, 1946 (No. 26 of 1946);
the expression "the Registrar" means the person appointed by the Minister to be registrar of the Court.
(2) The Interpretation Act, 1937 (No. 38 of 1937) applies to these Rules.

INVESTIGATION OF TRADE DISPUTE UNDER PART VI OF THE ACT

3. The Court may take such steps as it thinks fit for the investigation of a trade dispute in accordance with Section 67 of the Act.

4. In the event of the Court deciding to hold a formal sitting for the purpose of an investigation under Part VI the following rules shall, subject to the provisions of the Act, apply.

5. The Registrar shall make a public announcement of the place, date and time of the sitting and of the subject-matter of the investigation in such manner as the Chairman may direct. The Registrar shall also make a similar public announcement of any subsequent public sittings as the Chairman may direct.

6. (1) Persons claiming to be concerned in the dispute (hereinafter called the parties) shall inform the Registrar at or before the sitting of the Court of the names of the person or persons appointed to act as spokesmen on their behalf.
The chairman may, during the course of the proceedings, permit the appointment of additional or substituted spokesmen.

(2) A party may apply to the Court for leave to appear by counsel or solicitor, and the Court may grant such leave if it is of opinion that the matter in issue is of such a nature that the applicant ought to be assisted by counsel or solicitor.

7. Subject to the provisions of these Rules, the procedure to be observed at a sitting of the Court shall be regulated by the Chairman.

Labour Court Provisional (Part VI) Rules 1946

8. The appointed spokesmen shall address themselves to the Court.

9. (1) At any stage of the proceedings, the Court may take evidence on oath.

(2) When the Court decides to examine a witness on oath, the witness shall be entitled to be represented by counsel or solicitor, and any party may apply to the Court for leave to be represented by counsel or solicitor and the Court may at its discretion grant or refuse such leave.

(3) The Court may permit counsel or solicitor, appearing as provided by this Rule, to examine, cross-examine and re-examine a witness placed on oath.

10. The Court may of its own motion or on the request of any party at any time decide to hold a sitting or part of a sitting in private.

11. The Court may suspend or adjourn a sitting, whether public or private, for the purpose of private consultation with any one, or more than one, of the parties, or to allow for private consultation between the parties.

12. Any person whose conduct is in the opinion of the Court frivolous, vexatious or obstructive may be required by the Chairman to withdraw from the sitting.

13. The Court may announce its recommendation or award at a public or private sitting or otherwise as it thinks fit, and subject to the provisions of Part VI of the Act, shall take such steps as it may think proper to bring its decision to the notice of all persons affected thereby.

14. As soon as may be after the making of such recommendation or award, the Registrar shall enter in a Register to be kept for that purpose either a copy of such recommendation or award or such particulars of the making thereof as the Court may direct, and such Register shall be open to public inspection at the Office of the Court between the hours of 10 o'clock in the forenoon and 4 o'clock in the afternoon (Saturdays, Sundays and Public Holidays excepted).

15. Non-compliance with any of these Rules or with any practice for the time being in force in the Court, shall not render the proceedings void, unless the Court shall so direct.

INDUSTRIAL RELATIONS ACT 1946 REGULATIONS 1950

(S.I. No. 258 of 1950)

1. These regulations may be cited as the Industrial Relations Act, 1946, Regulations, 1950.

2. These regulations shall come into operation on the 9th day of October, 1950.

3. In these regulations—
"the Act" means the Industrial Relations Act, 1946 (No. 26 of 1946),
references to sections are to sections of the Act,
"the Court" means the Labour Court.

4. (1) Notices under section 38, under that section as applied by section 40, [...] and orders under sections 39 and 40, shall be published by the Court in *Iris Oifigiúil* and in at least one daily newspaper circulating in the State.

(2) Where, however, an order under section 39 or section 40 has been published by the Stationery Office, it shall be sufficient for the Court to publish in *Iris Oifigiúil* and in at least one daily newspaper circulating in the State a notice stating that the order has been made and so published, and indicating its contents and stating that copies may be purchased from the Stationery Office.

(3) The Court may take such other steps as it thinks proper to bring the said notices and orders to the knowledge of persons concerned, including the sending of copies of notices prepared under regulation 5 or 6 to employers who appear to the Court to be affected and whose names and addresses are known to the Court.

COMMENTARY

The words in square brackets in paragraph (1) of this regulation have been deleted by virtue of the repeal of section 43 of the 1946 Act.

5. The Court shall, as soon as possible after the publication, under regulation 4, of notice of proposals under section 42 in relation to remuneration or conditions of employment, cause to be prepared a form of notice containing full details of the proposals and requiring representations to the proposals to be lodged with the joint labour committee concerned within thirty days of publication of notice of the proposals under regulation 4.

6. The Court shall, as soon as possible after the publication, under regulation 4, of notice of the making of an employment regulation order cause to be prepared a form of notice containing full details of the order.

7. The Court shall supply any person, on request, with copies of a notice prepared under regulation 5 or 6.

8. Every employer who employs a worker to whom proposals under section 42 relate, and every employer who employs a worker to whom an employment regulation order relates, shall post up and keep posted up a copy of the notice prepared under regulation 5 or 6, as the case may be, relating to such proposals or order, in prominent positions, so as to ensure that the notice shall be brought to the knowledge of, and can conveniently be read by all workers employed by him who are affected by it.

9. Where a notice to be posted up by an employer under these regulations refers to some prior notice or notices and, to be properly understood, must be read therewith, the employer shall post up and keep posted up a sufficient number of copies of the prior notice or notices, in the same manner as, and together with, the first-mentioned notices, so that both or all the said notices may be read as one notice.

10. (1) The Court may from time to time embody notice of any two or more employment regulation orders, giving effect to the proposals of a particular joint labour committee in a consolidated notice.

(2) Regulation 8 applies to a consolidated notice as it applies to notices under that regulation.

(3) The posting up and keeping posted up, in accordance with these regulations, of a consolidated notice shall be sufficient compliance with regulation 9.

11. The fee to be paid for a copy of a registered employment agreement supplied under section 31 shall be [£0.12].

COMMENTARY

Despite this provision the practice of the Labour Court is to provide such copies free of charge.

12. The Industrial Relations Act, 1946, Regulations, 1946 (S.R. & O., No. 320 of 1946), are hereby revoked.

INDUSTRIAL RELATIONS ACT 1969

(Number 14 of 1969)

An Act to amend and extend the Industrial Relations Act, 1946.
[*3 June 1969*]

Be it enacted by the Oireachtas as follows:

Definitions

1.—In this Act—
"the Court" means the Labour Court;
"the Minister" means the Minister for Labour;
"the Principal Act" means the Industrial Relations Act, 1946.

Membership of the Court

2.—[(1) The Court shall consist of a chairman (in this Act referred to as the chairman), a deputy chairman or deputy chairmen and ordinary members.

(2) The number of deputy chairmen shall be equal to the number of divisions of the Court less one.

(3) The number of ordinary members shall be equal to twice the number of divisions of the Court and shall be divided equally among workers' members and employers' members.]

COMMENTARY

The words in square brackets were substituted by section 9 of the Industrial Relations Act 1976.

Divisions of the Court

3.—Whenever the chairman is of opinion that for the speedy dispatch of the business of the Court it is expedient that the Court should act by divisions, he may direct accordingly, and, until he revokes his direction—

(a) the Court shall be grouped into—

(i) a first division, consisting of the chairman (who shall be chairman of the division) and a workers' member and an employers' member selected by him,

Industrial Relations Act 1969

   (ii) a second division, consisting of the deputy chairman appointed under section 4(1) of this Act (who shall be chairman of the division), a workers' member and an employers' member, and
   (iii) if the direction so provides, a third division consisting of the deputy chairman appointed under section 4(4) of this Act (who shall be chairman of the division) and a workers' member and an employers' member;
  (b) the chairman shall assign to each division the business to be transacted by it;
  (c) for the purpose of the business so assigned to it, each division shall have all the powers of the Court and the chairman of the division shall have all the powers of the chairman and references in this Act to the Court and the chairman shall be construed as including references to a division and the chairman of a division respectively.

COMMENTARY

There are currently four divisions of the Court, the fourth consisting of a deputy chairman appointed under section 8(3) of the Industrial Relations Act 1976, a workers' member and an employers' member.

Deputy chairman of the Court

4.—(1) The Minister shall appoint a deputy chairman who shall hold office on such terms as shall be fixed by the Minister when appointing him.

(2) The deputy chairman appointed under subsection (1) of this section shall, in the absence of the chairman, act in his place and references in the Principal Act and this Act to the chairman shall be construed as including references to the deputy chairman aforesaid so acting.

(3) The deputy chairman appointed under subsection (1) of this section shall be paid such remuneration (by way of either fees or salary) and allowances as the Minister, with the consent of the Minister for Finance, determines.

(4) The Minister may appoint a second deputy chairman who shall hold office on such terms as shall be fixed by the Minister when appointing him.

(5) [. . .]

(6) No person shall be appointed to be a deputy chairman unless he is ordinarily resident in the State.

(7) Neither the Civil Service Commissioners Act, 1956, nor the Civil Service Regulation Acts, 1956 and 1958, shall apply to the office of deputy chairman of the Court.

COMMENTARY

Subsection (5)

This subsection was repealed by section 8(5) of the Industrial Relations Act 1976.

Superannuation for chairman and ordinary members of the Court

5.—(1) [The Minister may, with the consent of the Minister for Finance, make a scheme or schemes for the granting of pensions, gratuities and other allowances on cessation of office or death to or in respect of the chairman, a deputy chairman (whether appointed under section 4(1) or 4(4) of this Act or under section 8(3) of the Industrial Relations Act, 1976) who is required by the Minister to devote the whole of his working time to the duties of the office of deputy chairman, and the ordinary members of the Court.]

(2) The Minister may, with the consent of the Minister for Finance, at any time amend a scheme made by him under this section.

(3) A scheme made by the Minister under this section shall be carried out by the Minister in accordance with its terms.

(4) If any dispute arises as to the claim of any person to, or the amount of, any pension, gratuity or allowance payable in pursuance of a scheme under this section, such dispute shall be submitted to the Minister who shall refer it to the Minister for Finance, whose decision shall be final.

(5) Every scheme made by the Minister under this section shall be laid before each House of the Oireachtas as soon as may be after it is made and if either House, within the next twenty-one days on which that House has sat after the scheme is laid before it, passes a resolution annulling the scheme, the scheme shall be annulled accordingly, but without prejudice to the validity of anything previously done thereunder.

(6) The Minister shall grant and pay to Cathal O'Shannon, upon his retirement without re-appointment from membership of the Labour Court, a pension for his life of one thousand, one hundred and twenty-five pounds per annum and a gratuity of one thousand, six hundred and eighty-eight pounds.

(7) The Minister shall grant and pay to Ernest Edmonson Benson, upon his retirement without re-appointment from membership of the Labour Court, a gratuity of three thousand pounds.

(8) [The Minister shall grant and pay to Joseph Stapleton Quigley, upon his retirement without re-appointment from membership of the Court, a gratuity of an amount equal to one year's salary at the date of his retirement.]

Industrial Relations Act 1969

COMMENTARY

Subsection (1)

The words in square brackets were substituted by section 40 of the Industrial Relations Act 1990. The current scheme is the Labour Court (Members) Superannuation Scheme 1971 as amended.

Subsection (2)

The 1971 scheme was amended by the Labour Court (Members) Superannuation Scheme (Amendment) Scheme 1979 (S.I. No. 268 of 1979) and the Labour Court (Members) Superannuation Scheme (Amendment) Scheme 1983 (S.I. No. 216 of 1983).

Subsection (8)

The words in square brackets were substituted by section 10 of the Industrial Relations Act 1976.

Industrial relations officers

6. [...]

COMMENTARY

This section was repealed by section 7 of the Industrial Relations Act 1990.

Interpretation of employment agreements

7.—The Court may, at any time, on the application of the parties to an agreement between an employer or a trade union of employers and a worker or a trade union of workers relating to the pay or conditions of employment of any person to whom the agreement relates give its decision as to the interpretation of the agreement or its application to a particular person.

Investigation of trade dispute to be in private

8.—(1) An investigation of a trade dispute by the Court shall be conducted in private, but the Court shall, if requested to do so by a party to the dispute, conduct the investigation in public.

(2) Where an investigation of a trade dispute is being carried out by the Court in public, the Court may, if it is satisfied that any part of the investigation concerns a matter that should, in the interests of any party to the dispute, be treated as confidential, conduct that part of the investigation in private.

INDUSTRIAL RELATIONS ACT 1969

Inclusion of members of the Court on public service arbitration boards

9.—(1) The membership of any board established either before or after the commencement of this section to report on claims in relation to the pay and conditions of service and matters relating thereto of any person who—

(a) holds a position in the Civil Service of the Government or the Civil Service of the State,
(b) is a member of the staff of the Houses of the Oireachtas.
(c) is a member of the Garda Síochána,
(d) is a sub-postmaster,
(e) is employed by a county committee of agriculture, a vocational education committee or a local authority for the purposes of the Local Government Act, 1941,
(f) is employed as a teacher in a national, secondary, vocational or comprehensive school or in any similar school, or
(g) is employed by any such body established by or under statute and financed wholly or partly by means of grants or loans made by a Minister of State or the issue of shares taken up by a Minister of State as may be designated from time to time by the Minister for Finance,

shall include one workers' member of the Court and one employers' member of the Court who shall be selected by the chairman.

(2) Subsection (1) of this section shall come into operation on such day as the Minister may appoint by order.

COMMENTARY

No order has been made bringing subsection (1) into operation. In 1976, however, an interim arrangement, which still continues in operation, was arrived at whereby the various conciliation and arbitration schemes were amended to provide that, on the request of either side, a workers' member and an employers' member might be included as members. According to the Labour Court's *Forty-First Annual Report* (1987), members of the Labour Court (two in each case) are members of the Teachers', Gardai and Local Authorities' Arbitration Schemes, the Review Body on Higher Remuneration in the Public Sector, the Civil Service Arbitration Board and the arbitration machinery for clerical and administrative staff in the whole-time employment of Vocational Education Committees.

Breaches of registered employment agreements

10.—(1) If an employer or a trade union representative of employers affected by a registered employment agreement complains to the Court that an employer affected by the agreement has failed or neglected to comply with the agreement, the following provisions shall have effect—

(a) the Court shall consider the complaint, and shall hear all persons appearing to the Court to be interested and desiring to be heard,
(b) if, after such consideration, the Court is satisfied that the complaint is well founded, the Court may by order direct the said employer to do such things as will in the opinion of the Court result in the said agreement being complied with by the said employer.

(2) If, where an order is made by the Court under subsection (1) of this section, the direction contained in the order is not carried out, the person to whom the direction is given shall be guilty of an offence under this section and shall be liable on summary conviction to a fine not exceeding one [thousand] pounds, and, in the case of a continuing offence, a further fine not exceeding [two hundred] pounds for every day during which the offence is continued.

(3) If a person affected by a registered employment agreement fails or neglects to comply with the agreement, the person shall be guilty of an offence and shall be liable on summary conviction to a fine not exceeding [one thousand] pounds, and, in the case of a continuing offence, [...] a further fine not exceeding [two hundred] pounds for every day during which the offence is continued.

COMMENTARY

Subsection (2)

The figures in square brackets were substituted by section 4 of the Industrial Relations Act 1990.

Subsection (3)

The figures in square brackets were substituted by section 4 of the Industrial Relations Act 1990 and the words in square brackets were repealed by section 7 of the 1990 Act.

Fair employment rules

11. [...]

COMMENTARY

This section was repealed by section 7 of the Industrial Relations Act 1990.

Industrial Relations Act 1969

Enforcement of sections 10 and 11

12.—(1) An inspector for the purposes of Part IV of the Principal Act (in this section referred to as an inspector) may, for the purpose of enforcing the provision of section 10 [...] of this Act do all or any of the following things, that is to say—

(a) enter at all reasonable times any premises where he has reasonable grounds for believing that any person affected by a registered employment agreement [...] works,
(b) require the production of wages sheets or other records of remuneration kept by an employer and inspect and examine those sheets or records and copy any material part thereof,
(c) examine with respect to any matters under section 10 [...] of this Act or this section any person whom he has reasonable grounds for believing to be or have been a person affected by a registered employment agreement [...] and require such person to answer such questions (other than questions tending to incriminate such person) as the inspector may put relating to those matters and to sign a declaration of the truth of the answers to the questions.

(2) If a person—

(a) obstructs or impedes an inspector in the exercise of any of the powers conferred on the inspector by this section,
(b) refuses to produce any record which an inspector lawfully requires him to produce,
(c) prevents, or attempts to prevent, a person from appearing before or being questioned by an inspector, or
(d) [...] fails or refuses to comply with any lawful requirement of an inspector under subsection 1(b) of this section,

the person shall be guilty of an offence and shall be liable on summary conviction to a fine not exceeding [five hundred] pounds.

(3) An inspector may institute proceedings for an offence under section 10 [...] of this Act or this section.

COMMENTARY

Subsection (1)

The words in square brackets have been deleted consequent upon the repeal of section 11 of the Act.

Subsection (2)

The word in square brackets was deleted by section 55 of the Industrial

Relations Act 1990, and the figure in square brackets was substituted by section 4 of the same Act.

Subsection (3)

The words in square brackets have been deleted consequent upon the repeal of section 11 of the Act. Section 52 of the Industrial Relations Act 1990 provides that this section and sections 51 and 52 of the 1990 Act shall be construed as one section. Note that section 54 of the 1990 Act empowers an inspector to institute civil proceedings on behalf of a worker either where it appears that a sum is due from an employer to a worker to whom a registered employment agreement applies or where the employer has failed to comply with a condition of any such agreement with respect to the worker.

Rights commissioners

13.—(1) The Minister may from time to time appoint a person who shall be known as and is in this Act referred to as a rights commissioner to carry out the functions assigned to him by this section.

(2) Subject to the provisions of this section, where a trade dispute (other than a dispute connected with rates of pay of, hours or times of work of, or annual holidays of, a body of workers) exists or is apprehended and involves workers within the meaning of Part VI of the Principal Act, a party to the dispute may refer it to a rights commissioner.

(3) (a) Subject to the provisions of this section, a rights commissioner shall investigate any trade dispute referred to him under subsection (2) of this section and shall, unless before doing so the dispute is settled—

(i) make a recommendation to the parties to the dispute setting forth his opinion on the merits of the dispute, and
(ii) notify the Court of the recommendation.

(b) A rights commissioner shall not investigate a trade dispute—

(i) if the Court has made a recommendation in relation to the dispute, or
(ii) if a party to the dispute notifies the commissioner in writing that he objects to the dispute being investigated by a rights commissioner.

(4) A rights commissioner shall hold office for such period as the Minister may determine and shall be paid such fees and expenses as the Minister, with the consent of the Minister for Finance, may determine from time to time and shall hold office upon and subject to such other terms and conditions as the Minister may determine from time to time.

INDUSTRIAL RELATIONS ACT 1969

(5) (a) A rights commissioner may be removed from office by the Minister for stated reasons.
 (b) Neither the Civil Service Commissioners Act, 1956, nor the Civil Service Regulation Acts, 1956 and 1958, shall apply to the office of rights commissioner.

(6) A rights commissioner may provide for the regulation of proceedings before him in relation to an investigation under this section and may provide for the cases in which persons may appear before him by counsel or solicitor and, except as so provided, no person shall be entitled to appear by counsel or solicitor before him.

(7) The Minister, if he so thinks fit, may appoint more than one rights commissioner at the same time or appoint a rights commissioner at a time when one or more than one rights commissioner stands or stand appointed.

(8) An investigation by a rights commissioner shall be conducted in private.

(9) (a) A party to a dispute in relation to which a rights commissioner has made a recommendation may appeal to the Court against the recommendation and the parties to the dispute shall be bound by the decision of the Court on the appeal.
 (b) The Court shall hear and decide any appeal to it under this subsection and it shall convey its decision thereon to the parties.
 (c) A hearing under this subsection shall be held in private.

(10) The Court shall not investigate (except by way of appeal to it under subsection (9) of this section) a trade dispute in relation to which a rights commissioner has made a recommendation.

COMMENTARY

Subsection (2)

Section 8(10) of the Unfair Dismissals Act 1977 provides that a dispute in relation to a dismissal that is an unfair dismissal for the purposes of the 1977 Act shall not be referred to a rights commissioner under this subsection. As to the effect of section 8(10) of the 1977 Act see *Pat Russell Haulage Ltd.* v. *Sutcliffe* UD 389/1990 reported at [1991] E.L.R. 42.

Subsection (3)(a)(ii)

Section 36(3) of the Industrial Relations Act 1990 provides that a commissioner, in addition to notifying the Court, shall notify the Minister and the Labour Relations Commission of every recommendation made by him.

Subsection (3)(b)(ii)

By virtue of section 36(1) of the Industrial Relations Act 1990 any such objection shall be of no effect unless it is notified in writing to the commissioner within three weeks after notice of the reference of the dispute to the commissioner has been sent by post to that party.

Subsection (4)

Although section 34(2) of the Industrial Relations Act 1990 provides that the term of office of a rights commissioner appointed in pursuance of section 34(1) shall be a period not exceeding three years, section 34(3) empowers the Minister to re-appoint a rights commissioner for a further term or terms.

Subsection (7)

Section 34(1) of the Industrial Relations Act 1990 provides that where the Minister proposes to appoint a rights commissioner he shall request the Labour Relations Commission to submit to him a panel of persons and the Minister shall not appoint as a rights commissioner any person other than one included in such panel. Section 34(2) goes on to provide that the term of office of a rights commissioner appointed in pursuance of subsection (1) shall be a period not exceeding three years. There are presently four rights commissioners: Colin Walker, Robert Clarke, Stephen Tracey and Gerry Crowley. The first three are based in Dublin and the fourth in Cork. All were appointed under the 1969 Act. On the role of the rights commissioners see Kelly "The Rights Commissioner: Conciliator, Mediator or Arbitrator?" in *Industrial Relations in Ireland* (Department of Industrial Relations UCD, 1989) pp. 185–191 and Walker "An Analysis of Referrals and Results of Disputes and Claims to Four Rights Commissioners" (1986) 5 *J.I.S.L.L.* 67.

Subsection (9)

Section 36(2) of the Industrial Relations Act 1990 provides that an appeal under this subsection shall not be considered unless it is notified in writing to the Court within six weeks after the making of the recommendation. Although this paragraph provides that the parties will be bound by the Court's decision on appeal, the Act provides no sanction if one of the parties does not adhere to or implement the Court's decision. In *Fitzhenry* v. *Gallagher (Dublin) Ltd.* UD 419/1986, however, the Employment Appeals Tribunal said that, since the Court's decision was binding, it could not be "disregarded" by the Tribunal.

Prohibition on disclosure of information

14.—A rights commissioner shall not include in any recommendation any information obtained by him in the course of any investigation under this Act as to any trade union or as to the business carried on by any person which is not available otherwise than through evidence given at the investigation without the consent of the trade union or persons concerned, nor shall any person concerned in proceedings before a rights commissioner under this Act, without such consent, disclose any such information.

Amendment of section 23 of Principal Act

15. [...]

COMMENTARY

This section amends section 23 of the Industrial Relations Act 1946, which amendment is incorporated into the text of that Act.

INDUSTRIAL RELATIONS ACT 1969

Amendment of section 43 of Principal Act

16. [...]

COMMENTARY

This section amends section 43 of the Industrial Relations Act 1946, which amendment has since been repealed by section 7 of the Industrial Relations Act 1990.

Extension of Part VI of Principal Act

17. [...]

COMMENTARY

This section was repealed by section 7 of the Industrial Relations Act 1990.

Amendment of section 67 of Principal Act

18. [...]

COMMENTARY

This section was repealed by section 7 of the Industrial Relations Act 1990.

Amendment of section 68 of Principal Act

19. [...]

COMMENTARY

This section amends section 68 of the Industrial Relations Act 1946, which amendment is incorporated into the text of that Act.

Investigation of dispute by Court at request of parties

20.—(1) Where the workers concerned in a trade dispute or their trade union or trade unions request or requests the Court to investigate the dispute and undertake or undertakes before the investigation to accept the recommendation of the Court under section 68 of the Principal Act in relation thereto then, notwithstanding anything contained in the Principal Act or in this Act, the Court shall investigate the dispute and shall make a recommendation under the said section 68 in relation thereto.

(2) Where the parties concerned in a trade dispute request the Court to investigate a specified issue or issues involved in the dispute and undertake, before the investigation, to accept the recommendation of the Court under the said section 68 in relation to such issue or issues then, notwithstanding anything in the Principal Act or in this Act, the Court shall investigate such issue or

issues and shall make a recommendation under the said section 68 in relation thereto and, for the purposes of this subsection, subsection (1) of the said section 68 shall have effect as if the references therein to a trade dispute included references to an issue or issues involved in a trade dispute.

(3) Notwithstanding anything contained in section 8(1) of this Act, an investigation under this section shall be conducted in private and shall be given such priority over the other business of the Court as the Court considers reasonable.

Dissolution of Electricity Supply Board manual workers and general employees tribunals

21.—(1) The tribunal established under section 9 of the Electricity Supply Board (Superannuation) Act, 1942, and the tribunal established under section 3 of the Electricity (Supply) (Amendment) Act, 1949, are hereby dissolved.

(2) Subsection (1) of this section and section 23 of this Act (in so far as it repeals sections 9 to 11 of the said Electricity Supply Board (Superannuation) Act, 1942, and sections 3 to 6 of the said Electricity (Supply) (Amendment) Act, 1949) shall, in respect of any matter referred to either tribunal aforesaid before the passing of this Act, be deemed, unless a party concerned in the matter objects to its being determined by the tribunal to which it is referred, never to have been enacted.

Laying of orders before Houses of Oireachtas

22.—An order made by the Government or the Minister under this Act shall be laid before each House of the Oireachtas as soon as may be after it is made and, if a resolution annulling the order is passed by either House within the next twenty-one days on which that House has sat after the order has been laid before it, the order shall be annulled accordingly but without prejudice to the validity of anything previously done thereunder.

Repeals

23.—The Acts mentioned in the Schedule to this Act are hereby repealed to the extent specified in the third column of the Schedule.

Short title, construction and collective citation

24.—(1) This Act may be cited as the Industrial Relations Act, 1969, and shall be construed as one with the Principal Act.

INDUSTRIAL RELATIONS ACT 1969

(2) The Principal Act and this Act may be cited together as the Industrial Relations Act, 1946 and 1969.

SCHEDULE

(Section 23)

ENACTMENTS REPEALED

Year and Number	Short Title	Extent of Repeal
No. 17 of 1942.	Electricity Supply Board (Superannuation) Act, 1942.	Sections 9, 10 and 11.
No. 26 of 1946.	Industrial Relations Act, 1946.	Sections 10(2), 11, 12, 16 and 67(3).
No. 12 of 1949.	Electricity (Supply) (Amendment) Act, 1949.	Sections 3, 4, 5 and 6.
No. 19 of 1955.	Industrial Relations (Amendment) Act, 1955.	The whole Act.

INDUSTRIAL RELATIONS ACT 1976

(Number 15 of 1975)

An Act to amend and extend the Industrial Relations Acts, 1946 and 1969, to repeal the Agricultural Wages Acts, 1936 to 1969, and the Agricultural Workers (Holidays) Acts, 1950 to 1975, and to provide for other matters connected with the aforesaid matters.
[18 May 1976]

Be it enacted by the Oireachtas as follows:

Definitions

1.—In this Act—
"the Act of 1969" means the Industrial Relations Act, 1969;
"agricultural employer" means a person who employs other persons as agricultural workers;
"agricultural worker" means a person employed under a contract of service or apprenticeship whose work under the contract is or includes work in agriculture, but does not include a person whose work under any such contract is mainly domestic service;
"agriculture" includes horticulture, the production of any consumable produce which is grown for sale or for consumption or other use, dairy farming, poultry farming, the use of land as grazing, meadow or pasture land or orchard or osier land or woodland, or for market gardens, private gardens, nursery grounds or sports grounds, the caring for or the rearing or training of animals and any other incidental activities connected with agriculture;
"the Court" means the Labour Court;
"the Minister" means the Minister for Labour;
"the Principal Act" means the Industrial Relations Act, 1946.

Amendment of section 4 of Principal Act

2. [...]

COMMENTARY

This section was repealed by section 7 of the Industrial Relations Act 1990.

Consequential repeal

3. [...]

COMMENTARY

This section repeals section 66 of the Industrial Relations Act 1946.

Establishment of joint labour committee for agricultural workers

4.—(1) As soon as practicable after the passing of this Act the Court shall by order establish a joint labour committee to perform, in relation to agricultural workers and their employers, the functions assigned to it by Part IV of the Principal Act.

(2) Sections 35 to 40 of the Principal Act shall not apply to the joint labour committee established under this section but that committee shall, subject to section 5 of this Act, be deemed to be a joint labour committee within the meaning of section 34 of the Principal Act.

COMMENTARY

The Agricultural Workers' Joint Labour Committee was established on August 26, 1976: see Agricultural Workers Joint Labour Committee Establishment Order 1976 (S.I. No. 198 of 1976).

Modification of Second Schedule to Principal Act

5. [...]

COMMENTARY

This section was repealed by section 7 of the Industrial Relations Act 1990. See now paragraph 3 of the Fifth Schedule to the Industrial Relations Act 1990.

Repeal of Agricultural Wages Acts, 1936 to 1969

6.—(1) The Agricultural Wages Acts, 1936 to 1969, are hereby repealed.

(2) Notwithstanding subsection (1) of this section, any order made under section 17 of the Agricultural Wages Act, 1936, and in force at the commencement of this section shall continue in force and be deemed to be an employment regulation order.

(3) This section shall come into operation on the date of the making by the Court of the first employment regulation order under section 43 of the Principal Act following proposals to the Court under section 42 of that Act submitted by the joint labour committee established under section 4 of this Act.

COMMENTARY

The first Employment Regulation (Agricultural Workers Joint Labour Committee) Order was S.I. No. 61 of 1977 which was made on February 28, 1977 with effect from March 1, 1977.

Modification of section 49 of Principal Act

7.—Section 49(2) of the Principal Act, which relates to the posting by employers of certain notices, shall not apply to agricultural employers.

Additional divisions of the Court

8.—(1) Whenever the Minister is of opinion that for the speedy dispatch of the business of the Court it is expedient that there should be added to the Court another division or other divisions he may, notwithstanding anything in the Act of 1969, by order, made with the consent of the Minister for the Public Service, provide for such an additional division or divisions.

(2) A division of the Court provided for under this section shall consist of a deputy chairman of the Court (who shall be chairman of the division), a workers' member and an employers' member, and sections 3(*b*) and 3(*c*) of the Act of 1969 shall apply in relation to such a division as if it were a division under that Act.

(3) Whenever the Minister makes an order under this section he shall appoint a deputy chairman of the Court, and sections 4(4) to 4(7) of the Act of 1969 (as amended by this Act) shall apply in relation to a deputy chairman appointed under this Act as if the references in those sections to a deputy chairman were references to a deputy chairman appointed under this Act.

(4) A deputy chairman (whether appointed under this section or under section 4(4) of the Act of 1969) shall be paid such remuneration (by way of either fees or salary) and allowances as the Minister, with the consent of the Minister for the Public Service, determines.

(5) Section 4(5) of the Act of 1969 is hereby repealed.

COMMENTARY

The setting up of a fourth division of the Court was provided for by the Labour Court (Fourth Division) Order 1979 (S.I. No. 161 of 1979). Section 41 of the Industrial Relations Act 1990 provides that the Minister may amend or revoke an order made by him under this section.

Consequential amendment of section 2 of Act of 1969

9. [. . .]

COMMENTARY

This section amends section 2 of the Industrial Relations Act 1969, which amendment is incorporated into the text of that Act.

Amendment of section 5 of Act of 1969

10. [. . .]

COMMENTARY

This section amends section 5 of the Industrial Relations Act 1969, which amendment is incorporated into the text of that Act.

Repeal of Agricultural Workers (Holidays) Acts, 1950 to 1975

11.—(1) The Agricultural Workers (Holidays) Acts, 1950 to 1975, are hereby repealed.

(2) This section shall come into operation on the commencement of regulations under the Holidays (Employees) Act, 1973, providing for the application of that Act to agricultural workers.

COMMENTARY

The 1973 Act was applied to agricultural workers by means of the Holidays (Agricultural Workers) Regulations 1977 (S.I. No. 64 of 1977) which came into operation on February 28, 1977.

Short title, construction and collective citation

12.—(1) This Act may be cited as the Industrial Relations Act, 1976, and shall be construed as one with the Principal Act.

(2) The Industrial Relations Acts, 1946 and 1969, and this Act may be cited together as the Industrial Relations Acts, 1946 to 1976.

INDUSTRIAL RELATIONS ACT 1990

(Number 19 of 1990)

An Act to make further and better provision for promoting harmonious relations between workers and employers, and to amend the law relating to Trade Unions and for these and other purposes to amend the Industrial Relations Acts, 1946 to 1976, and the Trade Union Acts, 1871 to 1982.

[*18 July 1990*]

COMMENTARY

Reform of Irish trade union and industrial relations legislation has been high on the agenda of successive Ministers for Labour ever since the establishment of the Department of Labour in 1966. The general state of industrial relations was then, and for some time thereafter, perceived to be one of serious disorder—unofficial industrial action was widespread, there were frequent disruptions to essential services and there were a significant number of inter-union disputes. Two major Bills were produced by the newly created Department, but the Trade Union Bill 1966 did not receive its Second Reading until February 19, 1969 (see 238 *Dáil Debates* Cols. 1319 *et seq.*). This Bill provided, *inter alia*, that the rules of a trade union should be deemed to require that, before the service of a strike notice, a majority of the members entitled to vote and voting in a secret ballot should have approved of such service and the Bill further provided that members taking unofficial action would lose the immunities provided by the Trade Disputes Act 1906. The Bill evoked strong opposition from the trade union movement and was subjected to considerable criticism in the Dáil. Ultimately the Bill was not pursued, the Minister conceding that the only law that would work was that "in which the trade unions co-operate" (see 238 *Dáil Debates* Col. 2370). The other Bill which became the Industrial Relations Act 1969 was well received providing as it did for the enlargement and more flexible operation of the Labour Court and the establishment of the rights commissioner service. Two provisions in the Trade Union Bill were revived in the 1970s—tighter criteria for the granting of negotiation licences (Trade Union Act 1971) and improved machinery for amalgamations (Trade Union Act 1975).

In May 1978, the Minister appointed a Commission of Inquiry on Industrial Relations charged with considering and reporting on industrial relations generally and in particular on, *inter alia*, the relevance of statute law to industrial relations. The Commission of Inquiry (minus its trade union members), which reported in July 1981, concluded that voluntary means alone were incapable of imparting the required degree of order to the collective relations between unions and employers and made a number of controversial recommendations in relation to reform of the law (see McCarthy and von Prondzynski "The Reform of Industrial Relations" (1982) 29 *Administration* 220; Kelly and Roche "Institutional Reform in Irish Industrial Relations" (1983) LXXII *Studies* 221; and Murphy and Kelly "The Report of the Commission of Inquiry on Industrial Relations" in *Industrial Relations in Ireland: Contemporary Issues and Developments* (2nd ed., 1989) published by the Department of Industrial Relations UCD). None of these recommendations were implemented, although the Trade Disputes (Amendment) Act 1982 did remove the "trade or industry" requirement. Despite the lack of any major legislative reform, the state of Irish industrial relations progressively improved. Throughout the 1980s there was a considerable degree of trade union rationalisation culminating in the amalgamation on January 1, 1990, of the Irish Transport and General Workers' Union and the Federated Workers' Union of Ireland. There has also been a dramatic decrease in the number of days lost through strikes, with unofficial action now responsible for an insignificant proportion of them (3 per cent. in 1990).

Nevertheless the relatively healthy state of Irish industrial relations was not felt to justify complacency, and the Programme for National Recovery agreed in 1987 committed the Minister for Labour to holding discussions with the social partners about changes in the legislation which would provide "a better framework for collective bargaining and dispute settlement and help create conditions for employment-generating investment."

In February 1988 the Minister published a set of proposals (see *Industrial Relations News* 8, February 25, 1988) designed to form the basis for the "prolonged and intensive discussions" which took place in 1988 and 1989 (*Department of Labour Annual Report 1988* p. 7). In putting these proposals forward, the Minister said that he did not believe it was possible to achieve a complete consensus as to what the legislation should contain. His approach would be to address the major issues which he felt were required to be tackled and to devise arrangements which would be workable and with which both sides could live. The Minister also made it clear that, while he would engage in extensive consultations with both sides and attempt to achieve as much consensus as possible, he intended to have legislation enacted. The Minister himself had described his reform proposals as a "pragmatic package" (in the 14th Countess Markievicz Memorial Lecture "Industrial Relations in the 1990s: Consensus and Participation" delivered on November 6, 1989). While the Trade Disputes Act 1906 was to be repealed in its entirety, the immunities system would be retained. There was no question of moving to a system based on a positive right to strike (as proposed by Ruairi Quinn when he was Minister—on which see Quinn "The Reform of Trade Dispute and Industrial Relations Legislation" (1986) 5 *J.I.S.L.L.* 1; Kerr "Industrial Action: Rights or Immunities?" (1986) 5 *J.I.S.L.L.* 7; and Bonner "Industrial Relations and the Law: What next?" in the first edition of *Industrial Relations in Ireland: Contemporary Issues and Developments* published by the Department of Industrial Relations UCD in 1987). The position in relation to secondary picketing would be clarified; the immunity in the case of disputes between workers would be removed, as would the immunity in the case of disputes involving one individual worker where procedures had not been followed. There would also be a requirement for trade unions to include pre-strike ballot provisions in their rule books and linked to this would be restrictions on an employer's ability to obtain interim and interlocutory injunctions in trade disputes. Additionally, there would be a reform of the dispute settlement machinery by the creation of a Labour Relations Commission. Finally, there would be reform of the law relating to trade union organisation and Joint Labour Committees. This framework, the Minister said, was designed to make the collective bargaining system work better with the over-riding objective of minimising conflict and maximising co-operation. (For a detailed description of the 1988 proposals see Bonner "Industrial Relations Reform" in the second edition of *Industrial Relations in Ireland: Contemporary Issues and Developments* published by the Department of Industrial Relations UCD in 1989.)

It is a measure of the Minister's determination and the accuracy of his officials' assessment of what would be acceptable that the Act is largely unchanged from the proposals put forward in 1988. The Bill was generally well supported on all sides (see Deputy O'Sullivan at 396 *Dáil Debates* Col. 767) but there were occasionally sharp disagreements on some of the detail and the Workers Party were generally of the view that it would invite the intervention of the courts to a far greater extent than had been the position before (see Deputy Rabbitte at 396 *Dáil Debates* Col. 778). Most importantly there was support from across all the political parties for the proposition that, while legislation could have an impact on the conduct of industrial relations, on its own it was no answer to our problems. Good industrial relations was primarily a matter for the parties involved and the role of the law was merely to provide a framework within which collective bargaining could operate (see, for instance, the Minister at 126 *Seanad Debates* Col. 65) or, as Deputy Hillery put it (396 *Dáil Debates* Col. 845), "to help industry help itself."

On the Act generally see Wilkinson "The Irish Industrial Relations Act 1990—Corporatism and Conflict Control" (1991) 20 *I.L.J.* 21, and note that at the inaugural conference of the Irish Municipal, Public and Civil Trade Union an overwhelming majority of the delegates voted to call on the union to campaign for changes in the Act (see *Industrial Relations News* 19, May 16, 1991).

Be it enacted by the Oireachtas as follows:

PART I

PRELIMINARY

Short title

1.—This Act may be cited as the Industrial Relations Act, 1990.

Collective citations and construction

2.—(1) This Act (other than Part II) and the Industrial Relations Acts, 1946 to 1976, may be cited together as the Industrial Relations Acts, 1946 to 1990, and shall be construed together as one Act.

(2) Part II of this Act and the Trade Union Acts, 1871 to 1982, may be cited together as the Trade Union Acts, 1871 to 1990, and shall be construed together as one Act.

Interpretation

3.—(1) In this Act—
"the Minister" means the Minister for Labour;
"the Court" means the Labour Court;
"the Commission" means the Labour Relations Commission established by section 24.

(2) In this Act—

(a) a reference to a Part or section is to a Part or section of this Act unless it is indicated that a reference to some other enactment is intended;

(b) a reference to a subsection or paragraph is to the subsection or paragraph of the provision in which the reference occurs, unless it is indicated that a reference to some other provision is intended; and

(c) a reference to any other enactment shall, unless the context otherwise requires, be construed as a reference to that enactment as amended by or under any other enactment, including this Act.

(3) In any enactment other than this Act, a reference to the Trade Disputes Act, 1906 (repealed by this Act) or to any provision thereof shall, without prejudice to section 20(1) of the Interpretation Act, 1937, be construed as a reference to any relevant provision of Part II of this Act.

Increase of fines

4.—(1) A person convicted of an offence for which a penalty is provided in any enactment indicated in the First Schedule to this Act at any reference number shall, in lieu of the fine provided in that enactment, be liable to the fine specified in column (3) of that Schedule at that reference number, and that enactment shall be construed and have effect accordingly.

(2) Where it is provided in the First Schedule to this Act at any reference number that a person shall be liable to a daily default fine, he shall be guilty of contravening the relevant enactment on every day on which the contravention continues after conviction of the original contravention and for each such offence he shall be liable to a fine not exceeding the amount specified at that reference number instead of the fine specified for the original contravention.

(3) The provisions of this section shall not apply to any offence committed before the passing of this Act.

Summary proceedings for an offence

5.—Notwithstanding section 10(4) of the Petty Sessions (Ireland) Act, 1851, summary proceedings for an offence under the Industrial Relations Acts, 1946 to 1990, may be instituted within one year from the date of the offence.

Expenses

6.—The expenses incurred in the administration of this Act shall, to such extent as may be sanctioned by the Minister for Finance, be paid out of moneys provided by the Oireachtas.

Repeals

7.—The enactments referred to in the Second Schedule to this

INDUSTRIAL RELATIONS ACT 1990

Act are hereby repealed to the extent specified in the third column of that Schedule.

PART II

TRADE UNION LAW

Trade Disputes

Definitions for Part II

8.—In this Part, save where the context otherwise requires—
"employer" means a person for whom one or more workers work or have worked or normally work or seek to work having previously worked for that person;
"trade dispute" means any dispute between employers and workers which is connected with the employment or non-employment, or the terms or conditions of or affecting the employment, of any person;
"trade union" means a trade union which is the holder of a negotiation licence under Part II of the Trade Union Act, 1941;
"worker" means any person who is or was employed whether or not in the employment of the employer with whom a trade dispute arises, but does not include a member of the Defence Forces or of the Garda Síochána;
"industrial action" means any action which affects, or is likely to affect, the terms or conditions, whether express or implied, of a contract and which is taken by any number or body of workers acting in combination or under a common understanding as a means of compelling their employer, or to aid other workers in compelling their employer, to accept or not to accept terms or condition of or affecting employment;
"strike" means a cessation of work by any number or body of workers acting in combination or a concerted refusal or a refusal under a common understanding of any number of workers to continue to work for their employer done as a means of compelling their employer, or to aid other workers in compelling their employer, to accept or not to accept terms or conditions of or affecting employment.

COMMENTARY

"employer": this word was not defined in the Trade Disputes Act 1906 but its meaning was considered by the High Court in *Roundabout Ltd.* v. *Beirne* [1959] I.R. 423. Here the owner of a public house was in dispute with a trade union over the dismissal of union members. The pub closed and the plaintiff company was incorporated with the owner of the pub, his wife, his brother, his accountant and three former employees as directors. This company then took a yearly tenancy of the pub, the licence was transferred and when the pub reopened, the company sought an injunction to restrain the picketing of the pub. Dixon J. granted an injunction on the ground that, as the plaintiff company was a legal entity distinct from the owner and so far employed no employees, it could not be held to be an employer within the meaning of the 1906 Act. The definition in the Act does nothing to affect this reasoning and attempts during Committee Stage to amend the definition so as to cover the situation where a person acquires an undertaking for which one or more workers work or have worked were not successful (see 398 *Dáil Debates* Cols. 327–338). The circumstances in the *Roundabout* case were described by the Minister as being "quite exceptional" and he doubted if such an attempt to get around the provisions of the legislation would succeed today. Indeed it is likely that, were the *Roundabout* situation to be repeated, the courts would regard the formation of the company and the subsequent tenancy agreement as sham transactions and would go on to "lift the corporate veil" for the purpose of establishing who were in reality the parties to the dispute. Such an approach was adopted by the English Court of Appeal in *Examite Ltd.* v. *Whitaker* [1977] I.R.L.R. 312.

"trade dispute": this definition differs somewhat from that in the 1906 Act, in that it is both broader and narrower. As well as removing disputes between workmen from its ambit it also covers disputes connected with terms or conditions "of or affecting" the employment of any person. The definition is not limited to disputes between an employer and his or her workers, because worker is defined as any person who is or was employed "whether or not in the employment of the employer with whom a trade dispute arises." This proposition was accepted by the Minister as being correct both at Committee Stage and Report Stage (see 398 *Dáil Debates* Col. 335 and 400 *Dáil Debates* Col. 1782).

The phrase "employment or non-employment" has been extensively considered by the Irish courts. It has been held to be wide enough to cover any dispute arising out of the employment or dismissal of any person. It covers future termination as well as an immediate dismissal, and it does not matter whether the dismissal was lawful or fair: see Lavery J. in *Quigley* v. *Beirne* [1955] I.R. 62, 76. So in *Goulding Chemicals Ltd.* v. *Bolger* [1977] I.R. 211 the Supreme Court held that workers who had been made redundant were quite entitled, under the 1906 Act, to demand a sum greater than their statutory entitlement to redundancy pay and to take industrial action if the claim was refused (see, *per* Kenny J. at 238 and McWilliam J. in *Cleary* v. *Coffey* reported at (1985) 4 *J.I.S.L.L.* 70, 71). Nor can any distinction be drawn between the case of a dismissed employee and that of a person seeking initial employment (see *per* Hamilton J. in *McHenry Brothers Ltd.* v. *Carey* reported at (1984) 3 *J.I.S.L.L.* 80, 85). Thus a dispute over the hiring policies of an employer or his refusal to hire a particular person will be a trade dispute. McWilliam J. has held, however, in *J. Bradbury Ltd.* v. *Duffy* (reported at (1984) 3 *J.I.S.L.L.* 86) that there had to be some restriction on "the universality of the application of the term 'non-employment'." He took the "extreme case" of a person starting a new business for which ten employees were required and receiving fifty applications. McWilliam J. could not accept that the forty unsuccessful applicants were entitled to take any sort of industrial action simply because they had not been given jobs. Similar views were expressed by Costello J. in his *ex tempore* judgment delivered on May 31, 1991, in *Michael McNamara & Co. Ltd.* v. *Lacken* (1990 No. 17675P) when he said that there was a fair issue as to whether refusal of employment to the defendants was a trade dispute.

Under the 1906 Act the phrase "terms of employment or conditions of labour" (which has been replaced by the concept of terms or conditions of or affecting employment) was considered by the High Court in *Brendan Dunne Ltd.* v. *Fitzpatrick* [1958] I.R. 29. Budd J. interpreted "terms of employment" as meaning "all matters covered by the contract of employment either express or implied" and "conditions of labour" as meaning "the physical conditions under which a workman works." So in *Becton Dickinson & Co. Ltd.* v. *Lee* [1973] I.R. 1, the Supreme Court held that a dispute as to whether a trade union should be allowed to negotiate terms and conditions of employment was a dispute connected with "terms of employment" and was thus a trade dispute. See, further, Kerr and Whyte, *Irish Trade Union Law* (1985) pp. 271–274.

The dispute need only be "connected with" one or more of the above matters. Attempts to restrict the definition by inserting the word "directly" before "connected with" were unsuccessful (see 398 *Dáil Debates* Cols. 339–349). English and Northern Irish caselaw suggests that any connection will be sufficient, since it has been held by the House of Lords and the Northern Ireland Court of Appeal that, *absent* a requirement that the dispute be "wholly or mainly connected" and provided there is a real connection between the dispute and one or more of the specified matters, predominance of subject matter is irrelevant: see *NWL Ltd.* v. *Woods* [1979] I.C.R. 867 at 878 and 889 and *Crazy Prices (Northern Ireland) Ltd.* v. *Hewitt* [1980] N.I. 150 at 169. However, the decision of the former Supreme Court in *Esplanade Pharmacy Ltd.* v. *Larkin* [1957] I.R. 285 would suggest that the dispute must be *immediately* connected with one or more of the specified matters. See, further, Kerr and Whyte, *Irish Trade Union Law* (1985) pp. 267–269. It must be emphasised that a dispute will not cease to be a trade dispute merely because the workers' claims appear to be unreasonable (*per* McWilliam J. in *Cleary* v. *Coffey* reported at (1985) 4 *J.I.S.L.L.* 70, 71) or unrealistic (*per* Millet J. in *Associated British Ports* v. *Transport and General Workers' Union* [1989] I.R.L.R. 291, 299).

The fact that the dispute may be connected with the employment of "any person" means that there can be a trade dispute between employers and workers over the employment of persons who are not workers. This proposition was accepted by the Minister as being correct (see 398 *Dáil Debates* Cols. 342–343, 349) although it was not the view of the majority of the former Supreme Court in *Smith* v. *Beirne* (1954) 89 I.L.T.R. 24. See, further, Kerr and Whyte, *Irish Trade Union Law* (1985) pp. 275–276.

"trade union": there are at present 67 unions possessing negotiation licences catering for a membership of approximately 481,000. Such unions are hereafter referred to as "authorised trade unions." For the conditions as to the granting of negotiation licences, see the commentary to section 23.

"worker": This definition is almost identical to that of "workman" under the 1906 Act as amended by the Trade Disputes (Amendment) Act 1982. As originally drafted the definition also excluded persons who, under a contract for services, personally did work or provided services for another—the intention clearly being to exclude self-employed persons from the scope of the legislation. This proviso, however, was deleted at Committee Stage because it was realised that it "would also exclude various categories of workers it was not intended to exclude" (*per* the Minister at 398 *Dáil Debates* Col. 360). Persons who are seeking employment for the first time would not appear to come within this definition: see O'Higgins C.J. in *Goulding Chemicals Ltd.* v. *Bolger* [1977] I.R. 211, 230.

The failure to provide that a dispute to which a trade union is a party is to be treated as a dispute to which workers (or, as the case may be, employers) are parties leaves uncertain the status of a dispute between an employer and a trade union. It is clear that a dispute connected with one or more of the specified matters between an employer and a trade union representing that employer's workers will be a trade dispute (see, *per* Ó Dálaigh J. in *Smith* v. *Beirne* (1954) 89 I.L.T.R. 24, 38). What remains unclear is whether a trade union can raise a trade dispute with an employer, where none of the persons whose employment forms the subject matter of the dispute are members of the trade union concerned. This question was answered in the negative in *Ryan* v. *Cooke and Quinn* [1938] I.R. 512, *Doran* v. *Lennon* [1945] I.R. 315 and *Crowley* v. *Cleary* [1968] I.R. 261. In *Sheriff* v. *McMullen* [1952] I.R. 236, however, Murnaghan J., with whom Maguire C.J. agreed, said that there might be occasions on which members of a trade union might have a dispute with an employer even though none of the employer's workers was a member of the union, but he hastened to add (at 252) that "not every dispute with a trade union was a trade dispute." See, to similar effect, Lord Parker in *Larkin* v. *Long* [1915] A.C. 814, 833 and more recently Goulding J. in *Health Computing Ltd.* v. *Meek* [1981] I.C.R. 24, 32. Note also the difference of opinion on this point between Lords Diplock and Scarman in *N.W.L. Ltd.* v. *Woods* [1979] I.C.R. 867 at 877 and 887 respectively.

"industrial action" and "strike": these definitions are framed in terms of collective action. Action by one individual worker would not be covered. The strike or industrial action must be done as a means of compelling the employer, or aiding other workers in compelling their employer, to accept or not to accept terms or conditions of or affecting employment. Withdrawal of labour in protest against the continued imprisonment of Martin Foran would not be a strike as defined. Picketing (on which see the commentary to section 11) is clearly covered by the definition of industrial action (see the Minister at 398 *Dáil Debates* Col. 371). The definition of "industrial action" includes both lawful and unlawful industrial action and a number of Deputies expressed concern at its breadth (see Deputy Rabbitte at 398 *Dáil Debates* Cols. 370 and 374–376 and Deputy Quinn (a former Minister for Labour) *ibid.* at Cols. 373–374, the latter expressing the fear that we had entered "Ceaucescu land") in the context of the balloting requirement in section 14. An amendment to limit its application and specifically exclude "a refusal to carry out work or provide services which, if carried out, would frustrate a strike or industrial action engaged in by others" was defeated at Report Stage (see 400 *Dáil Debates* Cols. 1782–1794).

Application of provisions of Part II

9.—(1) Sections 11, 12 and 13 shall apply only in relation to authorised trade unions which for the time being are holders of negotiation licences under the Trade Union Act, 1941, and the members and officials of such trade unions, and not otherwise.

(2) Where in relation to the employment or non-employment or the terms or conditions of or affecting the employment of one individual worker, there are agreed procedures availed of by custom or in practice in the employment concerned, or provided for in a collective agreement, for the resolution of individual grievances, including dismissals, sections 10, 11 and 12 shall apply only where those procedures have been resorted to and exhausted.

(3) Procedures shall be deemed to be exhausted if at any stage an employer fails or refuses to comply with them.

(4) The procedures referred to in subsection (2) may include resort to such persons or bodies as a rights commissioner, the Labour Relations Commission, the Labour Court, an equality officer and the Employment Appeals Tribunal but shall not include an appeal to a court.

Industrial Relations Act 1990

COMMENTARY

Subsection (1) re-enacts section 11 of the Trade Union Act 1941. Thus the immunities conferred by sections 11 and 12 will only apply to members and officials of authorised trade unions and that conferred by section 13 will only apply to authorised trade unions, their trustees or officials and members thereof sued in a representative capacity. Workers who are not members or officials of such unions are only entitled to the benefit of the immunities conferred by section 10. In *Goulding Chemicals Ltd.* v. *Bolger* [1977] I.R. 211, the Supreme Court ruled that section 11 of the 1941 Act was not so restricted in application as to apply only to members and officials of authorised trade unions acting with the authority, or pursuant to a decision, of their union. The impact of that decision, however, has now been modified somewhat by section 17 of the Act.

As to who is a "trade union official" it must be noted that the definition contained in section 11(5) applies only for the purposes of that section. At Committee Stage amendments were moved by both the Fine Gael and Workers' Party spokespersons to include a definition of trade union official in section 8 (the section dealing with definitions for Part II of the Act). The former's provided that a "trade union official" meant "a person in the employment of a trade union or a person authorised in writing by a trade union to act for it for a purpose or purposes specified in the authorisation." The latter's provided that the term meant "any person in the employment of a trade union or any person appointed by a trade union to so act under the rules of that trade union." It was stated that the amendments were intended to clarify that the term did not just mean an officer in the employment of a trade union but also shop stewards and branch committee members who, although not employees of the union, were acting for the union in a particular dispute (see Deputy Mitchell at 398 *Dáil Debates* Cols. 349–350). The Minister repeatedly stated, however, (see 398 *Dáil Debates* Cols. 351 and 357) that, since the only area the issue arose was in section 11, he intended to put the definition there and not in section 8. Whilst, in a literal sense, it is true that the term "trade union official" only appears in section 11, the term "officials of such [*i.e.* authorised] trade unions" appears in section 9(1) and governs the availability of the immunities contained in sections 11 and 12. Moreover, section 13(1) refers to an action against a trade union "or official thereof" and section 14(2)(*b*) refers to constraint being imposed by the union or any of its officials. It would be unfortunate if the courts were to construe these expressions in a different manner to that provided for in section 11(5). Following the Minister's undertaking to look at the matter again before Report State the amendments were withdrawn and were not subsequently pursued.

Subsection (2) provides that none of the immunities will apply where "agreed procedures availed of by custom or in practice in the employment concerned, or provided for in a collective agreement, for the resolution of individual grievances" have not been resorted to and exhausted. This subsection was invoked for the first time in *Iarnród Éireann* v. *Darby and O'Connor* (*Irish Times*, March 23, 1991). Morris J. said that he was satisfied that the second named defendant was the only worker who had a dispute with the plaintiff. From the evidence, he had not gone through the agreed procedures and consequently the picket did not enjoy immunity. Subsection (4) further provides that the procedures referred to may include resort to such persons or bodies as a rights commissioner, the Labour Relations Commission, the Labour Court, an equality officer and the Employment Appeals Tribunal "but shall not include an appeal to a court." This list is not exhaustive and goes some way to meeting employer demands that disputes over individual statutory rights should not obtain the benefit of the immunities (as indeed was recommended by the Commission of Inquiry on Industrial Relations at paragraphs 701–704 of its *Report*).

Acts in contemplation or furtherance of trade dispute

10.—(1) An agreement or combination by two or more persons to do or procure to be done any act in contemplation or furtherance of a trade dispute shall not be indictable as a conspiracy if such act committed by one person would not be punishable as a crime.

(2) An act done in pursuance of an agreement or combination by two or more persons, if done in contemplation or furtherance of a trade dispute, shall not be actionable unless the act, if done without any such agreement or combination, would be actionable.

(3) Section 3 of the Conspiracy, and Protection of Property Act, 1875, and subsections (1) and (2) of this section shall be construed together as one section.

COMMENTARY

This section re-enacts the immunities concerning criminal and civil conspiracy formerly provided for in section 3 of the Conspiracy and Protection of Property Act 1875 and section 1 of the 1906 Act. In the case of civil conspiracy the retention of the wording of section 1 of the 1906 Act means that an agreement by workers to break their contracts of employment is actionable as a civil conspiracy despite section 10, as breach of contract is actionable if done by one person alone. An attempt to insert the words "in tort" after "actionable" in subsection (2) was not successful (see 398 *Dáil Debates* Cols. 495–497). Note also that section 17(1) provides that section 10 shall not apply in respect of proceedings arising out of or relating to a strike or other industrial action by a trade union or a group of workers in disregard of or contrary to the outcome of a secret ballot relating to the issue or issues involved in the dispute. Unlike the immunities contained in sections 11 and 12, the immunities herein conferred are available to persons who are neither members nor officials of authorised trade unions (see the commentary to section 9).

On the tort of civil conspiracy see Kerr and Whyte, *Irish Trade Union Law* (1985) pp. 227–230 and Sales "The Tort of Conspiracy and Civil Secondary Liability" (1990) 49 *Camb L.J.* 491. Following the decision of the Supreme Court in *Taylor* v. *Smyth* (unreported, July 5, 1990) it would appear that the paths of English and Irish law have gone their separate ways in this respect. According to the English Court of Appeal in *Metall und Rohstoff A.G.* v. *Donaldson Lufkin & Jenrette Inc.* [1990] 1 Q.B. 391, an agreement between A and B which is intended to and does cause economic loss to C is not actionable at the suit of C unless the sole or predominant purpose of A and B is to injure C's interests and not solely or predominantly to advance their own commercial interests, even if A and B adopt unlawful means in carrying out their purpose. McCarthy J. (with whom Finlay C.J. and Hederman J. agreed) was clearly impressed, however, with Eekelaar's comment (106 *L.Q.R.* 223 at p. 224) that it was "hard to defend an outcome in which conspirators who have caused injury by unlawful means are allowed to escape liability for conspiracy if they show that they were predominantly motivated by intention to further their own interests." To McCarthy J., it was "entirely logical" that when what was actionable when done by unlawful means, such as procuring a breach of contract, was actionable against an individual, even though his or her purpose was solely one of self interest, it should not cease to be actionable when done in combination by a group with a like purpose (see further Kerr, (1990) 12 *D.U.L.J.* (n.s.) 166).

Immunity is only provided where the agreement or combination is "in contemplation or furtherance of a trade dispute." This phrase, dubbed "the golden formula" by Lord Wedderburn in *The Worker and the Law* (1965) p. 222, also occurs in sections 11, 12 and 13. It is by the interpretation of this phrase, therefore, that the courts will determine the boundaries of lawful industrial action. The phrase is to be read disjunctively. The use of the word "contemplation" indicates that it is not necessary that there be a dispute in existence. The mere anticipation, however, of a possible dispute at some time in the future is not enough: see *Esplanade Pharmacy Ltd.* v. *Larkin* [1957] I.R. 285. It is necessary for the court to conclude that the dispute be "either imminent or actual": *per* Gibson L.J. in *Crazy Prices (Northern Ireland) Ltd.* v. *Hewitt* [1980] N.I. 150, 167. The word "furtherance" has given rise to considerable judicial debate in Britain. Some judges, such as Lord Denning, favoured an objective interpretation. In other words not only did a defendant have to show an intention to further a trade dispute but also that the acts done pursuant to that intention were reasonably capable of achieving the end. This interpretation was not accepted by the majority of the House of Lords in *Express Newspapers Ltd.* v. *MacShane* [1980] A.C. 672. Lord Diplock clearly favoured a subjective interpretation. "If the party who does the act honestly thinks at the time he does it that it may help one of the parties to the trade dispute to achieve their objectives and does it for that reason, he is protected by the section" (at 686). In other words the immunity merely depends on the *bona fides* of the defendant. Once it is shown that a trade dispute exists the person who acts, and not the court, is the judge of whether the acts will further the dispute. Lord Scarman confessed to being relieved at this conclusion. He said (at 694) that it would be a "strange and embarrassing task for a judge to be called upon to review the tactics of a party to a trade dispute and to determine whether . . . the tactic employed was likely to further, or advance, the party's side of the dispute." Lord Wilberforce, however, dissented. In his view, in order to obtain the immunity, the acts must be reasonably capable of furthering the dispute but he added that, in applying this test, the court must take into account the belief of the initiators of the action as to the capability of that action to achieve the objective. Where the initiators were "experienced trade union officials" the court should be reluctant to substitute its own judgment for theirs. In this respect, the provisions of section 13(2) should be noted. Here it is expressly provided that it shall be a defence that the act was done "in the reasonable belief that it was done in contemplation or furtherance of a trade dispute", where the action is against any trade union or its trustees or against any members or officials thereof in respect of any tortious act alleged or found to have been committed by or on behalf of the trade union.

Peaceful picketing

11.—(1) It shall be lawful for one or more persons, acting on their own behalf or on behalf of a trade union in contemplation or furtherance of a trade dispute, to attend at, or where that is not practicable, at the approaches to, a place where their employer works or carries on business, if they so attend merely for the purpose of peacefully obtaining or communicating information or of peacefully persuading any person to work or abstain from working.

Industrial Relations Act 1990

(2) It shall be lawful for one or more persons acting on their own behalf or on behalf of a trade union in contemplation or furtherance of a trade dispute, to attend at, or where that is not practicable, at the approaches to, a place where an employer who is not a party to the trade dispute works or carries on business if, but only if, it is reasonable for those who are so attending to believe at the commencement of their attendance and throughout the continuance of their attendance that that employer has directly assisted their employer who is a party to the trade dispute for the purpose of frustrating the strike or other industrial action, provided that such attendance is merely for the purpose of peacefully obtaining or communicating information or of peacefully persuading any person to work or abstain from working.

(3) For the avoidance of doubt any action taken by an employer in the health services to maintain life-preserving services during a strike or other industrial action shall not constitute assistance for the purposes of subsection (2).

(4) It shall be lawful for a trade union official to accompany any member of his union whom he represents provided that the member is acting in accordance with the provisions of subsection (1) or (2) and provided that such official is attending merely for the purpose of peacefully obtaining or communicating information or of peacefully persuading any person to work or abstain from working.

(5) For the purposes of this section "trade union official" means any paid official of a trade union or any officer of a union or branch of a union elected or appointed in accordance with the rules of a union.

COMMENTARY

This section replaces section 2(1) of the 1906 Act and effects major changes in the law on picketing. There was general agreement amongst Deputies that it was the most important section in the Bill (see the exchange between the Minister and Deputy Bell at 398 *Dáil Debates* Cols. 562–563). Subsections (1) and (2) purport to regulate what is generally referred to as "primary" and "secondary" picketing. Both subsections commence by averring that it "shall be lawful..." and thus, arguably, confer rights as opposed to immunities. The protection provided, however, is described hereafter and elsewhere in the text in terms of the latter.

Despite the many judicial *dicta* to the effect that picketing was only lawful on the conditions set out in the 1906 Act (see, for instance, Ó Dálaigh J. in *Esplanade Pharmacy Ltd.* v. *Larkin* [1957] I.R. 285, 298), picketing *per se* is not actionable at common law. This is so even if the picketing is secondary picketing, and it does not become actionable simply because it does not comply with the statutory provisions (see Kerr and Whyte, *Irish Trade Union Law* (1985) pp. 284–289, 297–298). Picketing is only actionable if it is tortious and the defendants, on ordinary principles, are responsible for the tort. What section 11 does is to establish quite clearly that attending for the purposes set out therein does not constitute a trespass to the highway or a common law nuisance.

Industrial Relations Act 1990

Neither subsection prescribes any limit to the number of pickets. Consequently mass picketing is not unlawful *per se* (although see *Thomas* v. *National Union of Mineworkers (South Wales Area)* [1985] I.C.R. 886) but as Walsh J. observed in *E.I. Co. Ltd.* v. *Kennedy* [1968] I.R. 69, 91:

> "Excessive numbers in pickets may also go beyond what is reasonably permissible for the communication of information or the obtaining of information and may amount to obstruction or nuisance or give rise to a reasonable apprehension of a breach of the peace".

Thus if more pickets are employed than are reasonably required for the stated purposes, the court may infer that it is not *bona fide* and hence not protected by the section. What is reasonable is a question of degree and, as Budd J. recognised in *Brendan Dunne Ltd.* v. *Fitzpatrick* [1958] I.R. 29, 44, depends on the size of the premises, the number of persons working or calling at them, the number of entrances and the confines and uses of the area in which the picketing takes place. The picketers must not only be attending "in contemplation or furtherance of a trade dispute" but they must also be "acting on their own behalf or on behalf of a trade union." Consequently the subsections apply both to official and unofficial picketing (although see the commentary to section 17 for the effect of subsection (1) of that section on the general proposition laid down by the Supreme Court in *Goulding Chemicals Ltd.* v. *Bolger* [1977] I.R. 211).

Under the 1906 Act the picketers could attend at or near a house or place where a person resided or worked or carried on business or happened to be. The width of this provision has been drastically curtailed. The picketers' attendance now must be "at, or where that is not practicable, at the approaches to, a place where their employer works or carries on business." Attendance at (or at the approaches to) a place where an employer who is not a party to the trade dispute works or carries on business is only permitted on the conditions set out in subsection (2). Unlike the equivalent legislation in Northern Ireland (Industrial Relations (Northern Ireland) Order 1976, Article 64A) the focus is not on where the picketers work but on where their employer works or carries on business. Picketers are thus quite entitled to attend at a place where they do not work provided that it is a place where their employer works or carries on business. The use of the present tense would suggest that pickets could not be placed on a place where the employer had worked or carried on business. The Minister assured Deputies, however, that it was not necessary to specifically refer to the past tense as the tense used was the "historic present" (see 398 *Dáil Debates* Cols. 556–559 and 400 *Dáil Debates* Cols. 1800–1801).

If the words "their employer" are interpreted strictly then it would seem that workers who have unsuccessfully sought employment with a particular employer will not be able to further that dispute by picketing the premises at which that employer works or carries on business because he will not be, in law, their employer. In *Westman Holdings Ltd.* v. *McCormack* unreported, May 14, 1991, the Supreme Court (Finlay C.J., O'Flaherty and Egan JJ.) were satisfied that there was a fair question of law to be tried on this issue. Here the defendants had been employed as bar staff in a Dublin licensed premises. These premises, together with fixtures and fittings and the benefit of the licence, were sold to the plaintiff and, before the sale was completed, the defendants and all the other members of staff were dismissed. The defendants unsuccessfully sought employment with the plaintiff and, when the premises re-opened, an official picket was placed. It was argued that, as none of the defendants had ever been employed by the plaintiff, it could not constitute "their employer" within the meaning of section 11(1). The Supreme Court upheld the decision of Lardner J. to grant an interlocutory injunction restraining the picketing because the plaintiff had raised a fair question to be tried at the hearing of the action and because the balance of convenience was in its favour. Assuming the case goes to trial it is likely to be decided on the basis that the European Communities (Safeguarding of Employees' Rights on Transfer of Undertakings) Regulations 1980 (S.I. No. 306 of 1980) apply and that, consequently, the employment relationships between the defendants and their previous employer (the vendor) were transferred to the plaintiff, despite the defendants' purported dismissal (see Case 101/87, *P. Bork International A/S* v. *Foreningen af Arbejdsledere i Danmark* [1988] E.C.R. 3057).

The meaning of the word "attend" was considered by the Supreme Court in *Ferguson Ltd.* v. *O'Gorman* [1937] I.R. 620 where it was submitted that the action of four to six persons patrolling in front of the plaintiff's premises was not "attendance". Sullivan C.J. said that there was nothing in the 1906 Act to limit the meaning of the word "attend" and make it inapplicable to prolonged and continuous action.

Much discussion took place in the Dáil (see 398 *Dáil Debates* Cols. 497–512, 545–554) on the question of multi-employment locations such as ports, airports, shopping centres and industrial estates. The Minister, responding to fears that the words "at the approaches to" would lead to picketing at the entrances to such locations, said that this ignored the words which came immediately before, namely "at, or where that is not practicable,". The test he predicted the courts would apply (see 398 *Dáil Debates* Cols. 499–500) was whether it was practicable to picket at the employer's place of business inside the location. If the owner of the location objected then the proviso would come into effect and the picket could then be placed outside. It is clear that nothing in the Act authorises an entry into private property against the will of the owner: see *Larkin* v. *Belfast Harbour Commissioners* [1908] 2 I.R. 214 and *McCusker* v. *Smith* [1918] 2 I.R. 432.

The question of picketing an industrial estate was considered by the English Court of Appeal in *Rayware Ltd.* v. *Transport and General Workers' Union* [1989] I.C.R. 457. The plaintiff company carried on business in a private trading estate. Some twenty other companies also had sites on the estate and the plaintiff's premises were on a private road approximately one kilometre from the entrance to the estate from the public highway. A dispute arose between the plaintiff and its employees and this lead to picketing at the gate leading from the highway on to the estate, this being, in the words of May L.J., "the nearest practicable point at which to do so without committing any act of trespass." The Court of Appeal refused to grant an injunction restraining the picketing because the picket was "at or near" the employees' place of work.

The 1984 Annual Conference of the Irish Congress of Trade Unions approved a number of directions in respect of picketing at ports and industrial estates. Where picketing is directed against a premises located within a port or an industrial estate the union engaged in the dispute should seek permission from the Port Authority or the owners of the industrial estate to picket outside the premises against which the picket is directed. In the event of permission being refused the picket will have to be maintained at the entrance to the port or industrial estate. In such an event the picket should clearly indicate the employment being picketed and every effort should be made to advise workers and their representatives at the port of industrial estate of the limit of the picket.

By virtue of subsection (2) secondary picketing is only to be permitted if it is reasonable for the picketers to believe "at the commencement of their attendance and throughout the continuance of their attendance" that the employer being picketed has "directly assisted" the employer in dispute "for the purpose of frustrating the strike or other industrial action." Subsection (3) expressly provides that any action taken by an employer in the health services to maintain life-preserving services during a strike or other industrial action shall not constitute assistance for the purposes of subsection (2). According to the Minister (see 398

Industrial Relations Act 1990

Dáil Debates Col. 564) merely filling a gap in the market left by a strike-bound employer could not give rise to lawful secondary picketing under the subsection. He said that the second employer must actively seek to frustrate the strike by direct assistance to the employer in dispute, such as by filling orders on behalf of the first employer or by providing services to the first employer's customers on behalf of the first employer.

The attendance must be "merely for the purpose of peacefully obtaining or communicating information or of peacefully persuading any person to work or abstain from working. "Full effect will be given to the word "merely." If the picketing is done for some other purpose the subsections cannot be relied on: see Kenny J. in *Newbridge Industries Ltd.* v. *Bateson* (a 1975 decision reported at (1988) 7 *J.I.S.L.L.* 191) and Henchy J. in *Becton Dickinson & Co. Ltd.* v. *Lee* [1973] I.R. 1, 44. However, the purpose or object to be obtained from the picketing must not be confused with the motive or reason for it: see O'Higgins C.J. and Kenny J. in *Goulding Chemicals Ltd.* v. *Bolger* [1977] I.R. 211 at 232 and 239 respectively. The dissemination of false or inaccurate information is not authorised by the section: see *Ryan* v. *Cooke and Quinn* [1938] I.R. 512.

Subsection (4) permits a trade union official, as defined in subsection (5), to accompany "any member of his union whom he represents" on a picket. Since the Interpretation Act 1937 provides, in section 11(a), that the singular imports the plural (unless the contrary intention appears), it would seem that more than one official can so attend. Such attendance, however, must be merely for the specified purposes — namely peacefully obtaining or communicating information or of peacefully persuading any person to work or abstain from working. If the official attends for some other purpose his or her immunity is lost (but not that of the picket itself). The official's immunity is also lost where the members he or she is accompanying go outside the ambit of subsections (1) and (2).

Removal of liability for certain acts

12.—An act done by a person in contemplation or furtherance of a trade dispute shall not be actionable on the ground only that—

(a) it induces some other person to break a contract of employment, or

(b) it consists of a threat by a person to induce some other person to break a contract of employment or a threat by a person to break his own contract of employment, or

(c) it is an interference with the trade, business, or employment of some other person, or with the right of some other person to dispose of his capital or his labour as he wills.

COMMENTARY

This section re-enacts section 3 of the 1906 Act (on which see Kerr and Whyte, *Irish Trade Union Law* (1985) pp. 258–261) with the addition of a provision granting immunity to persons who, in contemplation of furtherance of a trade dispute, threaten to induce a breach of a contract of employment or threaten to breach their own contracts of employment. The Irish courts had already held that, if it was not actionable to induce a breach of a contract of employment, it could not be actionable to threaten to induce such breach: *Becton Dickinson & Co. Ltd.* v. *Lee* [1973] I.R. 1, 31. The only extension of the law therefore is to grant a limited immunity where workers commit the tort of intimidation by threatening to break their own contracts of employment. This limited immunity is confined, like that in respect to the tort of inducement of breach of contract, to contracts of employment. Commercial contracts or contracts for services are not included. Inducements (or threats thereof) of breach of such contracts are not protected even if done in contemplation or furtherance of a trade dispute.

Significantly the section does not provide any immunity for the actual breach of a contract of employment. Nor does it in any way concern itself with the developing tort of "unlawful interference with trade or business": on which see most recently *Lonhro plc* v. *Fayed* [1990] 2 Q.B. 490. Consequently the issue of whether indirect inducement of a breach of a commercial contract is actionable, even where done in contemplation or furtherance of a trade dispute, remains to be decided. Judicial opinion in England was divided on this point (compare Lord Pearce in *J.T. Stratford & Son Ltd.* v. *Lindley* [1965] A.C. 269, 336 and Lord Diplock in *Hadmor Productions Ltd.* v. *Hamilton* [1983] 1 A.C. 191, 231) and it was only resolved when legislation (since repealed) expressly provided that an act rendered "not actionable" could not be regarded as the doing of an unlawful act or the use of unlawful means for the purpose of establishing liability in tort. To take an example. B Ltd. is in dispute over terms and conditions of employment with its employees. B Ltd. is party to a commercial contract with A Ltd., whereby A Ltd. has agreed to deliver goods to B Ltd. A trade union official, representing B Ltd.'s employees, induces A Ltd.'s employees to break their contracts of employment by persuading them to refuse to deliver the goods to B Ltd. Consequently there is a breach of the commercial contract. Can either party sue the trade union official? There has been no direct inducement of the breach of the commercial contract. The inducement is indirect, by means of the inducement of breach of the contracts of employment of A Ltd.'s employees. Ordinarily there would be sufficient unlawful means necessary to give rise to liability at the suit of either A Ltd. or B Ltd. However, the inducement of breach of the contracts of employment is rendered "not actionable" by section 12. Clearly the trade union official is rendered immune in respect of an action by A Ltd. in respect of the inducement of the breach of the contracts of employment of its employees. However, is the trade union official immune in respect of an action brought in respect of the indirect inducement of the breach of the commercial contract? Lord Diplock said that the trade union official would be immune in respect of an action brought by either A Ltd. or B Ltd. Lord Pearce, however, said that the trade union official would only be immune in respect of an action brought by A Ltd. In this jurisdiction the Supreme Court in its April 1981 *ex tempore* ruling in *Talbot (Ireland) Ltd.* v. *Merrigan* appears to have taken the view that the trade union official would possess no immunity as against either A Ltd. or B Ltd., but the Minister stated (see 400 *Dáil Debates* Col. 1978) that the phrase "shall not be actionable" meant that it shall not be actionable "by any person." The effect of section 12 was aired for the first time in *River Valley Products Ltd.* v. *Strutt* (1991 No. 1670P) but Costello J. is reported (*Irish Times* February 7, 1991) as having said that, since the proceedings were interlocutory, he was not required to make a final decision as to whether the section protected the defendants. (This case has now been settled, see *Industrial Relations News* 19, May 16, 1991.)

Restriction of actions of tort against trade unions

13.—(1) An action against a trade union, whether of workers or employers, or its trustees or against any members or officials thereof on behalf of themselves and all other members of the trade union in respect of any tortious act committed by or on behalf of the trade union in contemplation or furtherance of a trade dispute, shall not be entertained by any court.

(2) In an action against any trade union or person referred to in subsection (1) in respect of any tortious act alleged or found to have been committed by or on behalf of a trade union it shall be a defence that the act was done in the reasonable belief that it was done in contemplation or furtherance of a trade dispute.

COMMENTARY

Subsection (1) re-enacts, in substance, section 4 of the 1906 Act with an amendment to limit the immunity to torts committed in contemplation or furtherance of a trade dispute. The section does not prohibit actions against individual trade union officials in respect of their personal tortious liability, nor does it prohibit actions against an authorised trade union in its registered name where the tort was not committed in contemplation or furtherance of a trade dispute. Moreover the immunity only applies to actions in tort. It does not apply to actions for restitution (see *Universe Tankships Inc. of Monrovia* v. *International Transport Workers' Federation* [1980] I.R.L.R. 363), actions for breach of constitutional rights (see *Hayes* v. *Ireland* [1987] I.L.R.M. 651) and actions for breach of contract.

The continued use of the past tense may well revive the argument that the subsection does not prohibit injunctive relief against trade unions in respect of tortious acts that have not yet been committed. In respect of the 1906 Act the dominant judicial view was that trade unions were protected against actions being brought against them in which any form of injunction, including a *quia timet* injunction, was sought: see Meredith J. in *Irish Transport and General Workers' Union* v. *Green* [1936] I.R. 471, 480 and Winn L.J. in *Torquay Hotel Ltd.* v. *Cousins* [1969] 2 Ch. 106, 145–146.

The provisions of subsection (2) provide that it shall be a defence that the act was done in the reasonable belief that it was in contemplation or furtherance of a trade dispute. The subsection thus represents a compromise between the subjective approach favoured by Lord Diplock and the objective approach favoured by Lord Wilberforce in *Express Newspapers Ltd.* v. *MacShane* [1980] A.C. 672 (on which see further the commentary to section 10).

Secret ballots

14.—(1) This section shall come into operation two years after the passing of this Act ("the operative date").

(2) The rules of every trade union shall contain a provision that—

(a) the union shall not organise, participate in, sanction or support a strike or other industrial action without a secret ballot, entitlement to vote in which shall be accorded equally to all members whom it is reasonable at the time of the ballot for the union concerned to believe will be called upon to engage in the strike or other industrial action;

(b) the union shall take reasonable steps to ensure that every member entitled to vote in the ballot votes without interference from, or constraint imposed by, the union or any of its members, officials or employees and, so far as is reasonably possible, that such members shall be given a fair opportunity of voting;

(c) the committee of management or other controlling authority of a trade union shall have full discretion in relation to organising, participating in, sanctioning or supporting a strike or other industrial action notwithstanding that the majority of those voting in the ballot, including an aggregate ballot referred to in paragraph (d), favour such strike or other industrial action;

(d) the committee of management or other controlling authority of a trade union shall not organise, participate in, sanction or support a strike or other industrial action against the wishes of a majority of its members voting in a secret ballot, except where, in the case of ballots by more than one trade union, an aggregate majority of all the votes cast, favours such strike or other industrial action;

(e) where the outcome of a secret ballot conducted by a trade union which is affiliated to the Irish Congress of Trade Unions or, in the case of ballots by more than one such trade union, an aggregate majority of all the votes cast, is in favour of supporting a strike organised by another trade union, a decision to take such supportive action shall not be implemented unless the action has been sanctioned by the Irish Congress of Trade Unions;

(f) as soon as practicable after the conduct of a secret ballot the trade union shall take reasonable steps to make known to its members entitled to vote in the ballot:

  (i) the number of ballot papers issued,
  (ii) the number of votes cast,
  (iii) the number of votes in favour of the proposal;
  (iv) the number of votes against the proposal, and;
  (v) the number of spoilt votes.

(3) The rights conferred by a provision referred to in subsection (2) are conferred on the members of the trade union concerned and on no other person.

(4) Nothing in this section shall constitute an obstacle to negotiations for the settlement of a trade dispute nor the return to work by workers party to the trade dispute.

(5) The First Schedule to the Trade Union Act, 1871, is hereby extended to include the requirement provided for in subsection (2).

COMMENTARY

This section does not come into operation until July 18, 1992 (the operative date) and provides that the rules of every trade union must contain certain provisions relating to balloting in respect of strikes and other industrial action. To that end the First Schedule to the Trade Union Act 1871, which sets out certain matters which must be provided for by the rules of registered trade unions, is extended to include this requirement. Furthermore section 15 empowers a trade union's controlling authority "by memorandum in writing" to alter the union's rules so far as may be necessary to give effect to this section "notwithstanding anything in the rules of the union". Section 16 requires a trade union, not later than the operative date, to forward to the Registrar of Friendly Societies a copy of its rules incorporating the said provisions. Section 16 further provides that a trade union, which does not alter its rules so as to comply with section 14, shall cease to be entitled to hold a negotiation licence and its existing licence shall stand revoked on the operative date.

The required provisions in respect of balloting are very different from those required in Great Britain and Northern Ireland: on which see Ewing (1986) 5 J.I.S.L.L. 19. They are also very different from those contained in section 14 of the ill-fated Trade Union Bill 1966. There it was provided that the rules of a trade union should be deemed to require that, before the service of a strike notice, a majority of the members entitled to vote and voting in a secret ballot conducted by the trade union should approve of such service. Any vote to serve strike notice was then subject to approval by the union's controlling authority and the immunities conferred by the Trade Disputes Act 1906 were to be confined to acts done or committed with the authority of the trade union. The effect would have been to outlaw "unofficial action". The 1990 Act does not go that far. What is outlawed by section 17 is action taken in disregard of or contrary to the outcome of a secret ballot relating to the issue or issues involved in the dispute. The only consequence of union members taking "unofficial action" (*i.e.* without holding a ballot or by holding an invalid ballot) is that the restrictions contained in section 19 on the availability of interim and interlocutory injunctions will not apply.

Paragraph (d) of subsection (2) deals with the situation where there is more than one union in an employment and the members of one union vote against a strike or other industrial action but a majority of all employees vote in favour. In such circumstances, the union whose members voted against will be entitled to call on its members to support the strike or other industrial action. No formal arrangements for the aggregation of ballot results are required.

Paragraph (e) was added at Committee Stage to make it clear that a decision to support a strike (but *not* other industrial action) by another trade union will not be implemented until an "All-Out Picket" is authorised by the Irish Congress of Trade Unions. According to the Minister (see 399 *Dáil Debates* Col. 858) this will ensure that Congress retains its position of having control over whether picketing is extended to cover members of trade unions other than the one directly involved in the dispute. This control is exercised under a policy adopted by Congress in 1970 which was designed to identify pickets which had been placed as a result of democratic decisions of the trade union movement and to secure that these pickets, and only these, had the support of trade union members. Under this policy, if a trade union wishes to call on members of other trade unions to support a strike, it must submit a request to Congress. This request is circulated to all affiliated unions and the unions, whose members will be directly concerned, meet with the Industrial Relations Committee of Congress. Arrangements will be made for each union concerned to ballot their members on the application. Before an All-Out Picket can be granted, the Committee must be satisfied that the application procedures have been followed and that an aggregate majority of those trade union members participating in a ballot on the application (including the votes cast by members of the applicant union in the ballot authorising the strike) are supportive of the application. Where an All-Out Picket has been granted arrangements shall be made for a review of its operation after the dispute has been in progress for two weeks, or at the request of any union affected by the dispute. The Committee is also empowered to make special arrangements with regard to the position of security staff employed at a premises against which an All-Out Picket is authorised. Paragraph (e), however, goes further than the policy in that there was nothing in the policy which prevented a trade union from deciding to support the union in dispute even where an all out strike had not been authorised. Henceforward such supportive action must not only be sanctioned by a secret ballot but it must also be authorised by Congress.

Subsection (3) provides that the rights conferred by any of the provisions referred to in subsection (2) are conferred on the members of the trade union concerned and on no other person. Since an employer is not a party to the contract created by the trade union rule book, he would not have been able in any event to seek an injunction enforcing the provisions referred to in subsection (2). To expressly confine the rights conferred by any such provision to trade union members, however, does not mean that failure to hold a secret ballot will not give a person adversely affected by the strike or other industrial action grounds for legal action. Failure to hold a ballot as provided for by section 14 is unlawful as being in breach of contract and could thus be available as unlawful means for the purpose of establishing liability in tort for "indirect inducement of breach of contract" or "unlawful interference with trade or business".

The decision when and how to hold a ballot will be decided by the trade union's rules. The section, however, confers no legal right on trade unions to use the employer's premises for a secret workplace ballot. The decision as to the question or questions is also that of the union; there is no requirement that only "appropriate" questions be asked. Nor is there any limit as to how long the mandate conferred by the ballot is to last. The electorate is stated to be those members of the union whom at the time of the ballot it is reasonable for the union to believe will be called upon to engage in the strike or other industrial action.

Presumably the inclusion of persons whom it is not reasonable to believe will be so called upon will invalidate the ballot, as will the non-inclusion of those whom it is reasonable to believe will be so called upon. Great care will have to be taken, therefore, in relation to secondary action. Depending on the questions originally asked, a second ballot may be required and this time the electorate will have to include those union members employed in the premises to be secondarily picketed.

Power to alter rules of trade unions

15.—(1) The committee of management or other controlling authority of a trade union shall, notwithstanding anything in the rules of the union, have power by memorandum in writing to alter the rules of the union so far as may be necessary to give effect to section 14.

(2) In the case of a trade union which is a trade union under the law of another country having its headquarters control situated in that country, the committee of management or other controlling authority referred to in this Part shall have the same meaning as in section 17(2) of the Trade Union Act, 1975.

COMMENTARY

Section 17(2) of the 1975 Act refers to a controlling authority "every member of which is resident in the State or Northern Ireland and which is empowered, by the rules of the trade union, to make decisions, in matters of an industrial or political nature which arise out of and are in connection with the economic or political condition of the State or Northern Ireland, are of direct concern to members of the trade union resident in the State or Northern Ireland and do not affect members not so resident".

Enforcement of rule for secret ballot

16.—(1) Every trade union registered under the Trade Union Acts, 1871 to 1975, or a trade union under the law of another country shall, not later than the operative date, forward to the Registrar of Friendly Societies a copy of its rules incorporating the provisions referred to in subsection (2) of section 14.

(2) A trade union failing to comply with subsection (2) of section 14 or subsection (1) of this section shall cease to be entitled to hold a negotiation licence under Part II of the Trade Union Act, 1941, and its existing licence shall stand revoked on the operative date.

(3) A body of persons shall not be granted a negotiation licence unless, in addition to fulfilling the relevant conditions specified in section 7 of the Trade Union Act, 1941, and section 2 of the Trade Union Act, 1971, as amended by section 21 of this Act, it complies with subsection (2) of section 14 and for this purpose that subsection shall have effect from the passing of this Act.

(4) A body of persons which is a trade union under the law of another country shall not be granted a negotiation licence unless, in addition to fulfilling the conditions referred to in subsection (3) and section 17 of the Trade Union Act, 1975, it forwards, at the time of application for a negotiation licence, a copy of its rules incorporating the provisions referred to in subsection (2) of section 14 to the Registrar of Friendly Societies.

(5) Where the Registrar of Friendly Societies is satisfied, after due investigation, that it is the policy or practice of a trade union registered under the Trade Union Acts, 1871 to 1975, or a trade union under the law of another country persistently to disregard any requirement of the provisions referred to in subsection (2) of section 14 he may issue an instruction to the trade union to comply with the requirement. Where such an instruction is disregarded, the Registrar of Friendly Societies shall inform the Minister and the Minister may revoke the negotiation licence of the trade union concerned.

COMMENTARY

Section 7 of the 1941 Act and section 2 of the 1971 Act impose conditions in relation to deposits with the High Court, membership and advertising of applications. Section 17 of the 1975 Act requires foreign trade unions to have a controlling authority every member of which is resident in the State or Northern Ireland and which is empowered to make certain decisions: see further the commentary to section 15, *supra*.

The use of the expressions "may" and "shall" in subsection (5) suggests that, while the Registrar is obliged to inform the Minister that his instruction has been disregarded, the Minister has a discretion as to whether the negotiation licence should be revoked.

Actions contrary to outcome of secret ballot

17.—(1) Sections 10, 11 and 12 shall not apply in respect of proceedings arising out of or relating to a strike or other industrial action by a trade union or a group of workers in disregard of or contrary to, the outcome of a secret ballot relating to the issue or issues involved in the dispute.

(2) In the case of ballots by more than one trade union, the outcome of a secret ballot referred to in subsection (1) shall mean the outcome of the aggregated ballots.

(3) Where two or more secret ballots have been held in relation to a dispute, the ballot referred to in subsection (1) shall mean the last such ballot.

COMMENTARY

Since the secret ballot referred to here is not necessarily a secret ballot held in accordance with the rules of a trade union as provided for in section 14, it has come into immediate effect and to the extent as provided overrules the decision of the Supreme Court in *Gouldings Chemicals Ltd.* v. *Bolger* [1977] I.R. 211.

Non-application of sections 14 to 17 to employers' unions

18.—Sections 14 to 17 shall not apply to a trade union of employers.

COMMENTARY

In addition to the Construction Industry Federation (CIF) and the Federation of Irish Employers (FIE), fourteen other employers' associations are registered as trade unions (see *Report of the Registrar of Friendly Societies 1985–86* p. 27). All sixteen hold negotiation licences, although the Minister is in the process of revoking the licences of the Irish Flour Millers Association and the National Grocery, Dairy and Allied Trades Association on the grounds that those associations have been dissolved. In addition a number of the associations (such as the Petroleum Employers Association) are effectively defunct.

Restriction of right to injunction

19.—(1) Where a secret ballot has been held in accordance with the rules of a trade union as provided for in section 14, the outcome of which or, in the case of an aggregation of ballots, the outcome of the aggregated ballots, favours a strike or other industrial action and the trade union before engaging in the strike or

Industrial Relations Act 1990

other industrial action gives notice of not less than one week to the employer concerned of its intention to do so, that employer shall not be entitled to apply to any court for an injunction restraining the strike or other industrial action unless notice of the application has been given to the trade union and its members who are party to the trade dispute.

(2) Where a secret ballot has been held in accordance with the rules of a trade union as provided for in section 14, the outcome of which or, in the case of an aggregation of ballots, the outcome of the aggregated ballots, favours a strike or other industrial action and the trade union before engaging in the strike or other industrial action gives notice of not less than one week to the employer concerned of its intention to do so, a court shall not grant an injunction restraining the strike or other industrial action where the respondent establishes a fair case that he was acting in contemplation or furtherance of a trade dispute.

(3) Notice as provided for in subsection (1) may be given to the members of a trade union by referring such members to a document containing the notice which the members have reasonable opportunity of reading during the course of their employment or which is reasonably accessible to them in some other way.

(4) Subsections (1) and (2) do not apply—

(a) in respect of proceedings arising out of or relating to unlawfully entering into or remaining upon any property belonging to another, or unlawfully causing damage or causing or permitting damage to be caused to the property of another, or
(b) in respect of proceedings arising out of or relating to any action resulting or likely to result in death or personal injury.

(5) Where two or more secret ballots have been held in relation to a dispute, the ballot referred to in subsections (1) and (2) shall be the last such ballot.

COMMENTARY

Subsection (1) imposes certain restriction on the ability of employers to obtain *ex parte* injunctions. The Minister strenuously resisted opposition attempts to have this provision extended so that nobody could apply for an *ex parte* injunction restraining a strike or other industrial action, claiming (399 *Dáil Debates* Cols. 863–869) that he had been legally advised that third parties would be unlikely to establish the necessary *locus standi* and that in any event it was very difficult to cut off third parties without encountering constitutional difficulties. Considerable disquiet had been expressed at the abuse by some employers of the availability of *ex parte* relief but in recent years there has been a marked reluctance by some members of the judiciary to grant such relief unless the circumstances were truly exceptional: see in particular the decision of Murphy J. in *Waterford Co-Op* v. *Murphy* (1988 No. 733IP) reported in the *Irish Times* August 3, 1988; the comments of McCarthy J. in (1987) 6 *J.I.S.L.L.* 1, 7; the comments of Costello J. in (1989) 8 *J.I.S.L.L.* 1, 8–9; and the statement by Costello J. reported in the *Irish Times* June 14, 1990.

Subsection (2), which alters the law in relation to the granting of interlocutory injunctions in trade disputes, applies, however, whenever an injunction is sought restraining the strike or other industrial action. The position after July 18, 1992 will be that once a plaintiff establishes a *prima facie* entitlement to an interlocutory injunction (by showing that there is a fair question to be decided), the court must then go on to consider whether the defendants can establish a fair case that they were acting in contemplation or furtherance of a trade dispute. If they can the injunction will not be granted. If the defendants cannot, then the court must go on and consider (as it presently does) whether the balance of convenience is in favour of granting the injunction. On the present position regarding the granting of injunctions in trade disputes see Kerr and Whyte, *Irish Trade Union Law* (1985), chapter 11, though note the subsequent decisions of the Supreme Court in *Bayzana Ltd.* v. *Galligan* [1987] I.R. 241 and *Westman Holdings Ltd.* v. *McCormack* unreported, May 14, 1991.

Amendment of Trade Union Acts, 1941, 1971 and 1975

Change of deposit consequent on change in number of members

20.—(1) Within one month after the 31st December each year a trade union which is the holder of a negotiation licence shall send to the Minister a statement of the number of its members on the 31st December and, if it is necessary to increase or reduce a deposit under Part II of the Trade Union Act, 1941, as amended by section 2 of the Trade Union Act, 1971, by any amount in order to make it equal to the appropriate sum, such trade union shall, not later than four months after the 31st December, increase such deposit by such amount or apply for the return out of such deposit of such amount (as the case may require).

Subsection (1) shall take effect on 1st January, 1991.

(3) The "appropriate sum" in subsection (1) shall be the appropriate sum under—

(a) section 7(2) of the Trade Union Act, 1941, or
(b) section 2(4) of the Trade Union Act, 1971, or
(c) section 21(3) or section 21(4) of this Act,

for the time being, as the case may be.

(4) If, in relation to any trade union required to send a statement under this section, there is a failure to send a statement or there is sent a wilfully false statement, such of the members and officers of the trade union as consent to or facilitate to send a statement or the sending of the false statement and, in the case of a trade union registered under the Trade Union Acts, 1871 to 1975, the trade

union itself shall each be guilty of an offence under this section and shall be liable on summary conviction thereof to a fine not exceeding £500.

(5) Save in pursuance of this section, a trade union shall not, on account of a change in the number of its members, change the amount of a deposit under Part II of the Trade Union Act, 1941, as amended by section 2 of the Trade Union Act, 1971.

(6) Sections 14 and 16 of the Trade Union Act, 1941, shall apply in relation to a deposit made with the High Court under this Act or under the Trade Union Act, 1971, as it applies to a deposit under the Trade Union Act, 1941.

COMMENTARY

This section replaces the provisions of section 15 of the Trade Union Act 1941 under which unions were obliged to make triennial returns. The appropriate sum under the 1941 Act where the number of members does not exceed 500 is £1,000; where the number exceeds 500 but does not exceed 2,000, it is £1,000 together with £200 for each additional 300 members (or part thereof) in excess of 2,000; where the number exceeds 5,000 but does not exceed 10,000, it is £4,000 together with £200 for each additional 500 members (or part thereof) in excess of 5,000; where the number exceeds 10,000 but does not exceed 20,000 it is £6,000 together with £200 for each additional 1,000 members (or part thereof) in excess of 10,000; and where the number exceeds 20,000 it is £8,000 together with £200 for each additional 1,000 members (or part thereof) in excess of 20,000 but subject to an overriding maximum of £10,000. These figures were increased by the 1971 Act and the appropriate sum under that Act, where the number of members does not exceed 2,000, is £5,000; where the number exceeds 2,000 but does not exceed 5,000, it is £5,000 together with £200 for each additional 300 members (or part thereof) in excess of 2,000; where the number exceeds 5,000 but does not exceed 10,000 it is £7,000 together with £200 for each additional 500 members (or part thereof) in excess of 5,000; where the number exceeds 10,000 but does not exceed 20,000 it is £9,000 together with £200 for each additional 1,000 (or part thereof) in excess of 10,000; and where the number exceeds 20,000 it is £11,000 together with £200 for each additional 1,000 members (or part thereof) in excess of 20,000 but subject to an overriding maximum of £15,000. The appropriate sum under the 1990 Act is set out in the Third Schedule hereto. Under section 2 of the Trade Union Act 1947 (as amended by the Trade Union Act 1952) the Minister may by order declare that the sum required by the 1941 Act be deemed to be reduced to such extent not exceeding 75 per cent. as the Minister thinks proper.

Section 14 of the 1941 Act, which sets out various provisions in relation to deposits, envisages that certain matters will be governed by Rules of Court. The relevant rules in RSC 1986 (S.I. No. 15 of 1986) are contained in Part VIII of Order 77, reproduced *supra* at pp. 75–80. Section 16 provides that whenever a Court makes an order, decree or judgment for the payment of money by a trade union which is the holder of a negotiation licence to any person, the High Court may, on the application in a summary manner of such person, order such money to be paid to such person out of the deposit so maintained.

Amendment of section 2 of Trade Union Act, 1971

21.—(1) In this section "the Act of 1971" means the Trade Union Act, 1971.

(2) Section 2(1)(b) of the Act of 1971 (which refers to the minimum membership for the grant of a negotiation licence) is hereby amended, in relation to applications for a negotiation licence made after the passing of this Act, by the substitution for "500" of "1,000."

(3) In respect of a body of persons applying under section 9(1) of the Trade Union Act, 1941, for a negotiation licence after the passing of this Act, "the appropriate sum" referred to in section 2(1)(a) of the Act of 1971 shall be the sum appropriate to the number of members of the body in accordance with the Third Schedule to this Act or the sum deposited and kept deposited in the High Court before such passing in accordance with the said section 2(1)(a) and the Schedule to the Act of 1971, as the case may be.

(4) Whenever after the passing of this Act a trade union is formed consisting wholly or mainly of two or more trade unions which have been amalgamated and each of which, immediately before the amalgamation, had been the holder of a negotiation licence, "the appropriate sum" referred to in the said section 2(1)(a) shall be such sum as the Minister may determine in respect of the union so formed.

COMMENTARY

As the Minister observed at Second Stage (396 *Dáil Debates* Col. 745), it has been a policy of successive Ministers for Labour to encourage the rationalisation of the trade union movement. The amendments effected by sections 21 and 22 have the complementary goals of discouraging the formation of new or breakaway unions and further encouraging mergers between existing unions. The membership requirement for a new union seeking a negotiation licence is doubled from 500 to 1,000 and there is a substantial increase in the level of the High Court deposit required by such a union. The Minister said (*ibid*, Col. 746) that while the present membership and deposit requirements had worked well "to forestall the establishment of small, poorly financed or breakaway unions in areas already serviced by existing unions," experience in recent years suggested that "some tightening of the requirements" was necessary.

Amalgamations and transfers

22.—(1) Section 15 of the Trade Union Act, 1975 (which refers to a grant towards expenses of amalgamations or transfers) is hereby amended by the deletion of "were exceptional and".

(2) Whenever two or more trade unions engage in an unsuccessful attempt to amalgamate or to effect a transfer of engagements from one union to another the Minister may, with the consent of the Minister for Finance, make to one or more of those trade unions out of moneys to be provided by the Oireachtas a grant of such amount as the Minister thinks fit towards such expenses as he is satisfied were incurred, within the period of two

years immediately prior to the failure, by that trade union in the course of, or in contemplation of, such attempted amalgamation or transfer.

(3) Where an instrument of amalgamation takes effect the registration of any amalgamating union shall cease to have effect and on the granting of a negotiation licence to the new union any negotiation licence held by an amalgamating union shall cease to have the effect.

(4) Where an instrument of transfer of engagements takes effect the registration of any transferor union and any negotiation licence held by such union shall cease to have effect.

COMMENTARY

The Trade Union Act 1975 permitted the introduction of a system of grants towards expenses incurred by unions in a successful merger. Since it was thought that the prospect of a merger attempt being unsuccessful and the associated expenses might deter smaller unions from attempting a merger, the section now provides that unions which attempt a merger but fail may still claim expenses relating to the two year period prior to the failure.

PART III

INDUSTRIAL RELATIONS GENERALLY

"Worker"

23.—(1) In the Industrial Relations Acts, 1946 to 1976, and this Part, "worker" means any person aged 15 years or more who has entered into or works under a contract with an employer, whether the contract be for manual labour, clerical work or otherwise, whether it be expressed or implied, oral or in writing, and whether it be a contract of service or of apprenticeship or a contract personally to execute any work or labour including, in particular, a psychiatric nurse employed by a health board and any person designated for the time being under subsection (3) but does not include—

(a) a person who is employed by or under the State,
(b) a teacher in a secondary school,
(c) a teacher in a national school,
(d) an officer of a local authority,
(e) an officer of a vocational education committee, or
(f) an officer of a school attendance committee.

(2) In subsection (1) "local authority" means—

(a) a council of a county, a corporation of a county or other borough, a council of an urban district, the commissioners of a town, a health board or a port sanitary authority,

(b) a committee or joint committee or board or joint board appointed (whether before or after the passing of this Act) by or under statute to perform the functions or any of the functions of one or more of the bodies mentioned in paragraph (a), and

(c) a committee or joint committee or board or joint board of or appointed by one or more of the bodies mentioned in paragraphs (a) and (b) but not including a vocational education committee, a committee of agriculture or a school attendance committee.

(3) The Minister for Finance may from time to time—

(a) designate for the purpose of subsection (1) any persons (other than established civil servants within the meaning of the Civil Service Regulation Act, 1956) employed by virtue of section 30(1)(g) of the Defence Act, 1954, or employed by or under the State, and

(b) cancel the designation of any persons under this subsection.

(4) Any person who stands designated by virtue of section 17(2)(a) of the Industrial Relations Act, 1969, at the passing of this Act shall remain designated for the purpose of subsection (1) unless the designation is cancelled under subsection (3)(b).

(5) The Government may by order amend the definition of "worker" in subsection (1) and may by order revoke or amend any such order.

(6) Every order made under this section shall be laid before each House of the Oireachtas as soon as may be after it is made and, if a resolution annulling the order is passed by either House, within the next twenty-one days on which that House has sat after the order has been laid before it, the order shall be annulled accordingly, but without prejudice to the validity of anything previously done thereunder.

COMMENTARY

This section, which sets out the definition of "worker" for the purposes of the Industrial Relations Acts, replaces section 4 of the Industrial Relations Act 1946 (as amended). The meaning of the expression "a person who is employed by or under the State" (as used in the Unfair Dismissals Act 1977) was considered by the Employment Appeals Tribunal in *Hayes and Caffrey* v. *B & I Line Ltd.* UD 193 and 192/1979 where the argument was rejected that, because the company was wholly owned by the Minister for Finance, the claimants were persons "employed by or under the State." The Tribunal interpreted the phrase as meaning civil servants. As to who may be an officer of a local authority see *O'Callaghan* v. *Cork Corporation* UD 309/1978. Such workers are covered by separate schemes of conciliation and arbitration, the express purpose of which are "to provide means acceptable both to the State and to its employees for dealing with claims and proposals relating to the conditions of service." These schemes are not statutory schemes in the sense of having in some way the force of statute; according to Kenny J. in *McMahon* v. *Minister for Finance* High Court, unreported, May 13, 1963 they are merely contracts (an analysis accepted by Murphy J. in *Inspector of Taxes' Association* v. *Minister for the Public Service* High Court, unreported, March 24, 1983 and by the Supreme Court on appeal [1986] I.L.R.M. 296, 299).

The persons standing designated by virtue of section 17(2) of the 1969 Act comprise State industrial employees and civilian employees serving with the Defence Forces.

The Labour Court and the Labour Relations Commission

Establishment of the Commission

24.—(1) There shall be a body to be known as the Labour Relations Commission to fulfil the functions assigned to it by this Act.

(2) The Commission shall stand established on such day as the Minister by order appoints.

(3) The Commission shall consist of a chairman and six ordinary members who shall be appointed by the Minister.

(4) The Fourth Schedule to this Act shall apply to the Commission.

COMMENTARY

The Minister gave as one of the main reasons for establishing the Commission (396 *Dáil Debates* Cols. 747–748) the need to have a body with the primary responsibility for the promotion of *better* industrial relations. The Commission, he said, would be "well placed to make public pronouncements on industrial practices and procedures which need to be changed and to call for legislative or other changes if necessary." The Commission would also be able to highlight examples of good practice and encourage others to adopt similar practices. "Their pronouncements will carry the authority of a tripartite body and the collective experience of respected experts drawn from the industrial relations field." Another reason for establishing the Commission was "to encourage and facilitate a more active approach to dispute prevention and resolution" and to make provision for a number of new functions and services. Another "major objective" was to restore "the original purpose and status of Labour Court investigations and recommendations." The Minister noted (*ibid.* Col. 749) that during the 1970s, when the Court had a central role in the resolution of issues which arose in the context of the various national wage agreements, the parties to disputes had developed the habit of referring matters to the Court for adjudication and had found it difficult to revert back to settling their own problems. In his view there were still too many recommendations being issued by the Court "on relatively trivial matters" because the Court had become a court of first resort. This, he said, could only damage the status of the Court and ultimately the acceptability of its recommendations. He wanted the Court to revert to its originally intended function—that of being "the final authoritative tribunal in industrial relations matters" whose recommendations would once again be documents "with great moral authority"—with the main responsibility for dispute prevention and resolution shifted back to the parties themselves.

When the proposal to establish a Labour Relations Commission was first mooted in early 1988, it was the subject of a strongly worded submission by the Court. The Court said that it could not envisage the proposed Commission as establishing an improved dispute settling service on either qualitative or administrative grounds. The Court believed that such a Commission would profoundly diminish the Court's effectiveness by divorcing it from the right to determine the cases which it would hear and by separating it from the conciliation service which had always been regarded as an integral part of the Court. It was undeniable that the expansion and strengthening of the conciliation service could only be of benefit to industrial relations but what the Court found difficult to understand was how the effectiveness of the conciliation service or the quality of its work could be better achieved under the Commission than was possible under the Court, assuming the availability of the necessary resources and the development of an independent career structure for Court staff (see *Industrial Relations News* 19, May 13, 1988).

The Commission's Chairman is Dan McAuley (former Director General of the Federated Union of Employers). The other members are Kevin Duffy (assistant general secretary of the Irish Congress of Trade Unions); Philip Flynn (general secretary of the Local Government and Public Services Union); Finbarr Flood (managing director of Arthur Guinness & Son (Dublin) Ltd.); Turlough O'Sullivan (a director of the Federation of Irish Employers); Joyce O'Connor (Director of the National College of Industrial Relations); and Michael Keegan (former Secretary in the Department of Labour). The Commission was formally established with effect from January 21, 1991: see Labour Relations Commission (Establishment) Order 1991 (S.I. No. 7 of 1991). On the potential role of the Commission see the report (in *Industrial Relations News* 16, April 25, 1991) of the address to the Irish Association for Industrial Relations by the Commission's chief executive.

Functions of the Commission

25.—(1) The Commission shall have general responsibility for promoting the improvement of industrial relations and shall—

- (a) provide a conciliation service;
- (b) provide an industrial relations advisory service;
- (c) prepare codes of practice relevant to industrial relations after consultation with unions and employer organisations;
- (d) offer guidance on codes of practice and help to resolve disputes concerning their implementation;
- (e) appoint equality officers of the Commission and provide staff and facilities for the equality officer service;
- (f) select and nominate persons for appointment as rights commissioners and provide staff and facilities for the rights commissioner service;
- (g) conduct or commission research into matters relevant to industrial relations;
- (h) review and monitor developments in the area of industrial relations;

(i) assist joint labour committees and joint industrial councils in the exercise of their functions.

(2) The Commission may at the request of one or more parties to a trade dispute or on its own initiative offer the parties its appropriate services with a view to bringing about a settlement.

(3) Except where there is specific provision for the direct reference of trade disputes to the Labour Court, trade disputes shall first be referred to the Commission or to its appropriate services.

(4) The Commission may, if it thinks fit, on request or on its own initiative, provide for employers, employers' associations, workers and trade unions such advice as it thinks appropriate on any matter concerned with industrial relations.

(5) The functions referred to in subsection (1)(a), (b) or (d) shall be performed on behalf of the Commission by members of its staff duly appointed by the Commission.

(6) The Commission, a member of the Commission or any of its staff shall not include in any report any information obtained by it in the course of any proceedings before it under this Act as to any trade union or as to the business carried on by any person which is not available otherwise than through evidence given at the proceedings (including conciliation conferences and advisory meetings) without the consent of the trade union or person concerned, nor shall any member of the Commission or any of its staff or any person concerned in the proceedings, without such consent, disclose any such information.

(7) Subsection (6) shall not apply to a report to the Court under section 26(1)(a) or a notice to the Court under section 26(3)(a) or a report under section 48(3).

(8) Subsection (6) is without prejudice to section 8(2) of the Anti-Discrimination (Pay) Act, 1974, or section 14 of the Industrial Relations Act, 1969.

COMMENTARY

Most of the functions set out in subsection (1) were discharged by the Labour Court but the Minister during his Second Stage speech (396 *Dáil Debates* Cols. 750–751) emphasised the role the Commission would play in providing a new advisory service and in drawing up codes of practice. The Minister said, in respect of the latter, that it was his intention, as soon as the Commission was established, to draw a number of areas to its attention which he felt should be given priority. These included: a dispute procedure which would set out the procedural stages to be followed before industrial action is taken; provision of information to and consultation with employees on the activities of the undertaking and on decisions likely to affect employees; levels of cover to be provided in the case of disputes in essential services; and protection of and facilities for workers' representatives in the company. At a later stage he hoped the Commission would look at codes on individual grievance procedures and disciplinary procedures. Codes of practice are also specifically dealt with by section 42 *infra*.

For equality officers see section 37, for rights commissioners see section 34, for joint labour committees see section 39.

Subsection (3) provides that, except where there is "specific provision" for the direct reference of trade disputes to the Labour Court, trade disputes shall first be referred to the Commission or to its appropriate services. This is designed to ensure that as many issues as possible are settled without recourse to the Labour Court. This is reinforced by section 26, although the Court still has power to intervene in exceptional circumstances. Provision for direct references to the Court is contained in section 20 of the Industrial Relations Act 1969, namely, where the workers concerned or their trade union undertake to accept the Court's recommendations or where the parties concerned request the Court to investigate a specified issue or issues and undertake to accept the recommendation. In the period January 21–March 15, 1991 the number of conciliation conferences held under the Commission was 371, whereas the number of cases referred to the Court for a full hearing was just twelve (see *Industrial Relations News* 15, April 18, 1991).

Section 8(2) of the Anti-Discrimination (Pay) Act 1974 provides that any information obtained by an Equality Officer or the Labour Court in the course of an investigation or appeal under the 1974 Act as to any trade or person or as to the business carried on by any person which is not available otherwise shall not be included in any recommendation or determination without the consent of the trade union or person concerned, and nor shall any person concerned in proceedings before an equality officer or the Labour Court disclose any such information without such consent. Section 14 of the Industrial Relations Act 1969 refers in identical terms to rights commissioner investigations under the 1969 Act.

Investigation of dispute by Court

26.—(1) The Court shall not investigate a trade dispute unless—

(a) subject to subsection (3), it receives a report from the Commission stating that the Commission is satisfied that no further efforts on its part will advance the resolution of the dispute, and

(b) the parties to the dispute have requested the Court to investigate the dispute.

(2) The report referred to in subsection (1)(a) shall include information on the issues in dispute, the attempts made to resolve the dispute and any other information which the Commission considers of assistance to the Court.

(3) Notwithstanding subsection (1)(a), the Court may investigate a dispute if—

(a) the Chairman of the Commission (or any member or officer of the Commission authorised by him) notifies the Court that in the circumstances specified in the notice the Commission waives its function of conciliation in the dispute, and

(b) the parties to the dispute have requested the Court to investigate the dispute.

(4) The foregoing provisions of this section shall not apply in relation to an investigation of a trade dispute by the Court instituted by it before the establishment of the Commission or an appeal to the Court in relation to a recommendation of a rights commissioner or of an equality officer.

(5) Where the Court, following consultation with the Commission, is of opinion, in relation to a trade dispute which but for this subsection it would be precluded by virtue of subsection (1) from investigating, that there are exceptional circumstances which warrant it so doing, it may investigate the dispute.

COMMENTARY

Subsection (5) was added at Committee Stage because the Minister had become satisfied (see 399 *Dáil Debates* Col. 954) that the Court should have power to intervene, on its own initiative, when exceptional circumstances so warrant. The subsection is closely modelled on the now-repealed section 18 of the Industrial Relations Act 1969.

Procedure of the Commission

27.—(1) The Commission may act notwithstanding the existence of not more than two vacancies in its membership.

(2) The Commission may from time to time make rules regulating its own procedure and business (including the fixing of a quorum for its meetings) and shall furnish the Minister with a copy of any such rules as soon as may be after they have been made.

(3) The Commission shall in each year, at such date as the Minister may direct, make a report of its activities to the Minister including such observations as it thinks proper relating to trends and developments in industrial relations including pay and the Minister shall cause copies of the report to be laid before each House of the Oireachtas.

(4) The Commission shall supply to the Minister such information as he may from time to time require regarding its activities.

The chief executive

28.—(1) There shall be a chief officer of the Commission who shall be known as the chief executive.

(2) The first chief executive shall be appointed by the Minister and each subsequent chief executive shall be appointed by the Minister after consultation with the Commission.

(3) The terms and conditions of service of the post of chief executive shall be determined by the Minister with the consent of the Minister for Finance.

(4) The office of chairman and the post of chief executive may be held by the same person for such period and subject to such

conditions as the Minister with the consent of the Minister for Finance may determine.

(5) The chief executive may be removed from office by the Minister for stated reasons.

COMMENTARY

The Commission's chief executive is Kieran Mulvey, formerly general secretary of the Association of Secondary Teachers, Ireland.

Superannuation and gratuities for and in respect of the chief executive of the Commission

29.—(1) The Minister may, with the consent of the Minister for Finance, make a scheme or schemes for the granting of pensions, gratuities and other allowances on cessation of office or death to or in respect of the chief executive of the Commission.

(2) The Minister may, with the consent of the Minister for Finance, at any time amend a scheme made by him under this section.

(3) A scheme made by the Minister under this section shall be carried out by the Minister in accordance with its terms.

(4) If any dispute arises as to the claim of any person to, or the amount of, any pension, gratuity or allowance payable in pursuance of a scheme under this section, such dispute shall be submitted to the Minister who shall refer it to the Minister for Finance, whose decision shall be final.

(5) Every scheme made by the Minister under this section shall be laid before each House of the Oireachtas as soon as may be after it is made and if either House, within the next twenty-one days on which that House has sat after the scheme is laid before it, passes a resolution annulling the scheme, the scheme shall be annulled accordingly, but without prejudice to the validity of anything previously done thereunder.

Grants to the Commission and power to borrow

30.—(1) In each financial year there may be paid to the Commission out of moneys provided by the Oireachtas a grant of such amount as the Minister, with the consent of the Minister for Finance, may sanction towards the expenses of the Commission in the performance of its functions.

(2) The Commission may, with the consent of the Minister, given with the consent of the Minister for Finance, borrow temporarily by arrangement with bankers such sums as it may require for the purpose of providing for current expenditure.

Accounts and audits

31.—(1) The Commission shall, in such form as may be

INDUSTRIAL RELATIONS ACT 1990

approved by the Minister with the consent of the Minister for Finance, keep all proper and usual accounts of all moneys received or expended by it.

(2) Accounts kept in pursuance of this section shall be submitted annually at such times as the Minister, with the consent of the Minister for Finance, directs, by the Commission to the Comptroller and Auditor General for audit and those accounts, when so audited, shall (together with the report of the Comptroller and Auditor General thereon), be presented to the Minister, who shall cause copies of the audited accounts and the report to be laid before each House of the Oireachtas.

Staff of the Commission

32.—(1) The Minister, with the consent of the Minister for Finance, may appoint such staff as he thinks necessary to assist the Commission in the performance of its functions.

(2) Appointments under this section shall be on such terms as the Minister with the consent of the Minister for Finance determines and shall be subject to the Civil Service Commissioners Act, 1956, and the Civil Service Regulation Acts, 1956 and 1958.

Industrial relations officers and advisory service

33.—(1) The Commission may appoint members of its staff to act as industrial relations officers.

(2) The industrial relations officers shall perform any duties assigned to them by the Commission through its chairman or its chief executive officer and, in particular, they shall assist in the prevention and settlement of trade disputes.

(3) The Commission may appoint members of its staff, including industrial relations officers, to give advice on matters relating to industrial relations to management and workers or their representatives.

Rights commissioners

34.—(1) Where the Minister proposes to appoint a rights commissioner under section 13(1) of the Industrial Relations Act, 1969, he shall request the Commission to submit to him a panel of persons and he shall not appoint as a rights commissioner any person other than a person included in such panel.

(2) The term of office of a rights commissioner appointed in pursuance of subsection (1) shall be a period not exceeding three years.

(3) A rights commissioner may be re-appointed for a further term or terms by the Minister.

INDUSTRIAL RELATIONS ACT 1990

COMMENTARY

The office of rights commissioner was first created by the Industrial Relations Act 1969. At present there are four commissioners whose function under the 1969 Act is to investigate trade disputes which are not connected with rates of pay, hours or times of work, or annual holidays of a body of workers. Rights commissioners also have certain functions under the Unfair Dismissals Act 1977, the Maternity Protection of Employees Act 1981 and the Payment of Wages Act 1991. On the role of the rights commissioner, see Kelly "The Rights Commissioner: Conciliator, Mediator or Arbitrator" in the second edition of *Industrial Relations in Ireland* (Department of Industrial Relations, UCD) pp. 185–191 and Walker "An Analysis of Referrals and Results of Disputes and Claims to Four Rights Commissioners" (1986) 5 *J.I.S.L.L.* 67.

The Rights Commissioner Service

35.—(1) The rights commissioners shall operate as a service of the Commission and references to rights commissioners in the Industrial Relations Act, 1969, the Unfair Dismissals Act, 1977, and the Maternity Protection of Employees Act, 1981, shall be taken to be references to rights commissioners so operating.

(2) A rights commissioner shall be independent in the performance of his functions.

Objections and appeals

36.—(1) An objection under section 13(3)(*b*)(ii) of the Industrial Relations Act, 1969, by a party to a trade dispute to an investigation of the dispute by a rights commissioner shall be of no effect unless it is notified in writing to the commissioner within three weeks after notice of the reference of the dispute to the commissioner has been sent by post to that party.

(2) An appeal to the Court against the recommendation of a rights commissioner shall not be considered unless it is notified in writing to the Court within six weeks after the making of the recommendation.

(3) A rights commissioner, in addition to notifying the Court, shall notify the Minister and the Commission of every recommendation made by him.

(4) The Commission shall not exercise its function of conciliation on a dispute on which a rights commissioner has made a recommendation.

COMMENTARY

Section 13(3)(*b*)(ii) of the 1969 Act provides that a rights commissioner shall not investigate a trade dispute if a party to the dispute notifies the commissioner in writing that he objects to the dispute being so investigated.

Equality officers

37.—(1) The Commission may, with the consent of the Minister and the Minister for Finance, appoint members of its staff to be equality officers and a person so appointed shall be known (and is in this Part referred to) as an equality officer.

(2) The equality officers appointed before the establishment of the Commission under the Anti-Discrimination (Pay) Act, 1974, as adapted by section 18 of the Employment Equality Act, 1977, shall, after such establishment, perform their functions as officers of the Commission and not of the Court.

(3) An equality officer shall be independent in the performance of his functions.

(4) Section 6(1) of the said Act of 1974 shall cease to have effect on the establishment of the Commission but without prejudice to any appointments previously made under that subsection.

(5) References in the Anti-Discrimination (Pay) Act, 1974, and the Employment Equality Act, 1977, to equality officers shall be read as references to equality officers under this section.

COMMENTARY

For the role of equality officers under the Anti-Discrimination (Pay) Act 1974 and the Employment Equality Act 1977 see Curtin, *Irish Employment Equality Law* (1989).

Reference of dispute by Minister

38.—(1) Where the Minister is of the opinion that a trade dispute, actual or apprehended, affects the public interest, he may refer the matter to the Commission or the Court, which shall endeavour to resolve the dispute.

(2) Where the Minister is of the opinion that a trade dispute is a dispute of special importance, he may request the Commission or the Court or another person or body to conduct an enquiry into the dispute and to furnish a report to him on the findings.

COMMENTARY

This section complements section 24 of the Industrial Relations Act 1946 which provides that the Court shall consider any matter referred to it by the Minister concerning the employment conditions prevailing as regards the workers of any class and their employers and shall furnish a report thereon to the Minister together with such recommendations (if any) as the Court thinks proper. In the Department of Labour's submission to the Commission of Inquiry on Industrial Relations, it was argued that the Minister's powers under section 24 were "seriously inadequate" in that the section did not apply specifically to dispute situations, it did not apply to workers in the public service and the Court could comply with a Ministerial request merely by furnishing a report which simply consisted of a statement of the Court's unwillingness or inability to take any direct action. The Department proposed, accordingly, that the Minister should have the power to request the Court to investigate particular disputes. The Labour Court, however, was opposed to a change of this kind and the Commission in its *Report* (1981) did not recommend giving the Minister such a power. The Commission indicated (paragraph 527) that the intervention of a body such as the Labour Court in disputes at the direct behest of the Minister might lead workers and employers to doubt the extent of its independence in other matters.

Review of joint labour committees

39.—The Commission shall carry out a periodic review with a view to ascertaining whether, in the opinion of the Commission, new joint labour committees should be established or, as regards existing committees, whether any establishment order requires amendment or any committee should be abolished, and shall send a copy of the review to the Court and to the Minister.

COMMENTARY

The power to establish or abolish joint labour committees was conferred on the Labour Court by Part IV of the Industrial Relations Act 1946. See further sections 44–50 *infra*.

Superannuation and gratuities for and in respect of chairman, deputy chairmen and ordinary members of the Court

40.—Section 5 of the Industrial Relations Act, 1969, is hereby amended by the substitution for subsection (1) of the following subsection:

"(1) The Minister may, with the consent of the Minister for Finance, make a scheme or schemes for the granting of pensions, gratuities and other allowances on cessation of office or death to or in respect of the chairman, a deputy chairman (whether appointed under section 4(1) or 4(4) of this Act or under section 8(3) of the Industrial Relations Act, 1976) who is required by the Minister to devote the whole of his working time to the duties of the office of deputy chairman, and the ordinary members of the Court.".

Divisions of Court

41.—The Minister may amend or revoke an order made by him under section 8(1) of the Industrial Relations Act, 1976.

COMMENTARY

Section 8(1) empowers the Minister, whenever he is of the opinion that for the speedy dispatch of the business of the Court it is expedient that there should be added to the Court another division or other divisions, to provide by order for such an additional division or divisions. The setting up of a Fourth Division of the Court was provided for by the Labour Court (Fourth Division) Order 1979 (S.I. No. 161 of 1979).

Industrial Relations Act 1990

Codes of Practice

Codes of practice

42.—(1) The Commission shall prepare draft codes of practice concerning industrial relations for submission to the Minister, either on its own initiative or at the request of the Minister.

(2) Before submitting a draft code of practice to the Minister, the Commission shall seek and consider the views of organisations representative of employers and organisations representative of workers, and such other bodies as the Commission considers appropriate.

(3) Where the Minister receives a draft code of practice from the Commission he may by order declare that the code, scheduled to the order, shall be a code of practice for the purposes of this Act.

(4) In any proceedings before a court, the Labour Court, the Commission, the Employment Appeals Tribunal, a rights commissioner or an equality officer, a code of practice shall be admissible in evidence and any provision of the code which appears to the court, body or officer concerned to be relevant to any question arising in the proceedings shall be taken into account in determining that question.

(5) A failure on the part of any person to observe any provision of a code of practice shall not of itself render him liable to any proceedings.

(6) The Minister may at the request of or after consultation with the Commission by order revoke or amend a code of practice.

(7) Every order made under this section shall be laid before each House of the Oireachtas as soon as may be after it is made and, if a resolution annulling the order is passed by either House within the next twenty-one days on which that House has sat after the order has been laid before it, the order shall be annulled accordingly, but without prejudice to the validity of anything previously done thereunder.

COMMENTARY

This section replaces section 11 of the Industrial Relations Act 1969 which gave the Court power to draw up fair employment rules. The power was never availed of although consideration was given to the making of rules governing the employment of the disabled. The preparation of codes of practice is to be undertaken either on the Commission's own initiative or at the request of the Minister and the Minister indicated in the Dáil (396 *Dáil Debates* Col. 751) that it was his intention to draw a number of areas to the Commission's attention, including disputes procedures; information and consultation provisions; essential services; and protection of and facilities for worker representatives. One of the Commission's members, Kevin Duffy, is reported as having said that one of the Commission's first tasks should be to draw up a code of practice on worker involvement (see *Industrial Relations News* 1, January 3, 1991).

INDUSTRIAL RELATIONS ACT 1990

Subsection (4) provides that codes shall be "admissible in evidence" and that any provision of the code which appears to be relevant "shall be taken into account". Subsection (5) further provides that failure on the part of any person to observe any provision of a code of practice shall not in itself render him or her liable to any proceedings. It is thus clear that the status of these codes is purely evidential and that they cannot be used to circumvent the definition of "trade dispute" or otherwise impose legal sanctions.

Functions of Labour Court relating to codes of practice

43.—(1) The Court may on the application of one or more parties concerned give its opinion as to the interpretation of a code of practice, provided that in the case of an application by one party notice of the application has been given by that party to the other party.

(2) The Court may investigate a complaint that there has been a breach of a code of practice provided that the complaint has been referred to the Court by a party directly involved and that the complaint has first been considered by the Commission in accordance with section 26.

(3) Where the Court has investigated such a complaint, it may make a recommendation setting forth its opinion in the matter and, where appropriate, its view as to the action which a party in breach of the code should take or cease from taking in order to ensure compliance with the code.

COMMENTARY

This section confers the Labour Court not only with jurisdiction to give its opinion as to the interpretation of a code of practice but also to investigate a complaint that there has been a breach of a code. In relation to the latter jurisdiction, however, the complaint must have first been considered by the Commission under section 26.

Joint Labour Committees

Constitution and proceedings of joint labour committees

44.—The provisions of the Fifth Schedule to this Act shall have effect with respect to the constitution and proceedings of joint labour committees.

COMMENTARY

There are currently 15 joint labour committees covering approximately 58,000 workers in Aerated Waters and Wholesale Bottling; Agriculture; Brush and Broom; Catering; Contract Cleaning (City and County of Dublin); Hairdressing (Dublin); Hairdressing (Cork); Handkerchief and Household Piece Goods;

INDUSTRIAL RELATIONS ACT 1990

Hotels; Law Clerks; Provender Milling; Retail Grocery and Allied Trades; Shirt-making; Tailoring; and Womens' Clothing and Millinery. The largest and most recently established, is that for Retail Grocery and Allied Trades. This committee, which has been established since April 2, 1991 (S.I. No. 58 of 1991), is estimated to cover approximately 28,000 workers (see 407 *Dáil Debates* Cols. 1263–1265).

The provisions in the Fifth Schedule replace those that were contained in the Second Schedule to the Industrial Relations Act 1946 and are designed to improve the procedures governing the operation of the committees and make them more effective.

Making of establishment orders

45.—(1) The day for the holding of an enquiry into an application for an establishment order under section 38 of the Industrial Relations Act, 1946, to be set out in a notice under that section shall be not less than 30 days from the date of publication of the notice or later than 60 days from the receipt of the application by the Court and section 38(*b*)(ii) of the section shall stand amended accordingly.

(2) The Court shall make an establishment order, or make known its decision not to do so, within 42 days of the completion of the enquiry held in accordance with the said section 38.

Exclusion from scope of joint labour committee

46.—(1) The Court may by order exclude an undertaking to which a registered employment agreement applies from the scope of the functions of a joint labour committee at the request of the employer and the group of workers or their representatives in the undertaking provided that the remuneration and conditions of employment provided for in the registered employment agreement are not less favourable than those provided for in the relevant employment regulation order.

(2) An order under subsection (1) shall cease to have effect if—

(*a*) the remuneration and conditions of employment provided for in the registered employment agreement become less favourable than those provided for in the relevant employment regulation order, or
(*b*) the registered employment agreement is revoked.

COMMENTARY

Under Part III of the Industrial Relations Act 1946, the Labour Court may register an employment agreement, the primary effect of registration being to extend the coverage of the agreement to employers and workers who were not parties to the agreement. See further sections 51–55 *infra*.

Report for assistance of joint labour committee

47.—(1) The Court may, on its own initiative or at the request of a joint labour committee, arrange for the provision of a report on the industry or trade covered by the committee and the position of its workforce, having regard to the purposes for which the committee was established.

(2) A request for a report under subsection (1) may be made by the committee on the application of the chairman with the approval of a majority of the members of the committee.

Proposals for employment regulation order

48.—(1) Where a joint labour committee has formulated proposals for an employment regulation order, the committee shall publish a notice stating—

(a) the place where copies of the proposals may be obtained;
(b) that representations with respect to the proposals may be made to the committee within the period of 21 days after the date of such publication.

(2) The joint labour committee, having considered any representations made to it in accordance with subsection (1), may submit to the Court such proposals as it thinks proper for an employment regulation order.

(3) When proposals for an employment regulation order are submitted to the Court, the chairman of the committee shall submit a report to the Court on the circumstances surrounding their adoption.

(4) The Court may, as it thinks proper, by order give effect to the proposals from such date (subsequent to the date of the order) as the Court specifies in the order.

(5) (a) Where the Court is not satisfied that it should make an order giving effect to the proposals it may submit to the committee amended proposals which it is willing to accept.
(b) The Committee may, if it thinks fit, re-submit the amended proposals, with or without modifications, to the Court.
(c) The Court may, as it thinks proper, make an order giving effect to the proposals as so re-submitted from such date (subsequent to the date of the order) as the Court thinks proper and specifies in the order or refuse to make an order.

COMMENTARY

The specific function of a joint labour committee is to submit to the Labour Court proposals for fixing the minimum rates of remuneration or for regulating the conditions of employment of workers covered by the committee. When such proposals are confirmed by the Labour Court, through the making of an employment regulation order, they become statutory minimum remuneration and statutory conditions of employment and employers are bound under penalty to pay rates of wages and to grant conditions of employment not less favourable than those prescribed in the order. To some extent the section takes account of the concern expressed by the Supreme Court in *Burke v. Minister for Labour* [1979] I.R. 354.

Enforcement of employment regulation order by inspector by civil proceedings

49.—(1) An inspector may institute on behalf of a worker civil proceedings for the enforcement of any right of action of the worker against his employer in respect of the failure of the employer to comply with a condition of employment of an employment regulation order and in any such proceedings an order may be made for the payment of costs by the inspector but not by the worker.

(2) The power given by subsection (1) shall not be in derogation of any right of the worker to institute civil proceedings on his own behalf.

Amendment of section 52(2)(*d*) of Industrial Relations Act, 1946

50.—(1) Section 52(2)(*d*) of the Industrial Relations Act, 1946 (which refers to failure or refusal to comply with any lawful requirement of an inspector) is hereby amended by the deletion of "wilfully" before "fails".

Registered Employment Agreements

Records

51.—(1) The employer of any workers to whom a registered employment agreement applies shall keep such records as are necessary to show that the registered employment agreement is being complied with and shall retain the records for three years.

(2) If an employer fails to comply with a provision of subsection (1) he shall be guilty of an offence and shall be liable on summary conviction to a fine not exceeding £500.

(3) If any employer required by this section to keep records keeps or causes to be kept, or produces or causes to be produced or knowingly allows to be produced to an inspector, any record which is false in a material respect knowing it to be false, he shall be

guilty of an offence and shall be liable on summary conviction to a fine not exceeding £1,000 or imprisonment for a period not exceeding three months or to both.

Powers of inspection for enforcement of registered employment agreement

52.—The powers of inspection given to inspectors by section 12 of the Industrial Relations Act, 1969, shall be exercisable for the purpose of enforcing the provisions of section 32 of the Industrial Relations Act, 1946, and section 51 of this Act and the said section 12 and this section shall be construed as one section.

COMMENTARY

Section 12 of the 1969 Act empowers an inspector to enter at all reasonable times any premises where he has reasonable grounds for believing that any person affected by a registered employment agreement works; to require the production of wages sheets or other records of remuneration kept by an employer and to inspect and examine those sheets or records and copy any material part thereof; and to examine any person whom he has reasonable grounds for believing to be or have been a person affected by a registered employment agreement and to require such person to answer questions. Section 32 of the 1946 Act is concerned with complaints by a trade union that an employer has failed or neglected to comply with a registered employment agreement.

Proof of registered employment agreement and related matters

53.—(1) A copy of *Iris Oifigiúil* purporting to contain a notice published by the Court of the registration of an employment agreement shall be *prima facie* evidence of the making of that agreement.

(2) *Prima facie* evidence of a registered employment agreement or the variation of an agreement may be given by the production of a document purporting to be a copy of the agreement or of the variation and to be published by the Court.

(3) A copy of *Iris Oifigiúil* purporting to contain a notice or list published by the Court under section 31 of the Industrial Relations Act, 1946, shall be *prima facie* evidence of the contents of the notice or list, including any particulars published therewith.

COMMENTARY

Section 31 of the 1946 Act is concerned with the publication of notices of registration, variation and cancellation of registered employment agreements and the publication of lists of such agreements.

Enforcement of registered employment agreement by inspector by civil proceedings

54.—(1) An inspector may, if it appears to him that a sum is due from an employer to a worker to whom a registered employment agreement applies or that the employer has failed to comply with a condition of any such agreement with respect to the worker, institute on behalf of that worker civil proceedings for the recovery of that sum or the enforcement of that condition and in any such proceedings an order may be made for the payment of costs by the inspector but not by the worker.

(2) The power given by subsection (1) shall not be in derogation of any right of the worker to institute civil proceedings on his own behalf.

Amendment of section 12(2)(*d*) of Industrial Relations Act, 1969

55.—Section 12(2)(*d*) of the Industrial Relations Act, 1969 (which refers to failure or refusal to comply with a lawful requirement of an inspector) is hereby amended by the deletion of "wilfully" before "fails".

Failure to Attend Sitting of Court

Evidence of failure to attend sitting of Court

56.—(1) A document purporting to be sealed with the seal of the Court stating that—

(a) the person named in the document was, by a summons under section 21 of the Industrial Relations Act, 1946, summoned to attend as a witness before the Court on a day and at a place specified in the document,
(b) a sitting of the Court was held on that day and at that place, and
(c) the said person made default in attending the Court in pursuance of the summons,

shall, in a prosecution against the person so named for the alleged default, be received in evidence of the matters so stated without further proof.

(2) Section 18 of the Industrial Relations Act, 1946, shall apply to a document to which subsection (1) relates.

COMMENTARY

Section 18 of the 1946 Act, which is concerned with the Labour Court's official seal, provides that such seal shall be judicially noticed; that such seal, when affixed to any document, shall be authenticated by the signature of the chairman or the registrar or an authorised person; and that any document purporting to be

Industrial Relations Act 1990

sealed with an authenticated seal shall, unless the contrary be proved, be deemed to have been duly and lawfully sealed and shall be received in evidence without further proof.

First Schedule

(Section 4)

Increase of Fines

Ref. No. (1)	Section (2)	Fine (3)
	TRADE UNION ACT, 1871	
1	15	£200 per day.
2	16	£500, in lieu of five pounds.
		£1,000, in lieu of fifty pounds.
	TRADE UNION ACT, 1941	
3	6(2)	£1,000 and a daily default fine of £200.
4	12(2)	£100 and a daily default fine of £10.
5	13(2)	£100 and a daily default fine of £10.
	INDUSTRIAL RELATIONS ACT, 1946	
6	21(3)	£200.
7	32(4)	£1,000 and a daily default fine of £200.
8	45(1)	£750.
9	45(3)(a)	£750.
10	48(2)	£750.
11	49(3)	£500.
12	52(2)	£500.
13	52(3)	£1,000.
14	72(b)	£1,000.
	INDUSTRIAL RELATIONS ACT, 1969	
15	10(2)	£1,000 and a daily default fine of £200.
16	10(3)	£1,000 and a daily default fine of £200.
17	12(2)	£500.
	TRADE UNION ACT, 1975	
18	Section 10(8): Schedule, Paragraph 3(1)	£200.

INDUSTRIAL RELATIONS ACT 1990

SECOND SCHEDULE

(Section 7)

REPEALS

Session and Chapter or Number and Year	Short title	Extent of Repeal
38 & 39 Vict., c. 86	The Conspiracy, and Protection of Property Act, 1875	In section 3, the first paragraph, and the paragraph inserted by 6 Edw. 7, c. 47, section 1.
6 Edw., c. 47	Trade Disputes Act, 1906	The whole Act.
No. 22 of 1941	Trade Union Act, 1941	Section 11 Section 15.
No. 26 of 1946	Industrial Relations Act, 1946	Section 4 Section 23(2) Section 41 Section 43(1) Section 64 Sections 67, 69, 71 and 72 Second Schedule.
No. 14 of 1969	Industrial Relations Act, 1969	Section 6 In section 10(3) all words from "shall be liable on conviction" to "one hundred pounds and" Section 11 Section 17 Section 18.
No. 33 of 1971	Trade Union Act, 1971	Section 2(3).
No. 15 of 1976	Industrial Relations Act, 1976	Section 2 Section 5.
No. 15 of 1982	Trade Disputes (Amendment) Act, 1982	The whole Act.

THIRD SCHEDULE

(Section 21)

DEPOSITS

1. Where the number of members does not exceed 2,000, the deposit shall be £20,000.

2. Where the number of members exceeds 2,000 but does not exceed 5,000, the deposit shall be £20,000 together with £800 for each additional 300 members (or part of 300 members) in excess of 2,000 members.

3. Where the number of members exceeds 5,000 but does not exceed 10,000, the deposit shall be £28,000 together with £800 for each additional 500 members (or part of 500 members) in excess of 5,000 members.

4. Where the number of members exceeds 10,000 but does not exceed 20,000, the deposit shall be £36,000 together with £800 for each additional 1,000 members (or part of 1,000 members) in excess of 10,000 members.

5. Where the number of members exceeds 20,000 the deposit shall be £44,000 together with £800 for each additional 1,000 members (or part of 1,000 members) in excess of 20,000 members, but subject to an overriding maximum of £60,000.

FOURTH SCHEDULE

(Section 24)

LABOUR RELATIONS COMMISSION

1. The Labour Relations Commission shall be a body corporate with perpetual succession and an official seal and power to sue and be sued in its corporate name.

2. The chairman shall be appointed by the Minister after consultation with such organisations as the Minister considers to be representative of workers and of employers and shall be appointed for such period and on such terms and conditions as the Minister determines.

3. Of the ordinary members of the Commission—

(a) two shall be workers' members;
(b) two shall be employers' members; and
(c) two shall be nominated by the Minister.

4. The workers' members shall be the persons nominated for appointment by the Minister by such organisation or organisations as the Minister determines to be representative of trade unions of workers.

5. The employers' members shall be the persons nominated for appointment by the Minister by such organisation or organisations as the Minister determines to be representative of employers.

6. Each ordinary member shall be a part-time member of the Commission and shall be appointed on such terms and conditions as the Minister determines.

7. The chairman and each ordinary member may be paid, out of moneys provided by the Oireachtas, such allowances for expenses as the Minister, with the consent of the Minister for Finance, determines.

8. The chairman or an ordinary member may resign his office by letter addressed to the Minister.

9. The Minister may remove the chairman or an ordinary member from office for stated reasons.

10. (1) Where the chairman or an ordinary member of the Commission is nominated as a member of Seanad Éireann or as a candidate for election to either House of the Oireachtas or to the European Parliament he shall thereupon cease to hold office.

(2) A person who is, for the time being, entitled under the Standing Orders of either House of the Oireachtas to sit therein or who is a member of the European Parliament shall, while he is so entitled or is such a member, be disqualified from becoming the chairman or an ordinary member of the Commission.

11. The seal of the Commission shall be authenticated by the signature of the chairman or an ordinary member authorised by the Commission to act in that behalf and the signature of an officer of the Commission authorised by the Commission to act in that behalf.

12. Judicial notice shall be taken of the seal of the Commission and every document purporting to be an instrument made by the Commission and to be sealed with the seal (purporting to be authenticated in accordance with paragraph 11) of the Commission shall be received in evidence and be deemed to be such instrument without proof unless the contrary is shown.

FIFTH SCHEDULE

(Section 44)

CONSTITUTION AND PROCEEDINGS OF JOINT LABOUR COMMITTEES

1. In this Schedule—
"committee" means a joint labour committee;
"the Acts" means the Industrial Relations Acts, 1946 to 1990.

2. (1) Subject to paragraph 3, a committee shall consist of—

(a) one member (in this Schedule referred to as the independent member) appointed by the Minister and chosen as being an independent person, who shall be chairman of the committee, and

(b) members (in this Schedule referred to as representative members) appointed by the Court being—

   (i) such number as the Court thinks fit of persons (in this Schedule referred to as representative (employers) members) who, in the opinion of the Court, represent employers in relation to whom the committee is to operate, and

   (ii) an equal number of persons (in this Schedule referred to as representative (workers) members) who, in the opinion of the Court, represent workers in relation to whom the committee is to operate.

(2) Before appointing a representative member of a committee the Court shall, so far as is reasonably practicable, consult any organisation of employers or, as the case may be, workers concerned.

(3) The Minister shall appoint an independent person who shall act as independent member and chairman in the absence of the chairman and references in the Acts to an independent member or the chairman shall include references to a person so acting.

(4) The independent member of a committee shall hold office during the pleasure of the Minister.

(5) Where a representative member of a committee ceases, in the opinion of the Court, to be representative of the employers or, as the case may be, workers whom he was appointed to represent, the Court shall determine his membership.

(6) The Court may, in its discretion, determine the membership of any representative member of a committee.

(7) Where the membership of any representative member of a committee is determined, such member shall cease to be a member of the committee.

3. In the case of the joint labour committee for agricultural workers established under section 4 of the Industrial Relations Act, 1976—

(a) the independent member shall be appointed by the Minister with the consent of the Minister for Agriculture and Food;

(b) the representative (employers) members of the committee shall be appointed by the Court from a panel prepared and presented to the Court by the Minister after consultation with such organisation or organisations representative of agricultural employers as the Minister thinks fit and with the consent of the Minister for Agriculture and Food;

(c) the representative (workers) members of the committee (to a number equal to the number of representative (employers) members) shall be appointed by the Court from a panel prepared and presented to the Court by the Minister after consultation with such organisation or organisations representative of agricultural workers as the Minister thinks fit and with the consent of the Minister for Agriculture and Food;

(*d*) paragraph 2(2) shall not apply.

4. The proceedings of a committee shall not be invalidated by reason of any vacancy therein or of any defect in the appointment of a member.

5. In order to constitute a meeting of a committee the independent member and at least one-third of the whole number of the representative members must be present.

6. (1) Subject to the provisions of this paragraph, every member of a committee shall have one vote.

(2) If at any meeting of a committee the group of representative (employers) members present does not equal in number the group of representative (workers) members present—

(*a*) whichever of the said groups is in the majority may arrange that any one or more of its number shall refrain from voting so as to preserve equality,

(*b*) if no such arrangement is made, the chairman of the committee may adjourn the voting on any question to another meeting of the committee.

7. (1) A committee shall meet at such places and times as it may from time to time determine to be suitable for the discharge of its functions and may adjourn any of its meetings.

(2) A committee shall, save as otherwise provided by the Acts, adopt such procedure at its meetings and otherwise, as it may determine to be suitable for the discharge of its functions.

8. (1) A committee, with the consent of the Court, may appoint sub-committees to assist it.

(2) A sub-committee of a committee may consist of members of the committee and such other persons as the committee with the concurrence of the Court may appoint.

(3) A district trade committee established under the Trade Boards Acts, 1909 and 1918, established by a committee when it was a trade board shall be deemed to be a sub-committee appointed by the committee under subparagraph (1) of this paragraph.

9. Members of a committee or of a sub-committee, may be paid such remuneration and allowances (including compensation for

loss of time) as the Minister, with the consent of the Minister for Finance, may determine.

10. In the case of each joint labour committee existing at the passing of this Act, the independent members shall be entitled to continue in office until the appointment of the independent member of that committee under paragraph 2(1)(a) or 3, as the case may require.

Index

Note

References are to provisions of Acts and Regulations. References in *italics* refer to the author's commentary. Statutory forms are listed under **Forms.**

Accounts,
  Labour Relations Commission, 212
  trade unions, 5, *5*
Agreed disputes procedures, 186–187, *187*
Agreements, *see also* **Registered employment agreements.**
  trade union agreements, when not enforceable, 1–2
Agricultural employers, 175, 177
Agricultural Wages Acts 1936 to 1969,
  repeal of, 176
Agricultural workers,
  definition, 175
  employment regulation orders, *176*
  holidays regulations, 178
  joint labour committee, *134*, 176, 228–229
Agricultural Workers (Holidays) Acts 1950 to 1975,
  repeal of, 178
All out pickets, *197–198*
Alteration of union rules, *see under* **Rules of trade union.**
Amalgamations and transfers, 95–104
  appeals to High Court, 101
  application for registration, 110–111
  change of name of union, *see under* **Name of union.**
  complaints procedure, 100–101, 105–107
    appeal to High Court, 101
  conditions for, 97–98
  contents of instruments, 110, 111–112
  disposal of property on, 101–102
  fees, 115, 116
  foreign unions, with, *97*
    Irish members of, 99, *99–100*
  jurisdiction of Registrar, *96–97*

Amalgamations and transfers— *cont.*
  grants towards expenses, 104, 204–205, *205*
  negotiation licences, and, 89–90, *90*, 204, 205
  notice of proposed instrument, 97, 98
  offences and penalties, 106–107
  political fund and, *56*
  Registrar's approval, 98, 109
  registration of instruments, 98
    application for, 110–111
  regulations, 102, 109–114
  resolution of approval, 97, 98
    complaints, 100–101
    notice of vote on, 110, 113
    notice to members, 97–98
    voting on, 97, 98, 101
  unsuccessful attempts,
    grants towards expenses, *104*, 204–205
Appeals,
  amalgamations or transfers,
    complaints concerning, 100
  Circuit Court, to, 10–11, *11–12*, 12, 20
  decisions of Registrar, against, 52, *52–53*
  High Court, to, 101
  rights commissioner,
    recommendations, from, 169, *170*
Apprentices,
  employment regulation orders and, 142–143
  neglect by master, 17
Arbitration,
  reference of trade dispute to, 150
Audit,
  Labour Relations Commission accounts, 212
  trade union accounts, 5, *5*

231

Index

Authorised trade unions, 63, *185*
  certain immunities confined to, 186, *187*
  cesser of membership of, 64, 67
  deposits with High Court, *see under* **Deposits.**
  foreign-based, 62, 65–67
  inspection of register, 67, 73–74, 82–83
  negotiation licence, *see under* **Negotiation licence.**
  obligations of, 64–65
    foreign-based unions, 65–67
  register of members, 64, *65*, 66
  revocation of negotiation licence, 69, *197*, 199
  rules, provision for secret ballots in, 195–196
  tortious acts, 194, *195*

Ballot of members, *see also* **Secret ballot.**
  amalgamations or transfers, approving, 97, 98
  political fund, for, 53, 55–56
Bank of Ireland,
  transfers of trade union stock, 27–28
Branch of trade union,
  committee members, *187*
  property of,
    transfer of stock, *see under* **Transfer of stock.**
  vesting of, in trustees, 3
Breach of contract,
  actions for, *195*
  employment contract, *see under* **Contract of employment.**
  inducement of, *193–194*, 198
Breach of the peace, 15
Buildings,
  powers of trustees to purchase or lease, 3

Certificate of registry, *see under* **Registered unions.**
Certified unions, 52, *52*
Chairman of Labour Court, *see under* **Labour Court.**
Change of name of union, *see under* **Name of trade union.**
Chief executive of Labour Relations Commission, *see under* **Labour Relations Commission.**

Child,
  payment on death of, 27
Circuit Court,
  appeals to, 10–11, 20
Civil conspiracy, 15, 188, *188–189*
  tort of, *188–189*
Civil proceedings, *see also* **Immunities in trade disputes; Injunctions.**
  actions against trade unions, *195*
  actions by or against trustees, 4, *4–5*
  employment regulation orders, breach of, 145
  registered employment agreements, breach of, *168*, 222–223
  tortious actions of trade unions, 195, *195*
Civil servants, *206*
  arbitration boards, 165
  ordinary members of Labour Court, *120*
  staff associations, 61
Codes of practice, 217, 218, *217, 218*
  admissibility in evidence, 217
  breaches of, 217, 218
  complaints procedure, 218
  interpretation of, 218
  Labour Court, functions of, 218, *218*
  Labour Relations Commission, functions of, 208–209, *209–210*
  order to be laid before Oireachtas, 218
  preparation of, 217, *217–218*
  revocation or amendment by Minister, 217
Collective agreements, *see also* **Registered employment agreements.**
  disputes procedures, 186, *187*
Commercial contract, breach of, *193*
  inducement of breach, *193–194*
Commission of Inquiry on Industrial Relations, 179, *215*
Companies Acts 1963 to 1990,
  inapplicable to trade unions, 2

232

INDEX

Conciliation and arbitration boards, 82
 public service, for,
  inclusion of Labour Court members on, 165, *165*
Conciliation service, 150, 208
Conditions of employment, *see also* **Employment regulation orders.**
 disputes concerning, 183, *184*, 186
 negotiation rights, 60, *see also* **Negotiation licence.**
 statutory conditions, 134, 140, *221*
 failure to provide, 140, *141*
Conspiracy in trade disputes, 15
 civil 15, 188, *188–189*
 convictions for, 15
 criminal, 1, 15, *188*
 immunity from, 188, *188–189*
Conspiracy and Protection of Property Act 1875, 15–25
 breach of contract of employment, 16–17
 conspiracy in trade disputes, 15
 definitions, 21, 25
 intimidation or violence, penalties for, 17–18
 legal proceedings, 19–20
 neglect of apprentice, 17
 repeal of legislation, 21–24
 sea service, exemption for, 21
Constitutional rights, actions for breach of, *195*
Construction Industry Federation, *200*
Contract of employment,
 breach of,
  civil conspiracy, *188*, 189
  electricity workers, by, *16–17*
  gas or water workers, by, 16
  inducement of, 193, *193–194*
  injury, causing, 17
 employment regulation orders and, 139
 inducement of breach, 193, *193–194*
 registration of employment agreement and, 130
 trade union contracts, when not enforceable, 1–2
Counsel, *see under* **Legal representation.**
Court of summary jurisdiction, *see under* **District Court.**

Courts, jurisdiction of,
 enforcement of union contracts, 1–2
 see also individual court entries.
Criminal conspiracy, 1, 15
 convictions for, 15
 immunity from, in trade dispute, 15, 188, *188*
Criminal proceedings, 10, 19
 appeals to Circuit Court, 10–11, *11*, 19
 competence of witnesses, 19, *19–20*
 institution by Inspector, 145, 167
 offences, *see under* **Offences and penalties.**
 prosecutions by the Minister, 118
 reduction of penalties, 18–19
 summary proceedings, *6*, 9, 12, 19, 25, 28, 182
 time for institution of, 182
 trial on indictment, 16, 17, 18, 19

Defence Forces
 civilian employees, 206, *207*
Definitions, *see under* **Words and phrases.**
Deposits with High Court, 62
 appropriate sum, 62, 70, 90, 92 (1990 Act), *204*, 204, 225–226
 variation by Minister, 85–86, 87
 authorised securities, variation of, 75, 77
 change of, 202–203, *203*
 deficiency in, 69, 76
 false statements concerning, 202
 forms, 76–80
 income on securities, request for payment, 75, 77–78
 investment of, 75
  request form, 76
 judgment debts paid out of, 69
 offences and penalties, 202
 procedure for, 68
 requirement of, for negotiation licence, 62, 89
 return of, request for, 75–76, 78–79
 rules, 68, 75–76
 triennial returns, *203*
Deputy chairman of the Labour Court, *see under* **Labour Court.**
Disabled persons,
 employment at less than statutory minimum pay, permits for, 141–142

233

Index

Disclosure of information, prohibition on, 125
  Labour Relations Commission, 208–209, *209*
  rights commissioner, 170
Disorderly following, 18
Dissolution of union, 31
  notice of, 36, 49–50
District Court,
  appeals from decisions, 10–11, 19–20
  jurisdiction of, *6*, 10, 12, 25, 28, 186
  trials on indictment, 19

Edmonson, Ernest, 163
Electricity Supply Board,
  dissolution of tribunals, 172
Electricity Supply Board Staff Association, *52*
Electricity workers,
  breach of contract of employment, *16–17*
Employers,
  agricultural employers, 175, 177
  apprentices, premiums from, 142–143
  definition of employer, 183, *183–184*
  employment regulation orders,
    criminal liability, 143–145
    duties as to records and notices, 143, 145, 146
    enforcement powers of inspectors, 145–146, 221
    failure to comply with, 139–141, 143–145
  gas, water or electricity undertakings, in,
    duty as to posting of notices, 16
  health service, in,
    maintenance of life-preserving services, 190, *192*
  Labour Court, membership of, 119
  Labour Relations Commission, membership of, 226
  neglect of apprentice, 17
  picketing of, *see under* **Picketing.**
  registered employment agreements, *see also* **Registered employment agreements.**
    breaches of, 131, 165–166
    duty to keep records, 221
    enforcement by inspector, 222

Employers—*cont.*
  trade disputes, *see also* **Picketing; Trade disputes.**
    between union and employer, *185–186*
    restriction of right to injunction, 200–201, *201–202*
  trade union of, 119, 200
Employment agreements,
  definition, 126
  interpretation by Labour Court, 164
  registration of, 127–128, 154–155, *219*, *see also* **Registered employment agreements.**
Employment Appeals Tribunal, 186
Employment regulation orders, *see also*, **Joint Labour Committees,** 133, 137–138
  agent, criminal liability of, 143
  agricultural workers, *176*
  application of, determination of questions as to, 147–148
  apprentices or learners, and, 141–142
  benefits reckoned as payments, 142
  contract of service, adaptation of, 138
  disabled persons, permits for, 140–141
  enforcement of, 139–141, 144, 221
  inspector's powers, 144–145
  making of, 137, 220
  minimum wages, failure to pay, 139–140, 146
  notices in workplace, 164
  offences and penalties,
    false records, 146
    liability of agent and superior employer, 143–144
    minimum pay, 139–140, 146
    obstruction of inspector, 144–145
  proceedings for, 140, 146
  records, failure to keep, 143
  statutory conditions, non-provision of, 140, 141
  proposals for, 137–138, 159–160, 220
  publication of, 138, 159, 160
  records and notices, 142, 146, 164
  remuneration, computation of, 141

234

INDEX

Equality officers, *187, 208*
appointment of, 214–215
disclosure of information, prohibition on, *210*
independence of, 215
Establishment orders, *see under* **Joint labour committees.**
European Parliament,
candidates or members, 55, 227
Evidence,
codes of practice, of, 217
Labour Court documents, of, 122–123
Labour Court, in, 124, *125*, 154, 158
registered employment agreements, 222
***Ex parte* injunctions,** 201, *201*
Excepted bodies, 60–61, 81, 82
list of, *62*
Exemption from political fund, 53, 55, 56–57
form of notice, 58
Expenses,
administration of legislation, 60, 91, 105, 119, 182
amalgamations or transfers, complaint hearing, witness at, 106
grant towards, 104, *104*, 204–205, *205*
joint labour committees, 230
Labour Relations Commission, 212, 227
witness attending the Labour Court, of, 124

FAS, *127, 138*
FWUI,
amalgamation with ITGWU, *180*
Fair employment rules, *217*
Federation of Irish Employers, *200*
Fees,
alteration of rules, *14*, 116
inspection of documents, *14*, 116
negotiation licence applications, 63
register of members, inspection of, 64, 66
registered employment agreement, copies of, 160
registered trade unions, 7, *8*, *14*, 115, 116
Trade Union (Fees) Regulations 1983, 103, 115–116

Fines, *see also* **Offences and penalties.**
Industrial Relations Act 1990, 182, 224
Following,
penalties for, 17–18
Foreign unions,
amalgamations, jurisdiction of Registrar, *96–97*
amalgamations by Irish members, 99, *99–100*
members of, 60
cesser of membership, 65, 66–67
register of, 66, 67, 73
negotiation licence,
obligations under, 65–67
conditions of entitlement, 62, 104–105, 199
revocation of, 199
rules,
alteration to provide for secret ballot, 198
copies to be sent to Registrar, 199
secret ballot provisions, 198, 199
status of, *96*, *99, 100*
transfer of engagements,
Irish members, by, 99, *99–100*
Irish unions, with or from, 97
Forms,
amalgamations and transfers, notice of vote, 113
application for registration, 37–39
certificate of registry, 39
complete alteration of rules, 42
partial alteration of rules, 40
request to withdraw or cancel, 43–44
notice before withdrawal or cancellation, 43
withdrawal or cancellation, 44
change of name, notice of, 45
declaration to accompany application, 46
complete alteration of rules,
application for registration, 41–42
certificate of registry, 42
declaration accompanying alteration of rules, 40
deposits,
request for return of deposit, 78–79
request for variation of securities, 77

235

INDEX

Forms—*cont.*
  deposits—*cont.*
    request for investment of money lodged, 76
    requests for payments of income on securities, 77
    statutory declarations, 78, 79
  dissolution, notice of, 50
  negotiation licence, application for, 71–72
    notice of intention to apply for, 93
  partial alteration of rules, application, 39–40
    certificate of registry, 40
  political fund exemption notice, 58
  registered office, notice of change of, 45
  registered trade unions (1876 regulations), 37–50
  transfer of stock,
    application for direction, 47–48
    direction by Registrar, 49–50
    verifying declaration, 48–49
Fraudulent application of union property, 6
Freedom of association, *100*
Friendly Societies, Registrar of, *see under* **Registrar.**
Friendly Societies Acts, 1896 to 1977,
  applicability of, 2, 27

Gas workers,
  breach of contract of employment, 16
Government orders, 172
Grievance procedures, 186, *187*

Health services,
  maintenance of life-preserving services during strike, 190, *192*
High Court,
  appeals to,
    amalgamations or transfers, 101
    deposits of authorised unions, *see under* **Deposits with High Court.**
    negotiation licence declaration, 90–91
Highway, trespass to, *190*
Holidays regulations,
  agricultural workers, 178

IPU, *96, 99–100*
ITGWU,
  amalgamation with FWUI, *180*
Immunities in trade disputes, 186–195
  agreed procedures, need to exhaust, 186, *187*
  conspiracy, 15, 188, *188–189*
  contemplation or furtherance, meaning, *189*
  inapplicable where breach of ballot, *188*
  inducement of breach of contract, 193, *193–194*
  interference with trade or business, 193
  intimidation, *193*
  picketing, 189–190, *190–193*
  restrictions, 186, *187*
  secret ballot provisions, *197*, 200
  tortious acts of trade unions, 194–195, *195*
Inducement of breach of contract,
  commercial contract, *193–194*
  employment contract, 193, *193, 194*
  tort of, *193–194, 198*
Industrial action, *see also* **Picketing, Trade disputes, Strikes.**
  definition, 183, *186*
  disputes procedures, *209*
  secret ballot, *see also* **Secret ballot.**
    actions contrary to, *197*, 200, *201*
    requirement of, 195–198
  unofficial, *179, 180, 191, 197*
Industrial and Provident Society Acts, 1893 to 1977, 2
Industrial estates,
  picketing at, *192*
Industrial Relations Act 1946, 117–153
  definitions, 117–118, 126–127, 133–134, 147–148
  employment regulation orders, 137–147
  joint labour committees, 134–137
  Labour Court,
    establishment, officers and procedures, 119–126
  prosecutions by the Minister, 118
  registered employment agreements, 126–133

Index

Industrial Relations Act 1946— *cont.*
registered joint industrial councils, 147–149
regulations, 118, 159–160
repeals, 118, 151
standard wages for areas, 147
trade disputes, 149–151
schedule, 151

Industrial Relations Act 1946 Regulations 1950, 159–160

Industrial Relations Act 1969, 161–173, *179*
ESB tribunals, dissolution of, 172
Labour Court, 161–165, 171
laying of orders before Oireachtas, 172
repeals of legislation, 172
registered employment agreements, 165–167
rights commissioners, 168–169

Industrial Relations Act 1976, 175–178
agricultural workers' joint labour committee, 176
definitions, 175
Labour Court, additional divisions, 177
repeals, 176, 178

Industrial Relations Act 1990, 179–230
amalgamations and transfers, 204–205
background to passing of, *179–181*
codes of practice, 217–218
definitions, 183, *183–186*, 205–206
deposits with High Court, 202–203, 204, 225–226
employment regulation orders, 220–222
equality officers, 214–215
fines, increase of, 182, 224
joint labour committees,
  establishment, constitution and proceedings of, 216, 218–220, 227–230
Labour Court, 210–211, 215–216
failure to attend sitting of, 223
Labour Relations Commission,
  establishment, functions and procedure of, 207–214, 226–227
interpretation, 181–182

Industrial Relations Act 1990— *cont.*
registered employment agreements, 222–223
repeals, 225
rights commissioners, 213–214
schedules, 224–230
summary proceedings, 182
trade disputes, 183–202
  immunities, 186–195
  Labour Court investigation, 210–211
  picketing, 189–190, *190–193*
  reference by Minister, 215
  secret ballots, 195–200
  restrictions on right to injunction 200–201, *201–202*

Industrial relations advisory service, 213

Industrial relations officers, 213
mediation in trade disputes, 150

Industrial relations reform, *179–181*

Industrial relations research, 208

Industrial training committees, 82

Infirm or incapacitated persons, *see under* **Disabled persons.**

Information, disclosure of, *see under* **Disclosure of information.**

Injunctions, *180*
ex parte, 201, *201*
interlocutory, 201, *201–202*
restrictions where secret ballot held, 201, *201–202*
tortious acts of trade unions, *195*

Injury,
breach of contract causing, 17

Inquiries,
establishment order, into application for, 135–136, 219

Inspectors,
employment regulation orders, 144, 145–146, 221
registered employment agreements, 166–168, 222

Interlocutory injunctions, 201, *201–202*

Intimidation, 17–18, *18*, *193*

Iris Oifigiuil,
matters to be published in, 159
notices in, evidence of, *131*, 222

Irish Congress of Trade Unions,
all out strike, *197*

237

INDEX

Irish Congress of Trade Unions—*cont.*
  negotiation licence notification, 89, 90
  supportive actions, 196, *197*
Irish Nurses Union, *52*

Joint conciliation or arbitration boards, 82
Joint industrial councils, 209
  excepted body status, 81
  registration of, 148–149
    cancellation, 148
Joint Labour Committees, 134–137, *180*, 209
  abolition of, 137
  agricultural workers, *134*, 179, 228–229
  composition of, 228
  constitution of, 218, 227–230
  determination of questions as to operation of, 146–147
  establishment order,
    amendment of, 137
    application, 134–135
    inquiry into application, 135, 219
    making of, 136, 219
    publication of, 136, *136*, 159
    restrictions on making, 134
    revocation and variation, 136–137
  excepted body status, 61, 81
  exclusion from scope of, 218–219
  function of, *220–221*
  Labour Court report for assistance of, 219–220
  list of, *134*, *218–219*
  meetings, 229
  membership, 228–230
    vacancies in, 229
  power of Labour Court to establish, 134
  proceedings of, 219, 228–230
  proposals for employment regulation order, 137–138
  see also **Employment regulation orders.**
  remuneration and allowances, 230
  review provisions, *135*, 216
  trade boards, 146, *146*
Judgment debts,
  payment out of authorised union's deposits, 69

Judicial notice,
  Labour Court, seal of, 122
  Labour Relations Commission, seal of, 227

Labour Court,
  annual reports, 125
  appeals from rights commissioner recommendations, 169
  awards of, copy to be sent to Minister, 125
  chairman of, 119, 120
    superannuation scheme, 163
  codes of practice, functions in relation to, 218, *218*
  composition of, 119, *120*, 161
  copies of orders etc. to be furnished to Minister, 125
  decisions of,
    finality of, 122
    pronouncement of, 123, 154, 158
  deputy chairman, 162, 163
    additional appointments, 177
    office of, 162
  determination of certain questions, 123
  disclosure of information, prohibition on, 125
  divisions of, 161–162
    additional, 177, *177*, 216, *216*
  documents, authentication of, 122
  employments agreements, interpretation of, 164
    registered, *see under* **Registered employment agreements.**
  employment conditions, referrals by Minister, 126
  employment regulation orders, *see also* **Employment regulation orders.**
    determination of questions as to application of, 147–148
    making of, 138, 219–220
  establishment of, 119–120
  establishment orders, making of, 136, 219
    see also **Joint labour committees.**
  joint industrial councils,
    functions in relation to, 149–150
    registration of, 149–150
  joint labour committees, *see also* **Joint Labour Committees.**
    exclusion order, 219

INDEX

Labour Court—*cont.*
  joint labour committees—*cont.*
    power to establish, 134
    questions as to operation of, 147–148
    report for assistance of, 219–220
  Labour Relations Commission, submission on, *208,*
  members, *see* ordinary members (*below*)
  officers and servants, 121
  orders of,
    copies to be sent to Minister, 125
    proof of, 122–123
  ordinary members, 119, 120, *120*
    appointment and removal, 120
    inclusion on public service arbitration boards, 165
    nature of employment of, *120*
    superannuation, 164
    term of office, 120
  original function, *208*
  places for sittings and lodgment of documents, 121
  procedure, 122, 153–156, 157–158
    evidence on oath, 124, *125,* 154, 158
    formal sittings, 153–154, 157–158
    legal representation, 123, *124,* 154, 158
    private sitting, 154
    quorum for meeting, 123
    rules, 123, *123–124,* 153–158
    witnesses, 124, *125,* 154, 158, 223
  recommendations, 150, 158
    copies to be sent to Minister, 125
  Register of Joint Industrial Councils, 148
  Register of Employment Agreements, 127
  Registrar of Labour Court, 121, 153, 155, 156, 157, 158
  rules, 123, *123–124,* 153–158
  seal of, 122, *223*
  standard wages for areas, 148
  superannuation provisions, 163, *164,* 216
  technical assessors, 121

Labour Court—*cont.*
  trade dispute investigations, 186, 210–211
    exceptional circumstances, in, 211, *211*
    hearing to be held in private, 164
    mediator, appointment of, 150
    1990 Act provisions, 209, *210,* 210–211
    procedure, 157–158
    recommendation on, 150, 158
    reference of Minister, on, 215, *215–216*
    reference of dispute to arbitration, 150–151
    request of parties, at, 171–172, 210
    witnesses before, 124, *125,* 154, 158
    failure to attend sittings, 223
Labour Court Provisional (Part III) Rules 1946, 153–156
  procedure at formal sittings, 153–154
  registered employment agreements, 154–155
Labour Court Provisional (Part VI) Rules 1946,
  investigation of trade dispute, 157–158
Labour injunctions, *see under* **Injunctions.**
Labour Relations Commission, *180,* 226–227
  accounts and audits, 212–213
  advisory service, 208, 209, *209,* 212–213
  allowances and expenses, 227
  annual report to Minister, 211
  borrowing powers, 212
  chairman, 207, *207,* 211, 226
    removal from office, 227
  chief executive, 211–212
    superannuation, 212
  codes of practice, 208, *209–211,* 217, *217–218, see under* **Codes of practice.**
  composition of, 207, *207–208,* 226
  disclosure of information, prohibition on, 209, *210*
  disputes, reference by Minister, 215
  equality officers, appointment of, 214–215

239

Index

Labour Relations Commission—*cont.*
  establishment of, 207, *207–208*
  functions of, 208–209, *209–210*
  grants to, 212
  industrial relations officers, 213
  information to Minister, 211
  joint labour committees, review of, *135*, 216
  Labour Court submission on, *208*
  members, 207, *207–208*, 226–227
    disqualification from membership, 227
    removal from office, 227
    vacancies among, 211
  procedure, 211
  reports, 209
  rights commissioner recommendations, notification of, 215
  rights commisnioner service, *170*, 213, *214*
  rules, 211
  seal of, 227
    judicial notice of, 227
  staff, 213
  superannuation schemes, 212
  trade disputes functions, 208–209, *209*
    reference by Minister, 215
    reference of dispute to Labour Court, 209
    rights commissioner investigations and, 215
    waiver of, 210–211
Legal proceedings, *see under* **Civil proceedings; Criminal proceedings.**
Legal representation,
  Labour Court, before, 123, *124*, 154, 158
  rights commissioner, before, 168
Legislative reform, *179–181*
Life Assurance Companies Acts, 28
Local authority,
  definition, 205–206
  officers of, 205, *207*

Master,
  neglect of apprentice, 17
Mediation in trade disputes, 150
Members of Labour Court, *see under* **Labour Court.**

Members of Labour Relations Commission, *see under* **Labour Relations Commission.**
Members of trade union,
  agreements between, 1
  annual returns, entitlement to copy of, 9
  application for registration of union, 3
  ballots, *see* **Ballot of Members.**
  cesser of membership, specification in rules, 64, 65, 66–67
  foreign-based unions, 60, 65, 66–67
  fraudulent application of union money, 6
  minors, 29–30
  nominations, 30
    register of, 37–38
  political fund exemption, 53, *55*, 56–57, 58
  register of, 64
    inspection of, 64, *65*, 66, 67, 73–74, 82
  secret ballots, *see under* **Secret ballots.**
  treasurer's accountability to, 5
  withholding of union property, 6
Mergers, *see under* **Amalgamations and transfers.**
Minimum wages, *221*, *see also* **Employment regulation orders.**
  disabled employees, permits for, 141–142
  employer's failure to pay, 139–141, 145
  standard wages for areas, 147
  statutory minimum remuneration, 134, *221*
Minister for Agriculture and Food,
  joint labour committee for agricultural workers, functions in relation to, 228–229
Minister for Industry and Commerce,
  regulations, power to make, 7, 103
Minister for Labour,
  expenses of, 60, 91, 105, 119, 182
  functions and powers in relation to:
    amalgamations or transfers, 104, 204–205

240

INDEX

Minister for Labour—*cont.*
functions and powers in relation to—*cont.*
  codes of practice, 218
  deposits, 85–86, 87, 202
  equality officers, 214–215
  excepted bodies, 82
  inspectors, 145
  joint labour committees, 228, 230
  Labour Court, 119, 120, 121, 124, 125, 126, 162, 163, 165, 177, 216
  Labour Relations Commission, 211, 212, 213, 226, 227
  negotiation licences, 59, 61, 63, 64, 65, 66, 67, 69, 82, 89–90, 91
  prosecutions under 1946 Act, 118, *141*
  regulations, making of, *7*, 59, 118
  rights commissioners, 168, 169, *170*, 214
  trade disputes, reference of, 215, *215*
  inspection of register by officer of, 82–83
  orders of, laying requirement, 172
  powers and duties vested in, 7
Minors,
  trade union membership, 29–30
Misrepresentation,
  union property obtained by, 6
Municipal authorities, 25
  breach of contract by gas or water workers, 16

NUJ, *96, 99–100*
Name of union, 7, 33
  change of, 102
    application for approval, 35–36, 45–46
    forms, 45–46
    notice of, 35, 45–46
    registration of, 102, 103, 111
    rights or obligations unaffected by, 102
Negotiation licence, 60–69
  amalgamations or transfers and, 90, *90*, 204, 205
  application for, 63
  form of, 71–72
  notice of intention, 89, *90*, 93

Negotiation licence—*cont.*
  conditions of entitlement to, 62, 89–90, 203
  deposits, *see under* **Deposits with High Court.**
  foreign unions, 62, 104–105, 199
  membership requirements, 204
  definition, 60
  deposit requirements, *see under* **Deposits with the High Court.**
  excepted bodies, 60–61, 81
    certificate of Minister, 82
    list of, *62*
  exemption in certain cases, 81–82
  expenses of Minister, 60, 91
  fees for application, 63
  foreign unions, 60, 62
    conditions of entitlement, 104–105
    obligations of, 65–67
  grant of, 63
    conditions, 89–90, 199
    High Court declaration, 90–91
  High Court declaration, applicatiion for, 90–91
  inspection of register of members, 64–65, 66, 67, 73–74, 82–83
  membership requirements, 90, 204
  need for, 60
  notice of intention to apply for, 89, 90, 93
  obligations of holder, 64–65
    foreign unions, 65–67
  offences and penalties, 60, 64, 67
  regulations, 59–60, 71–79, 93
  restrictions on grant and holding of, 62, 89–90
  revocation of, 69
  secret ballot provisions, 199, *200*
  trade unions holding, *see under* **Authorised unions.**
Negotiations of wages or conditions, 60, *see also* **Negotiation licence.**
Nominations, 30
  register of, 37–38
Non-employment,
  disputes connected with, 183, *184–185*, 186
Nuisance,
  picketing as, *190*

Index

Offences and penalties,
amalgamations and transfers, witness in complaint hearing, 107
appeals to Circuit Court, 10–11, *11–12*, 12, 20
breach of contract of employment
 gas, water, electricity workers, 16–17
 injury to persons or property, causing, 17
criminal conspiracy, 15
deposits, false statements concerning, 202
District Court jurisdiction, *see under* **District Court**.
employment regulation orders, 139–141, 143, 144–145
false copies of union rules, circulation of, 9–10
fines, increase of, (1990 Act), 182, 224
fraudulent application of union property, 6
Labour Court order, failure to comply with, 132
Labour Court witness, 124
neglect of apprentice, 17
negotiating without a licence, 60
negotiation licences, holders of, 64, 67
obtaining union property by misrepresentation, 6
prosecutions, *see under* **Criminal proceedings**.
reduction of penalties, 18–19
registered employment agreement, connected with, 166, 167, 221–222
registered office, operating without, 8
registered unions, general statement of, 9
scheduled offences under Offences against the State Act, *18*
statutory conditions of employment, non-compliance with, 140
statutory minimum remuneration, failure to pay, 139–140, 145
summary proceedings, *see under* **Criminal proceedings**.
withholding of union property, 6
Offences against the State Act 1939,
scheduled offences, *18*

Oireachtas,
candidate or member, disqualification from membership of Commission, 227
trade union payments to, 54
matters to be laid before, 9, 118, 125, 172, 206, 217
O'Shannon, Cathal, 163

Pay, *see under* **Employment regulation orders; Minimum wages.**
Peaceful picketing, 189–193
Penalties for offences, *see under* **Offences and penalties.**
Persistent following, 17–18
Picketing, *186*, 189–190 *see also* **Industrial action, Secret ballot, Trade disputes.**
disorderly following, 18, *18*
employer's place of business, *191–192*
entry on private property, *191*
false information, dissemination of, *191*
industrial estates, *191*
intimidation, 17, *18*
legality of, 189–190, *190–191*
location of pickets, 189–190, *191–192*
mass picketing, *191*
multi-employment locations, *191–192*
1990 Act provisions, 189–190, *190–193*
nuisance, as, *191*
number of pickets, *191*
offences and penalties, 17–18
persistent following, 17, *18*
primary, 190, *190*
purpose of, 190, *192*
secondary, *180*, 190, *190, 191, 192*
secret ballot provisions, *199*
tortious, when, *191*
trade union officials, attendance of, 190, *192–193*
trespass to highway, as, *191*
violence, use of, 17, *18*
watching or besetting, 18, *18*
when actionable, *191–192*
Political fund, 53
amalgamations and, *56*
ballot approving resolution, 53
rules for conduct of, 55–56

INDEX

Political fund—*cont.*
complaints procedure, 53–54, *55*
exemption from, 53, *55*
  mode of giving effect to, 57
  notice, form of, 56–57, *58*
list of unions operating a, *56*
objections to contribution, 53, 56–57, *58*
political objects, 54, *55*
powers of Registrar, 53–54, *55*, 55–56, 56–57
resolution approving political objects, 53, 54
rules relating to, 53, 55–56
  breach of, 53–54
Political literature, distribution of, 54, *55*
Political party,
union support for, *55*
Primary picketing, 189, *189*
see also **Picketing.**
Programme for National Recovery, 1987, *180*
Property of trade union, *see under* **Trade union property.**
Public office, candidates for or holders of,
support from union funds, 54, *55*
Public service arbitration boards,
inclusion of Labour Court members on, 165

Quigley, Joseph Stapleton, 163

Register of Employment Agreements, 126, 127
inspection of, 156
Register of Joint Industrial Councils, 149
Register of members, 64, 66
inspection of, 64, *65*, 66, 67, 73–74, 82
Registered employment agreements, *126*, 126–133
application for registration, 127–128, 154–155
breaches of, 131–132, 165–166
  complaints procedure, 131–132, 156, 169–170, *226*
  powers of inspection, 226
cancellation of registration, 129–130, 131, 155
continuation in force, 129–130

Registered employment agreements—*cont.*
contract of service, consequential adaptation of, 130
copies of, 131
  fees for, 160
definition, 127
enforcement of, *133*, 165–168, 222–223
  civil proceedings, by, *168*, 223
  powers of inspector, 166–168, 222, *222*, 223
exclusion of undertaking from scope of joint labour committee, 219
inspection of Register, 156
interpretation of, 132
Labour Court orders, 132
objections to registration, 128
offences and penalties, 167, 222
proof of, 222–223
publication of particulars, 130–131, *223*
records,
  duty of employer to keep, 222
  false, 222
  inspection of, 177, *222*
registration procedure, 127–128
strike in breach of, 132
termination of, 130
variation of, 128–129, 131, 155
  proof of, 223
Registered joint industrial councils, 147–149
Registered office of union, 8
notice of change of, 35, 45
Registered unions, 3–10
alteration of rules, *see under* **Rules.**
amalgamations or transfers and, 205
annual returns to Registrar, 7, 8–9
appeals against Registrar's decisions, 52, *52–53*
application for registration, 7
  form 33, 37–39
authorised to negotiate, *see under* **Authorised unions,** *see also* **Negotiation licence.**
buildings, lease or purchase of, 3
certificate of registration, 7
cancellation or withdrawal of, 29, 35, 43–45, 52
effect of, 7
forms, 33, 39, 43–45

243

Index

Registered unions—*cont.*
certificates,
  complete alteration of rules, 43
  partial alteration of rules, 41
deposits, offences in connection with, 202
dissolution of, 30–31
  notice of, 36, 49
fees payable, 7, *8*, *14*, 115
  schedule of, 116
forms, 37–50
inspection of documents, fees for, *14*, 116
name of union, 7, 33
  change of, 35, 45–46
nominations, register of, 37–38
property of, 3–4
registered office, 8
  change of, 35, 45
registration, 3, 6–7
  appeals against decisions, 52, *52–53*
  cancellation or withdrawal of, 29, 35, 43–45, 52
  conditions for, 52
regulations, 7, 33–50
rules, *see under* **Rules.**
transfer of stock, 27–28, 36
  fees, 116
  forms, 46–50
withdrawal of certificate, 29, 35, 52
  appeals, 52
  forms, 43–45

Registrar of Friendly Societies, 9
amalgamations and transfers, 96, 97, 98, 100–101, 106, 109–110
  complaint hearing, 106–107
annual reports, 9
annual returns to, 8–9
authentication of documents by, 37
certification of unregistered unions, 52
change of name of union, 35–36, 45–46, 102, 103, 111
decisions of, appeals against, 52, *52–53*
foreign unions, jurisdiction, *96–97*
political fund,
  powers in relation to, 53–54, 55–56, 56–57
registration of union, 6–7, *see also* **Registered unions.**

Registrar of Labour Court, 121, 153
registered employment agreements, 153, 155, 156
trade dispute investigations, 157, 158

Registry of trade unions, 6–8

Regulations,
agricultural workers' holidays, 178
amalgamations and transfers, 103, 109–114
fees (1983), 103, 115–116
Industrial Relations Act 1946, under, 118, 159–160
inspection of register of members, 73–74
laying requirement, 118, 172, 206, 217
powers of Minister for Industry and Commerce, 7, 102
powers of Minister of Labour, 7, *7*, 59, 118
negotiation licences, 59–60, 71–79, 93
Registration of trade unions (1876), 33–50

Restitution, actions for, *195*

Restraint of trade, doctrine of,
union agreements and trusts excepted from, 1

Rights commissioners, 168–169, 208, 214
appeals against recommendations, *169*, 179
appointment and removal of, 168–169, *169*, 214
  re-appointment of, 214
disclosure of information, prohibition on, 170, *210*
disputes, investigation of, 178, 179, *169–170*
objections to, 214
private hearing, 169
function of, *214*
independence of, 214
legal representation before, 169
office of, 168–169
recommendations, 168, *169*
  appeals from, 169, *170*, 214
  notification requirements, 168, *170*, 215
regulation of proceedings, 169
service, 208, 214
term of office, 168, *170*, 218

INDEX

Riot, 15
Rules of Labour Court, 123, *123–124*, 153–158
Rules of the Superior Courts 1986, O. 77, part VIII,
  deposits with High Court, 75–76
  forms, 76–80
Rules of trade union,
  alteration of, 9, 33
    complete alteration, 33–34, 41–43
    fees for, *14*, 116
    foreign unions, 66
    forms, 39–43
    notification to Registrar, 9
    partial alteration, 33–34, 39–41
    secret ballot provision, to include, *198*, 199
    transfer of engagements, for, 98–99
  copies of, 8
    false copies, circulation of, 9–10
  foreign unions, 65, 66
  matters to be provided for, 8, 13–14, *14*, 30–31
    1990 Act, *14*
    authorised unions, 63–64, 65
    cesser of membership, 63–64
    conditions of entry, 63–64
    dissolution, manner of, 30
    foreign unions, 65
    political fund, 53–54
    secret ballots, 197, *198*, 199
  new rules, 9
  political fund ballot, approval of, 55–56
  pre-strike ballot provisions, *180*, 196, 199–200
  registered trade unions, 8
  restraint of trade, in, *2*

SIPTU,
  political fund ballot, *56*
School attendance committee,
  officers of, 205
School teachers, 205
Seamen, 21
Secondary picketing, *180*, 190, *190*, *191*, *192*
  health services, 190, *192*
  secret ballot provisions, *199*
Secret ballots,
  amalgamations or transfers, approving, 97

Secret ballots—*cont.*
  political fund resolution, approval of rules, 55–56
  strike or other industrial action, for, 196, *197–199*
    actions contrary to outcome of, *197*, 199
    aggregation of results, 196, *197*
    alteration of rules, *197*, 198
    electorate, 196, *198*
    enforcement of rule for, 199
    failure to hold, *198–199*
    notification of results to members, 196
    restriction of right to injunction, 200–201
    rules of union to provide for, 198
Self-employed persons, *185*
Shop stewards, *187*
Sit-in, *18*
Solicitors, *see under* **Legal representation.**
Spouse,
  competence as witness, 19, *19–20*
Standard wages, 147
State employees, 205, *206–207*, *see also* **Civil servants.**
State industrial employees, 206, *207*
Statutory conditions of employment, *221*, *see also* **Employment regulation orders.**
  definition, 134
  non-compliance with, 140
Statutory definitions, *see under* **Definitions.**
Statutory forms, *see under* **Forms.**
Statutory minimum wage, *see under* **Employment regulation orders; Minimum wages.**
Statutory objects of trade unions, 51, 52
Strike notice, *179*, *197*, 200
Strikes, *see also* **Immunity in Trade disputes.**
  all out strike, *197*
  breach of contract of employment, 16–17
  conspiracy, crime of, 15
  definition (1990 Act), 183, *186*
  electricity workers, by, *16–17*
  gas workers, by, 16

INDEX

Strikes—*cont.*
  injunction restrictions, 200–201
  injury to persons or property, involving, 17
  picketing, *see under* **Picketing.**
  pre-strike ballot provisions, *180,* 186, *187, see also* **Secret ballots.**
  registered employment agreement, in breach of, 132
  secret ballot, in contravention of, *187,* 200, *see also* **Secret ballots.**
  supportive action, sanction for, 196, *197*
  water workers, by, 16
Summary Jurisdiction Acts,
  definition, 12, *13*
Summary proceedings, *see under* **Criminal proceedings; District Court.**

Teachers, 169, 205
  organisations of, 61
Technical assessors, 121
Terms of employment,
  disputes concerning, 183, *184,* 186
Threat,
  inducement of breach of contract, 193, *194*
Tort,
  civil conspiracy, 188, *188–189*
  immunities, *see under* **Immunities in trade disputes.**
  inducement of breach of contract, commercial contract, *194*
    employment contract, 193, *193, 194*
    indirect, *194,* 198
  interference with trade or business, 193
  intimidation, *193*
  picketing as, *191*
  unlawful interference with trade or business, *193,* 198
Trade boards, 146, *see also* **Joint Labour Committees.**
Trade disputes,
  agreed procedures, 186, *187*
  arbitration, reference to, by Labour Court, 150
  between workmen, *180, 184*

Trade disputes—*cont.*
  codes of practice, *209*
  conditions of employment, concerning, 183, *185,* 186
  conspiracy in, 15
  contemplation or furtherance of, 188, *188–189*
  definition, 117–118, 183, *184*
  employer and trade union, between, *187*
  employment or non-employment, concerning, 183, *184,* 186
  "golden formula," *189*
  immunities in, *see under* **Immunities in trade disputes.**
  injunctive relief, restrictions on right, 200–201, *201–202, see also* **Injunctions.**
  Labour Court recommendation on, 150, 157, 158
  Labour Court investigation, 149, 150, 157–158, 186
  functions under 1990 Act, 209, *210,* 210–211
  private hearing, 164
  reference by Minister, 215, *216*
  request of parties, at, 171–172
  Labour Relations Commission, reference to, 186, 209, 215
  mediation by conciliation officer, 150
  picketing, *see under* **Picketing.**
  reference by Minister, 215, *216*
  rights commissioner investigations, 168, 169, *169–170*
    appeals against recommendations, 214
    objections to, 214
  secret ballot provisions, *see under* **Secret ballot.**
  strikes, *see under* **Strikes.**
  terms of employment, concerning, 183, *184,* 186
  unfair dismissals, concerning, *169*
Trade Disputes (Amendment) Act 1982, *180*
Trade Union Act 1871, 1–14
  criminal provisions, 1
  definitions, 12
  fees, 8, *14,* 115, 116
  legal proceedings, 10–12
  registered trade unions, 3–10
  Registrar, 9
  repeals, 13

Index

Trade Union Act 1871—*cont.*
schedules, 13–14
trade union accounts, 5
trade union contracts, 1–2
trustees of trade union, 3–5
Trade Union Act Amendment Act 1876, 27–33
certificate of registration, withdrawal or cancellation of, 29
definition of trade union, 12, *13*, 31
dissolution of union, 30–31
jurisdiction in offences, 28
membership of minors, 29–30
nominations by members, 30
penalty for failure to give notice, 31
Trustees, absence etc. of, 27–28
Trade Union Act 1913, 51–58
definition of trade union, 51–52
objects and powers of trade unions, 51
political fund, 53–58
political objects, 54
Schedule, 58
Trade Union Act 1941, 59–70
definitions, 59, 60
deposits with High Court, 62, 67, 69, 70
negotiation licences, 60–69
regulations, 59, *59–60*, 71–75, 93
rules, 75–79
schedule, 70
Trade Union Act 1941 (Application for Negotiation Licence) Regulations 1942, 71–73
Trade Union Act 1942, 81–83
inspection of register by officer of Minister, 82–83
negotiation licence, exemptions from requirement, 81–82
repeals, 83
Trade Union Act 1947, 85–86
deposits, variation of schedule, 85–86
Trade Union Act 1952, 87–88
Trade Union Act 1971, 89–92
deposits, 92
negotiation licence, grant of, 89–91
schedule, 92

Trade Union Act 1971 (Notice of Intention to Apply for Negotiation Licence) Regulations 1972, 93
Trade Union Act 1975, 95–107
amalgamations and transfers, 96–104
complaints procedure, 100–101, 106–107
change of name of union, 102
negotiation licence, foreign unions, 104–105
regulations, 103, 109–114
schedule, 106–107
Trade Union Amalgamations Regulations 1976, 109–114
application for registration, 110–111
approval of proposed instruments, 109
change of name, registration of, 111
contents of instruments, 110, 111–113
contents of notice of vote, 110, 113
Trade Union Bill 1966, *179*, *197*
Trade Union (Fees) Regulations 1983, 115–116
Trade union funds,
agreements for application of, 2
political fund, *see under* **Political fund.**
repeal of 1869 Act, 13
restrictions for political purposes, 53
trustees' liability, limitation of, 5
Trade Union (Inspection of Register of Members) Regulations 1942, 73–74
Trade union officials, 186, *187*, 190
attendance on picket, 190, *192–193*
definition, *187*, 190
personal tortious liability, *194*
TD or Senator, as, paid leave of absence for, 55
tortious acts of trade union, immunity in trade disputes, 194, *195*
Trade union property,
actions by or against trustees, 4
branch property, vesting in trustees, 3

247

INDEX

Trade union property—*cont.*
death or removal of trustees, 3–4, 27–28
disposal on amalgamation or transfer, 101–102
fraudulent application of, 6
liability of trustees, 4
  limitation of, 5
misrepresentation, obtained by, 6
powers of trustees, 3
transfer of stock, direction as to, 27–28, 36
  forms, 47–50
vesting in trustees, 3–4
withholding of, 6
see also **Political fund; Trade union funds.**

Trade unions,
accounts and audits, 5, *5*
agreements,
  restraint of trade, excepted from, 1
  when not enforceable by courts, 1–2
amalgamations, *see under* **Amalgamations and transfers.**
annual returns to Registrar, 7, 8–9
authorised unions, 62, *see also* **Authorised unions; Negotiation licence.**
High court deposits, *see under* **Deposits with High Court.**
obligations of, 63–65, 65–67
benefits to members, agreements to pay, 2
branch committee members, *187*
cancellation/withdrawal of registration, 29, 35, 43–45
certificate of registry, *see under* **Registered unions.**
certified unions, 52, *52*
change of name, 102
  application for aproval, 35–36, 45–46
  forms, 45–46
  registration of, 103, 111
constitution of, 51–52
contracts of, 1
  when not enforceable by courts, 1–2

Trade unions—*cont.*
definition, (1871 Act) 12–13, *13*; (1913 Act) *13*, 51–52; (1946 Act) 118; (1975 Act) 95; (1946 Act) 118; (1990 Act) 183, *185*
  foreign unions and, *96*
dispute with employer, *185–186*
dissolution of, 30–31
  notice of, 36, 50
employers' trade unions, 200, *200*
foreign, *see under* **Foreign unions.**
Friendly Societies Acts and, 2, 27
funds, *see under* **Political fund; Trade union funds.**
immunities, *see under* **Immunities in trade disputes.**
incorporation under Companies Acts disallowed, 2
judgment debts of,
  payment out of deposits, 69
legal status, 2
members of, *see under* **Members of trade union.**
name of, 7, 33, *see also* change of name (*above*).
negotiating without a licence, offence of, 60
negotiation licence, *see under* **Negotiation licence.**
nominations, register of, 37–38
notices, failure to give, 31
objects of,
  non-statutory, 51, 52
  political, 51, 52, 53–55, *see also* **Political fund.**
  statutory, 51–52
offences, *see under* **Offences and penalties.**
officials, *see under* **Trade union officials.**
payments on death of child, 27
political fund, *see under* **Political fund.**
political objects, 51, 52, 53–55
property of, *see under* **Trade union property.**
purposes of,
  in restraint of trade, 1
  unlawful, 3
rationalisation, *180*, *204*
register of members, 64, 66
  inspection of, 64, 66, 67, 73–74, 82

248

INDEX

Trade unions—*cont.*
registered employment agreement, breach of, 131–132, *see also* **Registered employment agreements.**
registered office of, 8
change of, 35, 45
registration, 3, 6–7, *see also* **Registered unions.**
restraint of trade and, 1, *2*
rules of, *see under* **Rules of trade unions.**
shop stewards, *187*
statutory objects of, 51, 52
statutory provisions inapplicable to, 2
tortious acts,
immunity in respect of, 195, *195*
injunctive relief, *195*
transfer of stock, *see under* **Transfer of stock.**
transfers of engagements, *see under* **Amalgamations and transfers.**
treasurer of, duty to render accounts, 5
trustees of, *see under* **Trustees of trade union.**
Trades Unions Funds Protection Act 1869,
repeal of, 13
Transfer of engagements, *see also* **Amalgamations and transfers.**
alteration of rules for, 98–99
contents of instrument, 110, 112–113
foreign unions, with, *96*, *97*
Transfer of stock, direction as to, 27–28, 36
fees, 116
forms, 47–59
Treasurer of trade union,
duty to render accounts, 5
Trustees of trade union,
absence of, 27–28
amalgamation or transfer, vesting of property on, 101–102
bankruptcy of, 27–28
capactiy to sue and be sued, 4, *4–5*
death or removal of,
survival of actions, 4
transfer of stock, 27–28, *see also* **Transfer of stock.**
vesting of property on, 3–4

Trustees of trade union—*cont.*
liability for union property, 4
limitations of, 5
power to sue treasurer, 5
treasurer's accounts, duty to submit to audit, 5
union property,
powers and duties in relation to, 3–5
vesting in, 3–4

Unfair dismissals disputes, *169*
Unlawful assembly, 15
Unofficial industrial action, *179, 180, 191, 197*
Unofficial picketing, *191*
Unregistered trade unions, *see also* **Foreign unions.**
trade union certificate, 52

Violence, 17–18
Vocational education committee,
officers of, 205

Wages,
minimum, *see under* **Employment regulation orders; Minimum wages.**
negotiations for fixing, 60, *see also* **Negotiation licence.**
Watching or besetting, 18, *18*
Water workers,
breach of contract of employment, 16
Witness,
amalgamations or transfers, complaint hearing, 106, 107
competence of, 19, *19–20*
Labour Court, before, 124, *125*, 154, 158
failure to attend, 223
Words and phrases,
agricultural employer, 175
agricultural worker, 175
agriculture, 175
any worker, *185*
appropriate sum, 62
attend, *191*
connected with, *185*
court of summary jurisdiction, 25
employer, 183, *183–184*

Words and phrases—*cont.*
employment agreement, 126
employment or non-employment, *184*
excepted bodies, 60–61, 81
furtherance, *189*
in contemplation or furtherance of a trade dispute, *189*
industrial action, 183, *186*
local authority, 205–206
maliciously, 21
member of trade union (Trade Union Act 1975), 95
member of unregistered union, 60
municipal authority, 25
negotiation licence, 60
political objects, 54
public office, 54
qualified joint industrial council, 148
registered employment agreement, 127
remuneration (Industrial Relations Act, 1946), 142
seamen, *21*
statutory conditions of employment, 134

Words and phrases—*cont.*
statutory minimum remuneration, 134
statutory objects (Trade Union Act 1913), 51
strike, 183, *186*
Summary Jurisdiction Acts, 12, *13*, 25
trade dispute, (1946 Act) 117–118; (1990 Act), 183, *184*
trade union, (1871 Act) 12–13, *13*; (1913 Act) *13*, 51–52; (1946 Act) 118; (1990 Act) 183, *185*
trade union official, *187*, 190
worker, 183, *184*, *185*, 205–206, *206*

Worker,
definition, 183, *184*, *185*, 205, *206*
excluded categories, 205
power of government to amend, 206

Young persons,
trade union membership, 29–30